A TRUE DELIVERANCE

A TRUE DELIVERANCE

Fred Harwell

ALFRED A. KNOPF   NEW YORK   1980

THIS IS A BORZOI BOOK
PUBLISHED BY ALFRED A. KNOPF, INC.

Copyright © 1979 by Fred R. Harwell, Jr.

All rights reserved under International and Pan-American
Copyright Conventions. Published in the United States by
Alfred A. Knopf, Inc., New York, and simultaneously in Canada
by Random House of Canada Limited, Toronto. Distributed by
Random House, Inc., New York.

Library of Congress Cataloging in Publication Data

Harwell, Fred, [date]   A true deliverance.

Includes index.
1. Little, Joan.   2.   Trials (Murder)--North Carolina--Raleigh.
I.   Title.
KF224.L52H37   1980   345'.73'02523   79–2233
ISBN 0–394–49989–1

Manufactured in the United States of America

FIRST EDITION

*For my parents
and for Mary*

I'm not one who objects to pre-trial publicity.

—JERRY PAUL
Chief Defense Counsel

The media shaped this case.
There's no doubt about it.

—WILLIAM GRIFFIN
Chief Prosecutor

CONTENTS

ACKNOWLEDGMENTS

This book could not have been written without the patient cooperation of many people directly involved in the case. Their names appear in the text and are too numerous to list here, but to all who gave me assistance I wish to express my sincere appreciation. The material, the views, and the conclusions in this book are based on my own observations, officials' records (some public and some not), and numerous interviews. I have made an effort to corroborate all information not received firsthand, and in several instances I have chosen to disregard claims and accusations that could be neither substantiated nor refuted upon further research. I wish to acknowledge the special assistance given to me by the chief prosecutor, William Griffin, and the chief defense counsel, Jerry Paul. Both granted extensive interviews and turned over case files and materials to me. My thanks also to the various courthouse officials in Beaufort County and Wake County who were always cooperative, and to the presiding judge, Hamilton Hobgood, without whose consent I could not have observed the trial so closely.

A portion of my research was financed by a grant from the Fund for Investigative Journalism, Washington, D.C.

F.H.

AUTHOR'S NOTE

At various times the defendant's name (pronounced "Jo-Ann") was spelled Joan, Joann, Joanne, JoAnn, JoAnne, and Jo-Anne in press accounts and defense statements. Her supporters wore "Free Joanne" buttons and shirts at the trial, and a fund-raising organization started on behalf of the defendant by her own attorneys was chartered as the "Joann Little Defense Fund." Originally her name was spelled "Joan," however, and it appeared in this form on most official documents. Upon inquiry the defendant indicated a preference for the original spelling, and it has been used throughout this book except where quoted sources employed a different version.

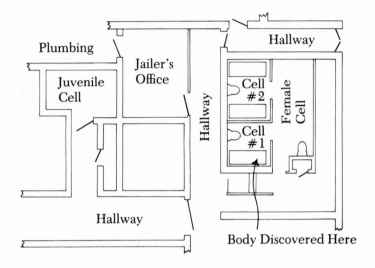

Beaufort County Jail

PART I

AUGUST 15, 1975

CHAPTER 1

A VERDICT WHICH SPEAKS THE TRUTH

It is a summer Friday, humid and hot even before 9:00 a.m., when court is to convene. The Wake County Courthouse in Raleigh, North Carolina, nine formidable stories of concrete and glass, is located on Fayetteville Street, the main street here, amid department stores, banks, office buildings, small shops, and state government warrens. Two blocks away the old domed state capitol building anchors one end of Fayetteville Street, as it has since before the Civil War. Just behind the capitol, through a small park, sprawls a modern legislative building, gleaming and contemporary, a symbol of the state's recent renaissance. Nearer the courthouse there is the crumbling shell of a once opulent hotel and a store with blackened windows where pornographic books and films are sold, symbols of another side of the same renaissance.

In Raleigh, the Old South and the New South compete for space. There are memories of mimosa here, but they are fast fading in the din of traffic and the gloom of brown smog that occasionally hangs in the sky. Raleigh is a community of dogwoods and high-rise apartments, of grassy lawns and crowded streets, of white mansions with columns and shanties where whole families huddle in a single room. It is neither urban nor rural, too small to be called a city and too large to be called a town. There is about

Raleigh, as there is about all of the South, a sense of uncertainty and transition, a lack of identity.

A small crowd has begun to gather outside the Wake County Courthouse, sensing that this will be the last day of a five-week trial that has probed and poked at this uncertainty. Reporters from all over the world have come here to test its procedures and personalities against their own perceptions of the South as it was and is. Yet most of the people on Fayetteville Street this morning seem oblivious to the trial, even uninterested in its outcome. Wake County jurors will decide the case, but they are the most anonymous of the actors on stage for this courtroom drama. Everyone else connected with it—the chief defense counsel, the district attorney, the judge, even the defendant—is from somewhere else. Moved here from a jurisdiction one hundred miles away, the trial has become front-page news across the country without disturbing the rhythm of the place where it is being held. The verdict may tell the people of Raleigh, and of the South, something about themselves, but what, they do not know and, along Fayetteville Street at least, do not seem to care.

Spectators at the trial, nearly half of them reporters, have already been admitted to the third-floor arena where it is being conducted in solemn security behind barred doors. They now occupy 112 seats in Superior Courtroom Number One and wait impatiently for the day's proceedings to begin. There are no squeaking chairs and whirring fans overhead, no artifacts to suggest torpid decadence and the ambience of wet decay that is, rightly or wrongly, often associated with courtrooms in the South. Instead, Superior Courtroom Number One seems sterile and oppressively functional. Even the recessed lights in the ceiling contribute to its artificial, air-conditioned environment by controlling the temperature as well as providing illumination. There is one small window, located high and to the side of the jury box. It is as if those in the courtroom have been sealed off from the outside world, locked by choice into the peculiar life-and-death reality of this small space.

The trial has been staged, like a theater production, as much for the benefit of those who observe as those who participate. Each phase has been elaborately orchestrated to produce an effect as well as a result, to render the appearance of justice as well as justice itself. Now the protagonists are assembling to perform a last essential ritual. The attorneys for both sides are present, as is the defendant, an enigmatic black woman named Joan Little. She has admitted that she stabbed a white jailer and fled from a county jail in rural eastern North Carolina. The prosecution has argued that the man's death was murder. The defense lawyers have insisted that Joan Little killed in self-defense. Racial hatred and sexual animosity have been kindled by the actions of both sides during the trial. Now, after the judge gives his instructions, the jury will decide the case.

"Oyez! Oyez! Oyez! This honorable Superior Court for the County of Wake is now in session, the Honorable Hamilton H. Hobgood presiding. . . ."

There is a shuffle as the spectators and the attorneys rise to their feet. The judge appears suddenly, a few minutes late, emerging from chambers with his long robe swirling behind him as he moves purposefully toward the dais of ersatz marble and stained veneer that commands one end of the small courtroom. At sixty-four, Hamilton Hobgood looks almost too much like a judge, gray-haired and scholarly, wearing spectacles, carrying a sheaf of papers in a manila folder. He has conducted this serious trial with firmness and restraint, often relieving the tension with folksy humor, but today his face is lined and he is not smiling.

". . . God save the state and this honorable court," the bailiff, a portly sheriff's deputy, intones with reverence and finality as everyone sits down. Each day of the five-week trial has opened with this same incantation. It is an ancient chant, echoing respected notions of fairness and justice. But it is also a refrain of historic misgivings, conjuring the sovereign's dread of disorder and anarchy, and it raises a question no less relevant today than it was centuries ago at the very incipiency of the common law. God save the state and this honorable court . . . from what?

Seated now, Judge Hobgood has the prosecution on his left, near the jury box, and the defense, the apparent threat to the sovereign, on his right. For weeks these defense attorneys have been challenging the state and the state's judiciary as institutions not of justice but of social and political oppression. They have seized an unaccustomed initiative, and they have often succeeded in making it seem that the court and the prosecution, rather than the defendant, have been on trial. The chief defense counsel is Jerry Paul, a hulking and sometimes pugnacious man whose previously modest reputation as an activist attorney has been vividly enhanced by publicity surrounding the case. There are other prominent lawyers in the room, but Paul's bulky figure dominates the defense table, overshadowing even the defendant herself, who is rigidly watching the jurors. Paul is hunched forward, his eyes on the judge, waiting for Hobgood to begin.

On the other side of the courtroom, two of the three prosecutors who have tried to establish Joan Little's guilt are also waiting. Lester Chalmers, of the state attorney general's office, is busying himself with paperwork. The chief prosecutor, District Attorney William Griffin, has his thin fingers pressed together in a contemplative peak. His eyes are focused beyond the wall at the judge's back, as if he is trying to project himself to a distant point somewhere outside the room. Lean and neatly dressed, Griffin offers a sharp contrast in appearance to Paul, a suggestion of other differences between the two men. At thirty-three, Griffin looks younger than his age, while Paul, also thirty-three, looks older. Both of them have practiced law in North Carolina for about six years, Griffin as a prosecutor and Paul, from the day he was admitted to the bar, as a defense attorney. Griffin believes as a result of his experience that the state's judicial system is essentially fair and just, while Paul is convinced after years of civil-rights activity that racism and sexism have saturated the state's courts and laws and lawmen. There are other differences between these two protagonists, one in particular that is fundamental to this trial. William Griffin believes Joan Little is guilty of murder. Jerry Paul believes she is innocent.

The courtroom has now been secured, and a heavy silence has fallen over the people locked inside. The jurors sit motionless, some looking on as Judge Hobgood shuffles and arranges his pile of papers, others studying the green carpet beneath their feet. They have been sequestered for five weeks, eating as a group in guarded isolation and sleeping in fortified motel rooms. They have long since been ready to decide the fate of the defendant. Bailiffs have overheard them expressing incredulity about the evidence against Joan Little, despite orders from the judge that they were not to discuss the case until after hearing all the witnesses and receiving his instructions.

For a moment there is no sound except the persistent scratching of three television sketch artists who continue to work furiously, oblivious to the gathering tension. The front rows of seats in the visitors' gallery have been assigned to authorized press representatives, placing them even closer to the trial than the family of the defendant. Reporters from many influential newspapers, from the international wire services, and from the three major television networks have joined local newsmen to cover the trial. Merely by their presence it has been infused with pomp and significance far exceeding its essential implications. The case involves no famous person, no heinous atrocity. The defendant is a heretofore obscure young woman who has been in and out of trouble with the law for several years. The victim was a sixty-two-year-old county employee, whose body was found partially unclad in a cell where the defendant had been incarcerated.

It has been more than eleven months since the killing, however, and in that time the case has become entangled in complex interpretations and convoluted subtleties. Imagination and indignation have overtaken the narrow issues of law, and one moment of conflict is now seen in a broad historical and sociological context. No longer is the question just what happened between two very different people in one small town in the South. The jury must now decide much more than whether the killing was murder and escape or rape and self-defense. Journalists have called the incident a quintessential act of bigotry and a paradigm of racism, sexism, and repression, raising in the media what has become perhaps the most compelling trial issue of all: How will the court and the jury handle the momentous and still unresolved social and political issues that are now inextricably confused with the basic question of the defendant's innocence or guilt?

Grasping the papers in his hand, Judge Hobgood disposes first of a few incidental matters and then turns briskly to the reading of his charge to the jury. The defendant has been accused of the unlawful killing of Clarence T. Alligood, he says, who was a night jailer at the Beaufort County jail in Washington, North Carolina, where Joan Little had been an inmate. She has entered a plea of not guilty. The trial has been long, the evidence complicated, and the arguments heated. It now remains for him to instruct the jurors on the applicable law and to explain how they might apply the law to make their decision in this case. "In the final analysis," he says solemnly, "you are the ones to determine the true facts and render a verdict which speaks the truth. . . ."

At the defense table there is almost no movement as the recitation of the formal charge begins. Jerry Paul and the other defense attorneys listen closely to Hobgood, shifting their attention only to make notes on points they may later object to as prejudicial. At the end of the table farthest from the judge and the jury, in what might seem the position of least importance, Joan Little sits with her cheek resting on a tightly clenched fist. Her large unblinking eyes are fastened hard on the judge; her mouth is set and firm. There is no expression on her face, no hint that the terms of her future are at last being enunciated in open court. She seems impassive, impervious to the drama unfolding around her; she has seemed so throughout the entire trial.

"The state has offered evidence," the judge reads in a monotone, "tending to show that the defendant, Joan Little, was a prisoner in the Beaufort County jail on the night of 26 August 1974 and that she had been a continuous inmate of said jail for several weeks prior to that date. . . . That . . . at five minutes to four a.m. on the twenty-seventh day of August 1974 Washington police sergeant Jerry Helms went to the jail, where he met Washington police officer Johnny Rose on the outside of the jail. Rose had arrested [a woman] for drunk and disorderly conduct and she was cursing and causing a disturbance. That the three went down a hallway to a steel door going into the jail and Officer Helms rang the buzzer several times.

"No one came to the jail door. . . ."

Contrary to the folklore of criminal procedure, the function of juries is not to distill truth from fiction, not to "determine the true facts" or to render a verdict that "speaks the truth" about a defendant's guilt or innocence. The jury makes no broad judgments about a defendant's culpability. It sits to determine not whether the accused is actually guilty but whether the prosecution has presented sufficient and persuasive evidence of guilt. The defendant is on trial, but it is the prosecution that must, at least procedurally, either win or lose. The jury decides only that guilt has been established or that it has not. "You are the ones to . . . render a verdict which speaks the truth in this case," Judge Hobgood has said, and now he adds, "The state must prove to you that she is guilty beyond a reasonable doubt. . . ."

By any measure, the prosecution of Joan Little has seemed skimpy and inconclusive. Although the judge has refused several times to grant defense motions for a general dismissal, he has dismissed a first-degree murder charge for lack of evidence of premeditation. Now the case will go to the jury on two lesser counts: second-degree murder and voluntary manslaughter. Joan Little no longer faces the gas chamber, the mandatory penalty for a capital crime in North Carolina, but still she could receive a sentence of life in prison if she is convicted.

The judge has been reading for nearly fifteen minutes and he is already beginning to grow hoarse. He pauses just long enough to take a sip of water before commencing his recitation of the prosecution's case. The state's evidence tends to show, he says, that the jailer's body was discovered inside a cell "lying on his side on the bunk and naked from the waist down except for his socks. . . . His trousers were hanging down from the bunk and he was holding the same with his left hand and his right hand was hanging over his body down toward the floor with an ice pick in his right hand with the point extending beyond his thumb." Medical evidence indicated that the man died of stab wounds, eleven in all, and that the wounds were probably inflicted with the ice pick found clutched in his right hand. A doctor who examined the body in the cell testified "that a string of seminal fluid extended from Alligood's penis to his left thigh . . . and that in his opinion there had been ejaculation just prior to or at the time of death and that he assumed it indicated sexual activity." A pathologist said that "in his opinion the length of life after the penetrating wound in the heart was approximately five minutes or not less than two minutes nor more than ten minutes, and in his opinion, from his autopsy examination, the deceased had ejaculated prior to death." Other witnesses testified about the investigation and about the activities of the jailer on the night he was killed. "The state contends," Hobgood reads finally, "that Joan Little took flight from the Beaufort County jail . . . after the death of Clarence Alligood." Then he skips a beat before continuing at the same cadence and in the same tone of voice. "On the other hand, the defendant contends . . . that she escaped because of fear of her own life and safety. . . ."

William Griffin regards Hobgood with respectful attention as the judge finishes his summary of the prosecution's evidence. Griffin has made no notes, and he will formally object to nothing the judge has said. He is aware that his case is weak. He has known that it would be since before the trial, even though he has maintained that it would be sufficient for the jury to return a guilty verdict. The state's case has been built entirely on circumstantial evidence, on a chain of circumstances and facts instead of on eyewitness accounts. Griffin's trial strategy, though, has been to rely primarily on Joan Little to convict herself, to force her to testify and then to shatter her on cross-examination. Now that strategy has clearly failed. She has withstood the test, has been ready with an answer for every question. Her words have brought tears to the eyes of many jurors, and her very appearance on the witness stand has, perhaps, sealed the case in her favor.

A good trial lawyer is a magician, a master of illusion. No charge can ever be proven or disproven to an absolute certainty, and so both the prosecutor and the defense counsel must try to create an illusion, one of guilt and the other of innocence. Items of evidence and snatches of testimony might mean different things to different people on the jury, and the advocate who can best and most convincingly interpret what the jurors see and hear will usually win the case. That is why pre-trial publicity about prior arrests and previous criminal activity is of such concern, especially to defense attorneys. It tends to dispel the illusion of innocence inside the courtroom.

In this case, however, some of the defense attorneys had inspired and encouraged pre-trial publicity, using it to shape the illusion that Joan Little stood for issues far transcending the question of her guilt or innocence. The defense attorneys themselves had no better idea than anyone else what had really happened between Clarence Alligood and Joan Little, but from the beginning they had been willing, even eager, to interpret the incident for the public. As Jerry Paul would later boast, media coverage of the case was artfully manipulated to make the facts seem incontestable and the implications manifest, with inevitable effects on public opinion and on the views of the jurors who would eventually sit in judgment. He had insisted before the trial that Joan Little's guilt or innocence was academic and that it was more important to consider some of the ramifications of the jailer's death than to determine exactly how and why he had died. In a real sense, phantom defendants were put on trial. Joan Little did not stand before the jury alone. She stood with every degraded woman, every persecuted black, every victim of racism and sexual oppression. While it was still unclear in this instance whether she was herself such a victim, her attorneys had made it seem that she was a symbol of them all.

"The defendant has offered evidence," the judge drones on, beginning his summary of the case presented by the defense, "tending to show . . . that she was in the Beaufort County jail from June 4 until August 27, 1974 . . . and . . . that she came to know all of the jailers well, but that only the deceased, Clarence Alligood, would come inside the cell bars." Hobgood has been reading for nearly three quarters of an hour, and there has been little movement in the hushed courtroom except the rustling of several small children who are squeezed in among the spectators. Even the sketch artists have silenced their chalks and are quietly watching the judge. The jurors are listening with fixed interest, all except one, who seems to be dozing.

Joan Little lowers her eyes momentarily and covers them with her hand as Hobgood begins to go over her testimony in detail, the first sign that she might show emotion as she sits stoically at the defense table. Then she raises her head and props her chin on her upraised palm, listening gravely as the judge reiterates what she has said about Clarence Alligood's death and her escape from the Beaufort County jail. Almost one year has passed since he appeared inside the cellblock that night, trapping her alone and defenseless inside her tiny cell.

"Give me some pussy," he had said, according to her testimony.

"I can't be nice to you that way," she had answered.

Then his shoes were off, left outside the cell, and suddenly he was standing in front of her, fondling her breasts with both hands. He removed her gown, then his trousers. And then the ice pick, appearing from nowhere, now in his hand.

". . . He sat down on the cot and pulled her to the floor in front of him," the judge says without inflection, "with the ice pick up at the side of her head. . . ."

As Hobgood reads on, Jerry Paul scans the faces of the jurors. He is confident that he will win this case, but how can he be certain? Will each of these twelve people, all meticulously chosen, perceive the evidence as he perceives it? Will they see the attempted subjugation of a young black woman, or will they see the seduction of a fatherly white custodian? Will they see the killing as a matter of self-preservation, or will they see it as murder?

". . . That she saw him loosen his grip on the ice pick," Hobgood reads, "and she grabbed for it as the ice pick fell to the floor and Alligood grabbed for the ice pick also. That she got the ice pick in her right hand and struck up at Alligood with it and he fell back on the bunk in a sitting position. That Alligood came up at her three or four times and she would strike him in the chest area. That Alligood finally grabbed her by her wrists and came up behind her and she exchanged the ice pick to her left hand. That she then struck him over her right shoulder on the side of his head and he turned her aloose [sic] and fell on the bunk and she saw blood on the right side of his face. That she immediately went to cell number two, took her blue jeans, blue pullover blouse and her pocketbook and as she went outside the control door she looked back and saw Alligood standing outside cell number one with a silly grin on his face."

More than an hour after he began, Hobgood is reaching the end of his charge to the jury. He has completed his review of the defense case and has gone on to explain the law, the elements of each offense, and the implications of Joan Little's plea of not guilty by reason of self-defense.

"Now, members of the jury," he says finally, "you may retire and select one of your members as a foreman, who may be either a man or a woman, to lead you in your deliberations. When you have reached a verdict, you may return to the courtroom to pronounce your verdict, which shall be one of the following three possible verdicts:

"One: Guilty of Second Degree Murder, or

"Two: Guilty of Voluntary Manslaughter, or

"Three: Not Guilty."

Then Hobgood lays down the last sheet of paper and folds his hands together. He smiles briefly toward the court reporter, who is sitting between him and the jury. "Let the record show that at this time the court excused the alternate jurors," he says in a coarse whisper, glancing up to allow his eyes to pass swiftly over the twelve people who will now decide the case. "All right—," he nods, "you may retire."

It is 10:33 a.m.

Shortly before noon the jurors—six blacks and six whites, seven women and five men—begin to emerge in single file from the conference room located directly behind the jury box. Their faces are tight, giving no clues to their verdict. They have been out for seventy-eight minutes, and have spent less than one hour in actual deliberation.

Quietly, at first unobtrusively, a number of uniformed officers have appeared and taken up positions at each exit and along the walls, ringing the spectators and newsmen on three sides as they bustle back to their seats. A few plainclothes state agents and several deputy sheriffs have also slipped in and are joining the other officers, and there are more than twenty-five armed lawmen in the courtroom. Judge Hobgood appears from chambers, marching toward the dais with his head thrust forward, and the bailiff shouts, "Court's in session, remain seated!"

Hobgood takes a while to settle himself and get organized, and then he peers into the back of the room, where the officers are standing at ragged parade rest, their eyes oscillating over the crowd. He frowns, and before turning to the jury he announces tersely that security has been tightened to prevent any breakdown in decorum. There will be no outburst, he says, no disturbance or demonstration of any kind. "If anyone out there feels that he or she can't control his or her emotions," he rattles, "the door is open and he or she may leave now." He pauses. No one moves.

There are fears of more than a boisterous reaction to the verdict, but Hobgood does not mention them in open court. The State Bureau of Investigation has received word from an informant that a trunkful of handguns has been smuggled into North Carolina and distributed to radicals for use if the jury votes to convict Joan Little. The informant has said that an assassination agenda has been drawn up, headed by the judge, the district attorney, and all of the jurors. He has also said, somewhat inexplicably, that Jerry Paul and Joan Little herself are on the list. The report is unconfirmed, but SBI agents have taken it seriously. William Griffin's bodyguard, Special Agent Dave Keller, has for several days carried a loaded pistol at all times, even in the evenings when accompanying the prosecutor to their motel pool for a swim.

Still no one has gotten up to leave the courtroom, and after a moment the trial is finally at its end. Juror number three, a lanky young man with pale skin and sunken cheeks, stands when the clerk asks if a foreman has been chosen. His face, like those of the other jurors, remains inscrutable. When the clerk asks if a verdict has been reached, he answers that it has. Then a faint smile crosses his lips, and he glances for the first time toward Joan Little and says, "We find the defendant not guilty."

. . .

Cases of champagne and ample supplies of party food had already been delivered to the defense headquarters at a downtown motel when the verdict was being announced, and by early afternoon a victory celebration is under way. Jerry Paul is not in attendance. Judge Hobgood has sentenced him to two weeks in jail for contempt of court because of remarks he made early in the trial. Some of the defense attorneys are at the courthouse now, arguing before another judge that Paul should be released pending a separate hearing on the contempt citation, while others are here with Joan Little, talking to reporters. She has told some of the newsmen that she would like to become a journalist herself, and that she will begin a series of speaking engagements during the coming weeks.

"I never liked being a symbol," she says to one reporter. "I always thought of myself as Joan Little."

William Griffin has hurried through the last of his administrative duties at the Wake County Courthouse and hopes to leave unobserved through a rear door, the same exit he has used throughout the trial. Always reluctant to deal with the press, Griffin has for weeks taken elaborate precautions to avoid contact with reporters. He has stayed at an out-of-town motel, keeping his location a secret for as long as possible, and he has rushed past newsmen and photographers outside the courthouse at each arrival and departure. Earlier today, while the jury was deliberating, he consented to his only press conference. Now, a few reporters overtake him before he can reach the elevator that will deliver him to his car in the garage in the courthouse basement. They ask their questions gently, as though they are speaking to someone who has just lost a friend.

"The case had to be tried," he tells one who has referred to assertions by the defense attorneys that Joan Little should never have been indicted.

They scribble in notebooks, and one asks what he might do differently if he had to try the case again.

"I have no regrets," he says sincerely, and receives skeptical glances.

"The integrity of the system was endangered by all the pre-trial publicity," he says to a third reporter as he steps into the waiting elevator. "The integrity of the system had to be preserved."

But has the "integrity of the system" been preserved, or only the appearance of integrity? In this unusual case the defense as well as the prosecution has assumed a burden of proof, and now the ultimate meaning of the verdict will depend as much or more on the clarity of the defense victory as on the certainty of the prosecution defeat. The district attorney has attempted unsuccessfully to knit threads of circumstance into a fabric of guilt. The defense attorneys have tried to infuse those circumstances with significance beyond the question of culpability. But have Joan Little's lawyers established that she was indeed innocent, that they were justified in contending she was on trial not because of evidence against her but because of her race and sex? Has this case changed the course of feminism and opened a window on prejudice and injustice? Or has the prosecution merely failed to prove that Joan Little was guilty? Has her trial left unanswered questions to spawn suspicion about the validity of the outcome? Have the jurors done anything more than choose between competing illusions?

PART II

MAY 1954
—
JUNE 1974

CHAPTER 2

SHE'S NO ANGEL

On May 17, 1954, the United States Supreme Court issued a decision titled *Brown* v. *Board of Education*, a landmark statement on the equality of citizenship that chipped flint over the kindling of a social revolution. The opinion consolidated appeals from lower courts in the states of Kansas, South Carolina, Virginia, and Delaware, all raising the same issue: "In each of these cases," wrote Chief Justice Earl Warren, "minors of the Negro race . . . seek the aid of the courts in obtaining admission to the public schools of their community on a nonsegregated basis." A simple proposition, but a profound question that raised doubts about the integrity of the existing order and sent a shudder through the whole country. In 1896 the Court had faced a similar issue and had ruled then that state laws establishing "equal but separate" public facilities were "reasonable regulations" and not unconstitutional. By 1954, however, there were different justices on the Court, men with a clearer vision of the Constitution, and the question was not whether black children could attend white schools but whether it was time to take the first step toward ending apartheid in the United States.

Joan Little was born in Washington, North Carolina, on May 8, 1954. Her mother was Jessie Ruth Little, a teenager, and her father was a laborer named Willis Williams. Nine days later the Supreme Court would acknowledge that the segregation of a people because of their race "generates a feeling of inferiority as to their status in the community that may affect their hearts and minds in a way unlikely ever to be undone." But it would be years before this message touched Joan Little directly, years before it would penetrate the staid and hidebound society of eastern North Carolina where she would grow up. Those historical attitudes necessary for the maintenance of a segregated social order had long since been adopted by people there, both black and white. The inferior status of blacks, no matter what the effect on their hearts and minds, had never seriously been challenged by either race, and would not soon be. When the challenge finally came, it would be accompanied by swift change, but in 1954 the social storm that would inevitably follow *Brown* v. *Board of Education* was only a squall on the distant horizon.

The town of Washington was already old and tired in 1954. Once it had been a busy upstream port for sailing traders from Europe and the West Indies, but now it slumbered and crumbled on the banks of the sluggish Pamlico River, a drowsy tobacco market, a county seat with a past but no future. Chartered before the Revolution, it claimed to be the first municipality named after George Washington, a dubious distinction contested by other towns in other states. Contingents of Washingtonians had twice fought and died for independence—once from King George and once from the United States Congress. Now the huffy matrons of Washington scrupulously traced their lineage in order to become Daughters of the American Revolution, and some of the young people—those who were white— were encouraged to join an organization called the Children of the Confederacy. During the Civil War the town had been occupied by Yankees for three years, then burned to the ground when they departed. Almost a century later the scars of the war were gone, but there was still a bronze monument—an infantryman standing lonely vigil over graves in the whites-only municipal cemetery—to recall the town's incineration and "Our Confederate Dead."

After the war Washington was rebuilt, a phoenix of shops and sheds strung along the waterfront and modest houses spreading back from the river along crude streets paved with broken oyster shells. Farther back from the river, in a jumbled collection of hutches and shanties, lived the blacks, now vested with all rights of citizenship but impoverished and isolated from power, freed but not really free. A breadbox courthouse with a tin roof, a steeple, and a big-faced clock painted with Roman numerals went up in the center of town, a place from which to run the business of Beaufort County. A few merchants and traders grew wealthy and built fine homes along the river and on Market Street, which ran from the river shore almost due north into the wilderness of woodlands and small farms surrounding the town. But not many prospered. Small industries were founded, only to fail, and the river bottom filled with silt, closing down the docks, closing down the area's only real link with the outside world. By 1900 the town had grown to a population of nearly ten thousand, but the river mouth had almost completely filled in and the strength of the state's economy had shifted to the more industrialized central and mountain regions to the west. Beaufort County was to remain what it had always been, a place of small farmers who raised vegetables, indigo, and tobacco. Washington stagnated, its period of expansion and vitality at an end, its racially segregated neighborhoods standing side by side, separate but unequal, two towns within one.

More than fifty years later, when the United States Supreme Court decided *Brown* v. *Board of Education* and when Joan Little was born, many blacks in Washington still lived in rough-hewn huts on dusty streets in an area referred to, even by blacks themselves, as "Niggertown." The rigid racial caste system that had supplanted slavery was not yet beginning to break down. Locked in by law and circumstances, blacks seldom openly defied this new but no less immutable discrimination, though it victimized them from birth until death. Like the divided neighborhoods where they still lived, the people of Washington existed side by side, separate but unequal. Their community was still a place where "niggers" and "white folks" watched each other across chasms of misunderstanding and mistrust, a place where the races were likely to be mixed only in hospitals and in the telephone directory.

In some ways the town and the county would change in the wake of *Brown* v. *Board of Education,* but such changes would begin to occur only ten years later, after specific civil-rights legislation forced both blacks and whites to accept compulsory desegregation. A pendulum was swinging in the country during the decade when Martin Luther King led his people first to the front of the bus and then to the forefront of political and social influence, but Washington and towns like it were near the top of the pendulum's arc, on the fringes of the liberation movement. The revolution would come too late for Joan Little, who would grow up a black child of the Old South, accustomed to the inferior status traditionally accorded those of her race and willing to accept it until tragedy and fate twisted her life and propelled it in unforeseen directions.

During these early years, Joan Little's family grew. Her mother had four more children by Willis Williams before she married Arthur Williams, who worked as a lumberman, and then four more by Arthur Williams. The youngest was nine when Joan turned twenty years of age. Sometime before, her father, Willis, had moved away from Beaufort County, eventually to find work as a security guard and settle in Brooklyn, New York. His departure had seemed to sadden Joan and may have contributed to the bitter feelings she would later express for her stepfather. Arthur Williams mistreated his family while she was growing up, she would say, and spent his money on liquor and good times. Their relationship was strained from the beginning, and later she would look back and recall that she had soon begun to hate the man her mother married.

As an adolescent, Joan Little drifted away from close ties with her mother, a woman whose spiritual needs often took her to "root doctors" and mystics for consultation. Jessie Williams was away much of the time, working as a domestic or in a local shirt factory. She often left her nine children in the care of their maternal grandmother, a woman Joan became very fond of. Jessie Williams tried to impose strict discipline on her household. More than once she ordered Joan to remain at home after school to take care of the other children. Much later, Joan would recall many evenings when she would crouch in a hallway, waiting for an opportunity to sneak out of the house. The often absent mother did not really get to know the daughter who was growing up fast and hard in the streets. By the age of fourteen, Joan had become a habitual truant. At sixteen, she simply left home and began living with a friend. At twenty, when she was charged with murder, she and her mother had already been strangers for years.

In the two decades between Joan Little's birth and Clarence Alligood's death, the place where they both lived underwent a mild but profound transformation. The superficial changes were most noticeable. There were no longer WHITE and COLORED signs in waiting rooms or above the public water fountains. There were some black clerks in the stores, some black tellers in the banks. Blacks and whites ate together in most restaurants, although some establishments still found ways to make black customers feel uncomfortable and unwanted. There were black policemen and there was a black deputy sheriff, a young officer who had been instructed for his own protection not to go into certain areas of the county where racial animosity still ran high. The schools had been desegregated, reluctantly but peacefully. Both blacks and whites had opposed desegregation, for similar reasons. Whites feared the social and economic leveling that would surely follow, feared the emergence of the black man as a competitor. Blacks were concerned about the loss of their homogeneity, their sense of community and of oneness with each other. A few years later, people of both races would be saying that desegregation had been neither as disruptive as had been feared nor as beneficial as had been hoped.

Desegregation brought fundamental and potentially far-reaching changes, however. Washington was still a small and out-of-the-way town, still flush with false snobbery and petty parochialism, but subtle forces had begun to dislodge long-held perceptions about color and caste. Attitudes were beginning to grind and shift, like sodden logs in a jam that would soon break up. Civil-rights laws, school integration, and the desegregation of public facilities had not eradicated racism in Beaufort County—and would not do so, there or elsewhere—but such legal, educational, and social innovations did begin to stir a reassessment of racial attitudes by both blacks and whites. Political perceptions began to adjust to new realities—a black man sat on the city council and would soon receive more votes from black and white constituents than any other candidate in a city-wide election. Economic conditions had improved—although still relatively poor, the county had recruited new industries, bringing in more jobs for blacks and whites and along with them the influence of managers and administrators from other parts of the country, the first infusion of fresh middle-class values since colonial times in a county long polarized between the very well-off and the very poor. Better jobs and the prospects for a decent future had begun to reverse trends that long had drained away the county's chief resource: The out-migration of youths— black and white—had slowed and would continue to decline each year. "Our young people used to feel they had to get out to make a living," a black social worker would say. "Now they're beginning to want to stay here and go to work."

But still there were those who wanted to get out, and Joan Little was one of them. In November 1968 her mother had asked a Beaufort County judge to send her to Dobb's Farm, a juvenile training school about an hour's drive from Washington. Jessie Williams had gone to the authorities after Joan refused to live at home, and then had asked to have her incarcerated when she failed to heed the judge's first order to move back under her mother's supervision. After only a month at Dobb's Farm, Joan told a faculty member she was going out to collect pine cones for a Christmas display and walked off the minimum-security campus and fled to the home of a cousin in New Jersey.

It was her first escape, but it would not be her last.

"It all started in 1973," Joan Little would later say. "It just seemed like a year of bad luck." Bad luck and hard times. During 1973 and 1974 she was picked up by police in three cities and charged with a variety of felonies. By the middle of 1974 she was a convicted felon, and by late summer, an accused murderer.

Joan Little lived in New Jersey until 1970 and refused to return until her mother promised not to have her sent back to Dobb's Farm. During the summer of 1970 she worked in tobacco and again tried living at home, but the situation there was no better. She began to drift in and out of Beaufort County, living for a while with relatives in Philadelphia, then wandering from North Carolina to New York, then back to Philadelphia, then to New Jersey, then "just around." To support herself she took jobs as a factory worker and a field hand. She attended school off and on in Newark and Philadelphia, where she was enrolled in the twelfth grade after telling officials at Simon Gratz High School that her scholastic records from North Carolina "had got burned up in a fire." But she never earned a high-school diploma. She left Simon Gratz before the end of the year and lost interest in completing her education when school officials in Beaufort County assigned her to the tenth grade because she had no academic credits to transfer from New Jersey or Pennsylvania.

She was almost eighteen when she came back to Washington and got a job as a café waitress. By then she was beyond the reach of her mother and the authorities, and she had no fear of being sent back to Dobb's Farm. She rented a small house and soon took a better job at a garment factory. Before long, she was spending time in the taverns and pool halls of a bawdy section of town called "Dodge City," the intersection of Fourth and Gladden streets, the highest crime area in Washington. It was there that she met Julius Rodgers at a poolroom called the Pic-Wic. A muscular man with a deep voice and wary, sallow eyes, Rodgers was fifteen years older than Joan Little. Within a few weeks she had quit her job and they were living together. He worked by day as an interior contractor, and at night he ran a small club of his own in "Dodge City." It was a place where "you could go in and buy beer, and we sold some liquor and it had psychedelic lights," she would recall. It was also a place that became known as a haven for whores, and it was there that her name was first linked with prostitution.

While still a teenager, Joan Little acquired a reputation that blended delinquency with promiscuity, a reputation that would be of some concern to her defense attorneys when she went on trial for murder. "She's no angel," one of them would say, and another would predict that the prosecutor "will try to show her to be a sex maniac with horns." Sexually experienced at an early age, she was treated for syphilis by county health officials when she was fifteen and again when she was seventeen. The county health department began supplying her with birth-control pills when she was sixteen and with a birth-control device some time later. Although she was never arrested on a morals charge of any sort, local police suspected that she was involved in a prostitution ring operating near the Camp Lejeune marine base in Jacksonville, North Carolina, about an hour's drive from Washington. Blacks in Beaufort County said she was reputed to have been engaged in prostitution there as well. Joan Little persistently denied these accusations, saying she had never been "on the stroll," but she could not deny having lived with Julius Rodgers and having helped to operate his night club. There was no defense for guilt by association. She was there almost every night, and her name became inextricably linked with an establishment known widely in the black community as a place to find women who would sell themselves for pleasure.

Early in 1973, she began to get into serious trouble with the law. Police in Jacksonville stopped a car for making an illegal turn and found a sawed-off shotgun under the front seat. Joan Little, the driver, was charged with possession of a dangerous weapon, but the charge was dropped when she was arrested on other charges in Beaufort County. Later she would deny having known the gun was there.

In Greenville, a college town about twenty miles from Washington in neighboring Pitt County, she was arrested during the spring and charged with shoplifting. She spent several nights in jail before appearing in court to plead guilty and receive a six-month suspended sentence and a fine. She would insist later, however, that she had not tried to steal anything: "You see, it was like this. I was with the people, and I knew what they was going in there for, and like when you with somebody and they in the act of it, and you know they in the act of it, you just as guilty as they are."

In November, Washington police arrested her on larceny charges after a woman from Pitt County accused her of stealing some clothing. The case was never tried because the woman who filed the complaint did not show up to testify. Joan Little explained that the clothes had been left in the back seat of the car she was driving, and that she had forgotten about them when she left Greenville to return home.

Some time thereafter she was arrested again in Washington and accused of shoplifting, but this case was dismissed when the investigating officer testified he had never actually seen her with any stolen merchandise. "They never saw me with a shopping bag," she would later say, "because I knew a lot of girls that were working in that shopping center and I talked to them that night. I walked around and talked with them, and even helped them straighten up some things in the store, you know. . . . And when it came down, they said, well, did you catch Joan Little with anything, you know? Did you see Joan Little pick up anything? And it all boiled down to who had the merchandise. And so they didn't have no other charges, and they *nol-prossed* it."

The shoplifting case was dismissed on January 10, 1974, and by then Joan Little had been living with Julius Rodgers in a small apartment near his club for many months. The house she had rented was being occupied by her nineteen-year-old brother, Jerome, and his girlfriend, Melinda, who was about fourteen. Rodgers was working on an apartment project in Greenville, and he had employed Joan there as an apprentice sheet-rock finisher. "That way," she said, "we didn't have to pay no taxes on what he paid me."

January 14, the following Monday, was clear and cold. In Sawyer's Trailer Park, near Washington, a black woman named Mary Brooks heard a dog bark around noon and went to her window to investigate the noise. She was expecting a delivery of kerosene fuel oil, but instead of a truck she saw three people standing outside her neighbor's house trailer. There were "two girls and a man," she would testify later. She did not recognize any of them, but she would recall that "one girl had on a short black-and-white fur, fuzzy-looking coat" and that "one had on a wide hat."

Three break-ins were reported to the Beaufort County Sheriff's Department later that day, all at the residences of black people. A rifle, a small chest, and a television set were missing from one home. Clothing, kitchen appliances, a television set, and a piggy bank full of change were gone from another. Food, clothing, jewelry, a vacuum cleaner, and a phonograph had disappeared from the third, a house trailer belonging to Roland Rhodes, who was a neighbor of Mary Brooks. Rhodes was in luck. Mary Brooks had seen strangers outside his trailer and was able to give him a description. He guessed at once who had been there. He had known Joan Little "quite a while," he would testify, and he had often seen her wearing a "little white fur coat."

By 7:30 that evening, sheriff's deputies had found some of the stolen items in the back seat of a car being driven by Jerome Little, and later that night Joan and Jerome showed the officers where some of the other stolen property had been dumped in a junkyard. Both of them were arrested and released immediately on bail. According to the com-

plaint prepared by a deputy sheriff, Joan Little "did unlaw-
fully, wilfully, and feloniously steal, take and carry away 2
televisions 1 30/30 rifle 6 pairs of shoes 1 stero [sic] copects
[sic] set men and women wearing aperal [sic] cook ware 1
vacum [sic] cleaner 1 automatic mixer and other House
Hold Goods the personal property of Mr. & Mrs. Ronnie
Johnson Roland Rhodes Pat Mills and James Keys Rt 5
River Road and Chocowinity NC breaking and entering
the premises were used as dwellings." In all, she and
Jerome were charged with breaking into three homes and
stealing property valued at more than $1,300. Jerome's girl-
friend, Melinda, was not charged.

In 1974 Joan Little became a hunted fugitive for the first
time. She failed to appear for her trial in March and eluded
the sheriff and the bail bondsman in April when they tried
to apprehend her in Chapel Hill, where she and Rodgers
had found work and were both earning more than $200 a
week. She said later that she did not realize she was due in
court in the spring, but testified at her murder trial that she
wanted to stay out of Beaufort County because authorities
there were pressuring her to give information about criminal activities and "asking a lot of questions about Julius." In
June, however, she gave up. Accompanied by Rodgers and
several friends from Chapel Hill, she surrendered to a
bondsman at a shopping center in Washington and was
placed in the Beaufort County jail. The next day she and
Jerome Little went on trial.

Both of them were charged with larceny and with breaking and entering, and Jerome was charged in addition with
receiving stolen property. The prosecution's case against
him was formidable, since the deputies had found some of
the missing property in his possession, but against Joan the
evidence was less concrete. Halfway through the morning,
when it looked as though Jerome might be convicted on
the more serious larceny charge unless he spoke up, he
changed his plea to guilty of receiving stolen goods and
agreed to testify against his sister.

"What did you do after that?" the prosecutor, a young

assistant district attorney, asked after establishing that
Jerome had talked to Roland Rhodes on the night of the
break-ins.

"I told him what had happened."

"What did you tell him had happened?"

"I told him that it was Joan that went out and took his
stuff."

"You told him that?" Joan's attorney, LeRoy Scott, interrupted.

"Her and Julius," Jerome mumbled.

"Huh?"

"Her and Julius—and how they had planned it out."

In the afternoon Joan Little came to the witness stand
wearing a pants suit and a wig of straight, short hair. In her
hands she clutched a book, holding it so that the jurors
could see the words HOLY BIBLE emblazoned across the
cover. She denied everything.

"Now, on the fourteenth of January, did you go out to any
trailers?"

"No, sir, I did not."

"How about to a trailer park?"

"No, sir, I did not."

"Did you, particularly, did you go in Mrs. Rhodes's trailer
—Mr. Rhodes's trailer?"

"No, sir."

"Did you go in any other trailer?"

"No, sir."

"Did you take any objects of clothing or a television?"

"No, sir."

"Or a rifle out of any one of those trailers?"

"No, sir."

After deliberating thirty minutes, the jury of nine
women and three men acquitted Jerome of the larceny
charges and found Joan Little guilty on three separate
counts of breaking and entering and larceny. And almost
at once an odd thing occurred. Jerome's attorney informed
the judge that Joan had confessed to him while the jury was
out, naming the people who were involved in the break-ins

and the people who were not. "It hadn't been half an hour ago," the lawyer told the incredulous judge, "that she said she sent them down there and she went further than that and said that Rodgers didn't have anything to do with it. That was her motivation."

For a moment the judge seemed indecisive. Following Jerome's testimony he had issued a bench warrant to have Julius Rodgers taken into custody. Now Joan Little was saying that Rodgers had had nothing to do with the break-ins.

"I'd like to clear this up," LeRoy Scott prodded.

"All right, let her come around to the witness stand," the judge said finally. "Remember you are still under oath, young lady."

This time her testimony was different. "I asked Rodgers could I have the keys to the car and he said yes. So Melinda, Jerome, and I went out to Mr. Roland Rhodes's house and knocked on the door and he wasn't there. So, we left from there and then we went over to the next trailer. That door was locked. Mr. Roland Rhodes's door wasn't locked. So, I was the one standing at the front door. The car was parked round in back and we went in and we went over to the house and I called Pat's name and Pat didn't come to the front door, so at that time I told Melinda I was going out to the car to see if there was anybody looking, so I went out to the car.

"So, I opened up the door and Melinda was passing out the stuff and . . . that's when the dog started barking when we first came up, so that's where the lady heard the dog barking at when we first came up. So, we took the stuff out of Roland Rhodes's trailer, it wasn't . . . all I can remember it was the razor and it was, I think it was that vacuum cleaner right there and Melinda picked up Pat's coat, it was a tweed middy coat and said, 'Joan, can I have this?' And I said, 'I don't care what you have.' So, she picked up that and took it to the car. So we left and that was all . . . but there was no component set in that house. If there was one in there somebody must have went in before we got there because there wasn't none in there.

"We left from there and we went next door. That door was locked, so we went around to the side of the building and Melinda found a stick and stuck it up under the window and so I picked Melinda up and let Melinda get through the window and she came to the back door and opened up the back door and that's where the three of us went in. We checked the refrigerator, and they didn't have nothing much in there, so Melinda was in the kitchen and that's how all the popcorn and everything got all over the floor in there and everything when Melinda checked the kitchen. The food or nothing did not come from Roland's, it came from the other man's trailer, Johnson's trailer, that's where it came from. I was in the bedroom, Melinda was in the kitchen and . . ."

She went on, explaining how the stolen property had been hidden in one location, then moved to another, and finally scattered in a field to get rid of it before the deputies could find them. Julius Rodgers had known nothing about the break-ins, she said, until after the warrant for her arrest had been issued. "I went back to the place," she testified, "and that's when I told Rodgers what really happened."

Then Joan Little stepped down. Having confirmed the jury's judgment about her own guilt, she had implicated her brother in the break-ins and had indicated that both of them might have committed perjury. More importantly, she had absolved Julius Rodgers of any complicity in the crimes. Her mother, who came to the stand voluntarily to plead for leniency for her daughter, told the judge that Rodgers was "the whole problem to all of us."

"Do you think your daughter is trying to get Julius out of it by what she said—trying to take the blame for herself and take it off Julius?" the solicitor asked.

"I think she's really trying to take all of it herself."

"Trying to keep Julius from being implicated?"

"Right . . ."

Why had Joan Little changed her testimony so abruptly? It would often be reported in connection with the jailer's death that she had confessed at this earlier trial in order to get a lighter sentence, an explanation which under the circumstances might have suggested that she was less interested in disclosing the truth than in currying favor with the judge. But nothing in the trial record supported such an interpretation. She had told Jerome's attorney that her "motivation" was to confirm "that Rodgers didn't have anything to do with it," and her mother had insisted from the witness stand that her daughter was "trying to take the blame . . . off Julius." Joan Little's only intention, it seemed, was to exculpate Julius Rodgers, a potentially important bit of circumstantial evidence that was never disclosed at the murder trial. In Raleigh the defense attorneys won its exclusion by arguing that Joan Little's change of testimony under oath could not be introduced as secondary evidence of bad character, a procedural victory that had little to do with what she had actually said at the trial in Washington nearly one year earlier. The prosecution attorneys, already lean on substantiation for their theory that Joan Little killed Clarence Alligood because she longed for Julius Rodgers, did not even suggest to the judge that the testimony itself might be substantive evidence of motive.

In any event the confession, which undercut the judge's intention to have Julius Rodgers charged in connection with the break-ins, did not seem to help Joan Little. She was sentenced on the spot to a prison term of seven to ten years and to five years of probation following her release. During that period, the judgment order would state, she was not to "associate with, be in the company of, have any dealings with or communicate with Julius Rodgers unless she [was] legally and lawfully married to him" and she was not to be "seen in the vicinity of 4th and Gladden streets, Washington, North Carolina." She would be eligible for parole within two years, but even then she was to be banished from "Dodge City."

As soon as the sentence was announced, an elderly bailiff stepped forward. The defense lawyers began to gather their books and papers at once, and the young prosecutor opened a new file and prepared to call his next case. William Griffin, who was in the courthouse to take care of administrative matters, had observed the last few minutes of the trial from the doorway of an anteroom. Now he watched as the prisoner was escorted to an elevator that would take her down three floors to the ground level of the courthouse, to the cellblock she would occupy in the women's section of the Beaufort County jail. It did not occur to him that he would ever see Joan Little again.

PART III

JUNE 1974
—
AUGUST 1974

CHAPTER 3

PRAY TO GOD
I'LL BE OUT VERY SOON

By the mid-1970s, community leaders in Washington were proud people. Their town had once risen from the ashes of war, and now it was beginning to rise from the sludge of economic stagnation. Experts had been brought in to study the area's problems, and government and private agencies had set to work with federal, state, and local money to implement ambitious programs for improvement. Between 1964 and 1974, much had been accomplished. Urban renewal had removed some of the blight and decay. Slums had been toppled and the business district had been refurbished. Much of the effort had gone into the "West End Neighborhood," where two thirds of the town's black people lived. Gradually the borders of "Niggertown" were shrinking. The old shack where Joan Little had grown up was gone, and her family now lived in a neat brick house in Chocowinity, a hamlet just outside town. "Dodge City" still stood at the geographical heart of the neighborhood, but it too was marked for destruction.

As part of the rejuvenation, a new courthouse and jail had replaced the antiquated facilities the city and county had been using jointly for more than a hundred years. Even in 1974 many jails in North Carolina were wretched places —cramped, hot, unsanitary, unsafe. But the jail in Beaufort County had been built just three years before Joan Little was sent there following her conviction. Unlike most other lockups in the area, it was modern, reasonably comfortable, and well maintained. Located on the ground level of the new courthouse, it was clean, well lighted, relatively spacious, and air-conditioned. The corridor walls were cinder block, painted pastel green. Overhead were paperboard acoustical panels, a false ceiling above which all the electrical wires, steam pipes, and air-conditioning ducts were hidden. The floor was terrazzo, a speckled tile.

The Beaufort County jail had entirely separate facilities for men and women. The women's section, a large room containing an enclosed cellblock with two individual cells inside, was secured by a heavy metal door which could be opened with a key carried by the jailer. Access to the cellblock, however, was controlled by an automatic door, operated from a switchbox on a nearby wall. The door had to be closed manually, and a spring-pressured bolt was thrown forward to engage the lock whenever it was pushed completely shut. The smaller of the two women's cells, cell number one, was situated just inside this doorway and had a single bunk attached to the left wall and a stainless-steel toilet and sink at the rear. It was about five feet wide and seven feet deep. The bunk was only twenty-seven inches across. It was here that Clarence Alligood's body would be found.

The new jail had been equipped with all the latest security gadgets, even an intercom system (that seldom worked) between the cells and the jailer's office and an array of television monitors covering both the men's and women's cellblocks as well as all corridors. On a wall inside the women's section, mounted between windows of frosted glass that let in refracted sunlight, there was a small television camera angled to project a continuous image of a portion of the cellblock interior. In theory this system made it unnecessary for a custodian to enter the area to observe the activities of the inmates, yet it kept them under continual scrutiny. But the camera in the women's section had never been put into regular use because, the head jailer would testify, all the jailers were men. During the summer of 1974, while Joan Little was still a prisoner, it was removed to replace a faulty unit somewhere else in the jail.

The television monitor screens, sixteen in all, were arrayed on a wall inside the jailer's small office, which was located about thirty feet from the entrance to the women's section. The office stood directly in front of the main jail door, a heavy metal barrier with an eye-level glass window which was usually covered by a piece of cardboard. Inside the office there were several chairs, a big clock advertising Dr. Pepper soft drinks, a bulletin board where notices were neatly tacked up, a telephone on the "booking counter" beside a police radio with a platform microphone, and a new three-drawer metal desk. Inside the middle drawer, there was an ice pick.

Beaufort County employed four jailers, all white, all male, all over forty years old. These men had virtual autonomy over what went on behind the main jail door. The county sheriff had been hospitalized for some time, and the acting sheriff, Chief Deputy Ottis "Red" Davis, had decided that he would "just stay out of there and let the jailers run it as they saw fit." They were paid $6,600 a year and worked in three eight-hour shifts with one man rotating through the cycle while the others took their days off. In July, however, the regular night jailer became seriously ill, and the swing man replaced him. Thereafter the three jailers worked the same shifts every day, seven days a week.

The night shift routinely began at 10:00 p.m. and ended at 6:00 a.m. The jailer who assumed this duty in July was a sixty-two-year-old farmer and lifetime resident of Beaufort County who had been a truck driver before joining the jail staff early in 1973. White-haired and stocky, he was about six feet tall and weighed around 185 pounds. He was in good health and looked fit. He had been married forty-four years, had six children, and was a great-grandfather. He lived quietly with his wife, who had been ill for some time, on their farm outside Washington. He was a member of the Beaver Dam Church of Christ, which was located near his home, and he belonged to the men's club in the church. He had friends in Washington, but he was not widely known in the community. After his death there would be mixed recollections of him. Some people would say he was an upstanding citizen and a good family man. Others would report that he was bitterly prejudiced against blacks, that he was a ladies' man, and that he often spoke of "going out to get some. . . ." His name was Clarence Alligood.

The jail was informally run and orderly. Conditions could have been better—there were complaints about a scarcity of sheets and towels, and about the food—but they also might have been much worse. Prisoners were not generally confined in individual cells, and visitors came and went all during the day. Candy, cigarettes, and soft drinks were available, and male and female inmates were permitted to pass books, magazines, and personal notes back and forth. Jailers and prisoners usually got along well, and it was customary for them to call each other by first names.

But time inside the Beaufort County jail was still close arrest. There were no exercise facilities, and except for the trusties, who were permitted some freedom to assist the jailers and perform housekeeping chores, prisoners never left their cellblocks except to go upstairs to the courtroom. Even the modest comfort could quickly become tedious. In the summer of 1974 there were two attempted escapes, and later in the year three prisoners overpowered a night jailer and broke out. Ordinarily the situation was not tense, but the potential for violence was always present.

Joan Little was confined in the Beaufort County jail for twelve weeks, longer than most prisoners were held in county lockups and longer than she had thought it would take for her to get out. Immediately after her conviction she had sent word to the clerk of court asking to remain in Washington while she tried to arrange for release on bail pending appeal. Her request had been granted, although county officials would have preferred, for reasons of security and economy, to have her transferred immediately to the state prison for women in Raleigh. But LeRoy Scott had then refused to represent her any longer unless she paid him a retainer of $1,000, and the ten-day deadline for filing notice of appeal, a necessary step if she was to obtain release on bail, passed without any action being taken. Julius Rodgers had disappeared, and Joan Little could not raise the money alone.

Scott seemed to have little interest in handling the case further, but at the end of the ten-day filing period he wrote to District Attorney William Griffin anyway, saying that "just as a matter of precaution" he had prepared a notice of appeal and asking Griffin to accept it even though he was no longer required to under the state's rules of court procedure. Griffin did not see the letter until a week later, at which time he decided to waive his objection after talking to the clerk of court in Beaufort County. Scott's request was forwarded directly to the trial judge, and on June 29, two weeks past the statutory deadline, Judge Robert Martin signed an exceptional order allowing the defense sixty days to prepare an appeal and setting bond pending appeal at $15,000.* Because of the timing of the jailer's death the ten-day statutory deadline and Judge Martin's unusual order might have become important links in the chain of

---

*Scott never "perfected" the appeal by filing the appropriate motions, however, and it was routinely dismissed in October 1974 by Superior Court Judge Joshua James. An evidentiary hearing in December before the same judge revealed that Jerry Paul had filed a motion for an extension by mail just prior to the dismissal and resulted in a finding that "the order dismissing the appeal was improvidently entered and that in the interest of justice it should be rescinded." Judge James also made the following findings of fact regarding the circumstances of the original trial:

> LeRoy Scott, attorney, had been employed by one Julius Rogers [sic] to represent the defendant at the trial and paid Mr. Scott $100.00 on behalf of the defendant, although Mr. Scott was not the defendant's choice of attorneys and she did not know that he would represent her until the trial was called; nor was Mr. Scott employed by the said Julius Rogers until very shortly before trial commenced, at which time Mr. Scott was not fully informed by Rogers of the exact nature of the charges against the defendant.

circumstantial evidence against Joan Little, but both were simply overlooked during the investigation and neither was specifically mentioned to the jury at the murder trial. At least one of the prosecutors was not even aware of the terms of the order, an oversight the district attorney would later be unable to explain.

Joan Little spent the whole summer of 1974 languishing in the women's section of the jail, sleeping during the day and doodling in crossword-puzzle books while she listened to a portable radio at night. She had few visitors except her mother, who fretted helplessly about the future of her errant and uncontrollable daughter. The jailers would remember Joan as a quiet and cooperative prisoner. They had no complaints about her conduct, and until much later she would have no complaints about theirs. After more than two months she had written to a friend in Chapel Hill saying she was comfortable and being treated well: "I have everything I need for right now. My mother brings me some of my clothes plus I had packed a small suitcase. The jailers are very nice to me so I am feeling a lot better now." Further on, she mentioned that she wanted to contact Julius Rodgers and referred again to the jailers: "When I wrote to him the last time I told him he could call me anytime after 10:00 p.m. The jailer would let me talk to him. They all are very nice." She would insist at the murder trial, however, that she had been abused while she was in jail and that she had first been accosted by Clarence Alligood more than a month before this letter was written.

In June, she began to keep a haphazard diary in the crossword-puzzle books and paperback novels she was accumulating. She frequently jotted notations on the covers or in the margins, recording incidents and emotions that seemed important, making notes that said nothing about abuse or uncomfortable circumstances but did indicate that she was on good terms with all the custodians except Ellis Tetterton, the sixty-four-year-old head jailer, who was never mentioned. She knew Tetterton least of all, perhaps because she was often asleep when he was on duty. He paid less attention to her than the others, and she was not fond of him. At the trial she would testify with bitterness in her voice that he had never announced himself before coming into the women's section. He would say that the only reason he ever went into the area without a female deputy preceding him was to serve meals.

She seemed to think more of David Watson, forty-eight, the evening jailer, whose duty extended beyond the departure of the daytime staff at the sheriff's office. In one entry in a puzzle book she referred to him as a "crazy, funloving guy," and at the trial she would testify that he had always banged on the door or called out before entering the women's section and that he had occasionally permitted her to make telephone calls. He would testify that he had refused to let her make calls, and in fact she had written in the margin of one of her books: "David won't let me make a phone-call to you, Baby. . . ."

It was the night jailers who were mentioned most frequently, those on duty from 10:00 p.m. until 6:00 a.m. She seemed to get along with Robert Flemming, the regular jailer who was taken ill halfway through the summer. In one place she recorded that he had given her the name of a bondsman, and in another she wrote: "Robert came back here to get some cups, nice guy. . . ." Flemming was also the only jailer mentioned in an entry that had sexual connotations: "Tonight Robert brought me a banana, said I would need it before I got out of here (smile) He [sic] been pretty nice since I've been in here."

The name of the other night jailer, Clarence Alligood, came up most often of all. He was referred to in five different entries, four of which were dated, none of which suggested provocative behavior. Contrary to the testimony Joan Little would give at the trial, her notes depicted Alligood as a passive man who would occasionally visit her in the women's section, who would often permit her to make telephone calls, and who would sometimes share a sandwich with her out of the bag he received each night from a twenty-four-hour hamburger stand called the Chuckwagon: "Mr. Alligood brought me a sandwich (H.L.T.) Had a headache so he included aspirins. 3:30 a.m. Wed. morning listening to music." . . . "Mr. Alligood just received his 3:30 snack. So far this week I received one ea. night. Thank God for that."

Random and apparently inconsequential entries such as these were the only written record of what might have been going on in the Beaufort County jail during the summer of 1974. At her trial Joan Little would paradoxically insist that she had noted everything of significance. "I wrote down close to everything that happened," she testified at one point, and later she told the court, "Well, whatever happened during those times I always wrote it down."

On cross-examination, William Griffin would ask about a note dated August 4, 1974, which said: "Mr. All. came back here talked Odds & Ends for about 20 min. I'm going home soon." Had she been referring to Clarence Alligood, Griffin wanted to know, and had he "made any advances on you on that occasion?"

"If he had done that," she would answer after objections from the defense attorneys had been overruled, "I would have put that in the book also."

But much of what Joan Little claimed had happened during that summer was not to be found "in the book," and her testimony regarding Clarence Alligood would conflict with the record she had made of his activities and habits while she was in jail. Did he come to the women's section infrequently, as her notes suggested, or had he spent a great deal of time there, as she testified? Were his sandwiches and his permission to use the telephone kind gestures, as she seemed to believe at the time, or were they favors for which he would want something in return? Did she appreciate the snacks he brought her, as an entry in one of her books indicated, or did she resent them, as she would testify at the trial? "Did you like him bringing sandwiches back there to you?" "No, most of the time I just took them and I would put them in the cell because he had told me on numerous occasions that he didn't want to let the other jailers see the bag or the sandwiches because it would get him in trouble."

Perhaps the most puzzling thing about these notes was the absence of any reference to an incident she insisted had occurred just "two or three weeks" following her confinement. On a night late in June (and, she said, only on that night prior to August 27) Clarence Alligood had gone to the control box inside the women's section, unlocked the mechanical door, and entered the cellblock.

"When Mr. Alligood came back in at that time, did he say anything to you?" Jerry Paul asked.

"He was talking about how nice I looked in my gown," she replied, "and that he wanted me to have, you know, sex with him."

"What did you say? . . . What did you say to him?"

"I told him to leave and that if he didn't that I was gonna tell Mr. Ellis when he came on."

No mention of this incident could be found in Joan Little's notes or in the other evidence offered by either the defense or the prosecution, but when the district attorney pressed for an explanation, she testified that she had made a notation of it in one of the three paperback novels she had while she was in jail.

"What was the novel?" Griffin asked.

"I think it was *Ben Hur,* I think."

"*Ben Hur*—and you said there is a notation to that effect in that particular novel?"

"I did not say that it was in that particular novel. I said it was in one of my books, which I haven't seen either of those books."

The novel, an abridged version, was then produced in court, but no reference to the incident could be found. The defense attorneys pointed out that at least seventy-two pages were missing from the battered book, and suggested that they had been purposely misplaced to prevent verification of the defendant's testimony. The mystery remained unsolved. Where were these pages? What, if anything, had Joan Little written on them? How and why had they been lost?

None of these questions was answered, nor was the peculiar incident in June satisfactorily explained. It had ended abruptly, Joan Little would testify. The door buzzer sounded, indicating that someone wanted access to the jail, and Alligood rushed out so hurriedly that he forgot to push the mechanical door shut even though he did stop to lock the outer door with his key. But why had she failed to mention Alligood's behavior to Ellis Tetterton as she had threatened, or to David Watson, who testified about finding the cellblock door unlocked some time after she said this incident had happened? "You had the evidence right there to show them, didn't you?" Griffin asked, referring not only to the open door but to the sandwich bags as well.

"Mr. Griffin," she replied firmly, "sometimes you have evidence and you tell people the truth, but then they twist it in a way that makes it seem that you're not telling the truth, and in Washington, North Carolina, coming up as a black woman it's different in saying what you did and having your word to go against a white person's. It is not acceptable." The answer was not precisely responsive, but it did serve as an effective distraction. William Griffin failed to point out, then and later on summation, that she had already said Alligood himself told her "on numerous occasions that he didn't want to let the other jailers see the bag or the sandwiches because it would get him in trouble."

On July 5, Julius Rodgers unexpectedly resumed contact, first with Jessie Williams and later with Joan Little herself. "Jessie R. said you called today," she wrote in a puzzle book. "I was to know she could reach you. Was getting worried. Feel a lot better now. Still have you as I always did. Pray to God I see you soon." Then, that afternoon, she got a telephone call from Chapel Hill, and Rodgers was on the other end of the line.

The call came from the office of Roger Bernholz, a young Chapel Hill attorney who practiced in an influential law firm that represented a number of black clients. After speaking to Jessie Williams that morning, Julius Rodgers had walked in off the street and asked to see any lawyer who was available. Referred to Bernholz, the firm's junior man, Rodgers was unable to explain exactly why he had come. Bernholz got the impression that he wanted to arrange representation for Joan Little, presumably on terms more favorable than those demanded by LeRoy Scott. Rodgers told Bernholz that Joan Little was being "railroaded" into jail, that she was innocent, and that her confession was untrue. She had testified against herself, he said, only to help her brother.

Bernholz had no transcript of the trial and no way to check what Rodgers was telling him, but he listened sympathetically and soon began to suspect that Joan Little was being mistreated by the authorities in Beaufort County. He had never practiced law in eastern North Carolina, but he was prepared to assume that there might be a frontier disregard for civil liberties in the area. While Rodgers was still in his office, Bernholz decided to call the Beaufort County jail and speak directly to the young woman he was being asked to represent. He did so mainly because he "just wanted to let Julius talk to her," but he also hoped to find out about her local attorney. He was concerned about the ethics of invading another lawyer's case if he decided to take on the appeal.

"Rodgers called today," Joan Little wrote later on July 5. "Said every. Fine. Don't worry Still Loves me. Doing everything he can to get me out. Keep writing same place. Lawyer says it is a possibility I can get out if it be the Lord's will." At the time she seemed more buoyed by the reappearance of Julius Rodgers than by the intervention of Roger Bernholz, but at the trial she would emphasize her conversation with Bernholz and testify that he had said he could arrange for her release from jail. She had realized even then, however, that his interest would not solve the problem foremost in her mind—raising money to make bond. ". . . Still trying to figure out how to get out of here," she wrote at the bottom of the same page. "Robert [Flemming] says give Wilson bondsman a call to check him out. Good Luck!"

Actually, she had no reason to be encouraged by anything Bernholz had said, but the jury would never find that out. After consulting with several of the senior members of his firm, he told Rodgers that he could represent Joan only on certain conditions. The preparation of an appeal brief would be time-consuming and costly, he explained, and before any work began, a retainer would have to be deposited. The amount required would be $1,000.

June had been a month of anxious hopefulness for Joan Little, with Julius Rodgers drifting in and out of contact. Now July turned into grim and growing despair. Roger Bernholz did not call, and it seemed that Julius might have abandoned her again. "Everyone is still trying to reach Rodgers. I wonder myself what's up. He must have found himself a new love. Smile . . . I guess its all over between Rodgers and me. But All Things come to an end sometime. . . . Well I guess Rodgers has run out. . . . So I have to bear it alone. So Fuck it. I guess I'll never see him any more so I'll have to make the best of everything everyone said he was going to run out and he did!"

In August, though, she finally got more word from Chapel Hill, a disturbing letter about Rodgers's state of mind. She wrote back at once:

"I knew Rodgers was going to do a lot of drinking. . . . I gave up on him a good while ago but I'm not saying I have forgotten him. I loved him before coming here and I love him now but he is letting me down and himself. I know he doesn't have the money to get me out but at least he can work so that I could have something to come back to. Rodgers has that don't-care mind now. . . . Rodgers has let me down but he is not my husband and I can't put my problems all on him, so I guess if I go to court I have to go alone but I'm not afraid anymore. . . . I have him there in my heart and even though he hasn't called or anything I haven't lost faith in him."

Joan Little seemed caught in the rapid flow of conflicting emotional currents. Realizing that there was no "money to get me out," she still fantasized about a new trial and another chance to be with Julius Rodgers. "They are having court for two weeks," she wrote to her friend in Chapel Hill. "I will be home real soon. I'll call you next week and I will have good news for him I am sure. Court is going on this week, high court. I will explain better after I call."

But there would be no "good news," and she would not make the predicted call. The two weeks passed. Prisoners came and went, shuttling between the jail and the courtroom, but Joan Little was not among them. Then, on August 23, she heard again from Roger Bernholz and for the first time in almost two months she spoke to Julius Rodgers.

Rodgers had again appeared at the lawyer's office in Chapel Hill without an appointment. He never explained why he had come that day, and once more Bernholz would be left with the impression that he really did not know why he was there. Nothing had changed since July 5. He had not been able to raise the money to post Joan Little's bond or the $1,000 retainer Bernholz needed to begin working on the appeal. But they had another long talk about the case anyway, and while Rodgers was there Bernholz again decided to phone Beaufort County. By then, however, he was more skeptical about what Rodgers had told him and more interested in making a professional assessment of the case uninfluenced by his first sympathetic response to the situation Rodgers had described. Before dialing the jail, he called Bessie Cherry, the clerk of court in Beaufort County.

At the murder trial almost a year later, testimony about the calls on August 23 would be essential to the acquittal. Motive would be the only real issue for the jury. The prosecution would use Joan Little's notes to argue that her longing for her lover became so intense that she was moved to plot seduction and murder in order to escape and reunite with him. The defense would claim that she expected to be released from jail within a few days and that she had no reason to be planning an escape on the night Clarence Alligood was killed.

What had Roger Bernholz told her that afternoon? Paul would ask.

"That he was going to bring some papers for me to sign," Joan Little would answer, "because he wanted to know whether or not there was another lawyer that was representing me and that he wanted—that he didn't want to put his own self in jeopardy, and so I told him I would sign the papers and he said that he could get me out on bond."

"With reference to getting out on bond is what you're talking about?" the judge would interrupt.

"Yes."

"And this was about the twenty-third of August?"

"Yes, sir."

"Now, Miss Little," Paul would continue, "on the night of August 26, 1974, what was your knowledge or status of mind in relationship as to when your case on appeal would be heard and when you would get out on bond?"

"In my estimate," she would answer, "in my mind I knew I was going to court that week."

"You were going to court that week?"

"Yes."

"Why did you think you were going to court that week, please?"

"Because they were having a session of Superior Court that week and they had extended it, you know, not for just that two weeks but another third week because it was so crowded."

"What was your status of mind as to when you were going to get out on bond?"

"In a few days."

"In a few days?"

"Few days."

"And this was on August the twenty-sixth?"

"Yes."

"Now what did you base that belief on, if you can tell us?"

"From what the attorney had told me and my mother was working on it and my whole family was working on getting me out on bond."

A verdict would hang in the balance. If the jury believed Joan Little—believed that she thought court was still going on and that a lawyer was arranging for her release—then the state's theory of seduction and escape was implausible. If the jury did not believe her, then the case would hinge on other evidence and the outcome would be far less certain.

In the end, the prosecution weakened but failed to break this crucial testimony. Eventually it was established that the two-week court term had ended on schedule on Friday, August 23. But whether Joan Little could have remained oblivious to the adjournment was left unclear. She had known how long the session was due to last, but on the witness stand she was unable to recall who had told her there would be an extension. She said first that David Watson might have mentioned it, then that she had discussed it with Clarence Alligood, the only jailer who could not be called for corroboration and also the one least likely to know the court schedule since his was the only shift that did not involve transferring prisoners to and from the courtroom. (Notes prepared by the defense attorneys indicated, however, that it was Ellis Tetterton who said she might be able to get a new trial while court was going on in August, and that he had made the remark prior to August 11, the first day of the regular session.) In her letter to a friend in Chapel Hill, moreover, she had complained of having "almost too much company" because the cellblock was filling up with prisoners awaiting trial. But by the time of the adjournment there were no other women inmates in jail.

Still, there was the call from Roger Bernholz. ". . . And I told him I would sign the papers and he said he could get me out on bond." The significant timing of Joan Little's conversation with the Chapel Hill attorney never struck the prosecutors, and they neglected to bear down on it at trial. Bernholz appeared briefly for the defense, and his testimony seemed to corroborate the statements Joan Little had already made on the witness stand. It was not pointed out that on August 23 he and Bessie Cherry, the clerk of court, had discussed both the terms of Judge Martin's appeal order and the fact that the August term of criminal court in Beaufort County had adjourned earlier that day.

Then Roger Bernholz had called Joan Little.

Most of the notes Joan Little scribbled in her crossword-puzzle books while she was in jail were introduced at the trial by the prosecution, but they shed no real light on the character of the jailer or on the guilt or innocence of the defendant. If there were significant nuances (the only dated entries mentioning Alligood's visits, for example, referred to nights when there were other female inmates in the jail), they were never emphasized. On the questions that really mattered the notes were silent, and only in silence could they have had any meaning. If they disclosed anything, they disclosed what did not happen at the jail that summer rather than what did. There was about them yet another unanswered question: Were they ghostly corroboration for testimony that could have come only from the grave?

There were two references to Clarence Alligood recorded in these notes late in August. Along the top of a page Joan Little wrote: "8–19–74 Monday 1:00 A.M. Alligood Here." Elsewhere, she mentioned the night jailer in writing for the last time: "This book belongs to 'Taurus' Miss Joan Little: age 20 5–8–54 Chocowinity, N.C. I been in here now 78-days [sic]. Today is August 22nd 1974. Time 10:25 p.m. Alligood just came on duty. Pray to God I'll be out very soon."

Five days later, she was.

CHAPTER 4

I WANT YOU TO HAVE SEX WITH ME

August 26 was an ordinary, humid Monday. Along Market Street ripples of heat rose and undulated above the pavement, and for hours the temperature hovered near a hundred degrees. Sweating pedestrians hurried from building to building, breathlessly seeking relief in artificial environments. In the afternoon there was a sudden cloudburst and large raindrops pelted down for about twenty minutes. Nightfall brought no relief, only damp darkness. Crickets chirruped in the stiff grass, mosquitoes buzzed madly, and down by the briny river frogs honked in revelry.

Although more rain was predicted before morning, the sky was clear and the stars were out when the night jailer arrived for work. Before going on duty, Clarence Alligood got a status report from David Watson. Everything was quiet, but an undershirt had been stuffed into a toilet and some of the pipes were clogged. The ice pick the jailers sometimes used to extract paper and gum from cell-door locks would be useless. A plumber would have to be called in the morning. Alligood said he would pass that information along to Ellis Tetterton.

There were four male inmates in the jail that night, including Terry Bell, an amiable teenager with a long police record who was scheduled for transfer to Polk Youth Center, a state prison in Raleigh. When Alligood arrived, Bell was sitting in the jailer's office having a soft drink. There was also one female inmate, the young black woman who had been confined there for the past eighty-four days and nights: Joan Little.

As soon as Watson was gone, Clarence Alligood set off to make a quick inspection of the premises. He left Terry Bell alone in the office, having no fear that Bell would reach for the ice pick kept in the desk drawer. All of the jailers considered this young man trustworthy and usually gave him the run of the place.

Joan Little was dressed in jeans and a sweater when Alligood reached the women's section and walked in. Standing outside the bars, he told her about the clogged pipes and asked if she was having any trouble with the three toilets inside the cellblock. She said she was not, and asked if she could make a telephone call.

This may or may not have been an unusual request. At her trial Joan Little would testify on direct examination that Alligood permitted her to make telephone calls frequently, whenever she wished. But then she would say on cross-examination that she could remember using the telephone only four times during the twelve weeks she was confined, and that at least three of those calls occurred while Alligood was not on duty. She was never asked why she had encouraged Julius Rodgers to call her "anytime after 10:00 p.m.," as if she had reason to believe that the night jailer would always let her receive telephone calls during his watch.

Alligood told Joan Little she could use the telephone, and a few minutes later he released her from the cellblock and escorted her to the office, where Terry Bell was still nursing his soft drink. She stepped in front of Bell, picked up the receiver, and placed a long-distance call to Chapel Hill. When her party answered, she turned away from the others and faced the jail door across from the booking counter. She spoke in a low voice, so that neither Bell nor Alligood could hear what she was saying. It was during this telephone call, the prosecutors would argue at her trial, that Joan Little took the ice pick out of the desk drawer. But there would be conflicting evidence about whether she was ever alone in the office.

While she was talking, at least four people came to the jail door and knocked or rang the buzzer to gain entry. The first was Billy Woolard, who had dropped by to ask whether he could harvest a few fresh vegetables from Alligood's garden. Sheriff's deputies Bobby Jackson and Willis Peachey also entered the jail on business, but left within a few moments. The fourth visitor was a woman who wanted to swear out an assault warrant against her husband. Clarence Alligood went outside to give her assistance, telling Bell to keep an eye on things while he showed the woman to the magistrate's office on the other side of the building. Beverly King, the radio dispatcher on duty that night in the communications room, would later recall seeing Alligood at the doorway of the magistrate's office shortly after 10:00 p.m.

Of the people who were inside the jail or at the jail door during Joan Little's call, only three testified at the trial. Willis Peachey said he had been there only momentarily and had left while she was still talking. Joan Little could not recall even seeing him inside the jail, so there was no conflict in their testimony. But she and Billy Woolard had different recollections about which one of them had gone out of the jailer's office first. She testified on direct examination that when Bobby Jackson left the jail Clarence Alligood "went to lock the door behind him and came back [and] told Terry to finish his soda. . . ."

"All right," Jerry Paul asked, "who was present at that time?"

"At that time?"

"When Mr. Alligood told Terry to hurry up and finish his soda, who was there at that time?"

"A white man [was] sitting there."

"Then what did Mr. Alligood do?"

"He left and went down the hallway with Terry and then he came back."

"All right, while he was gone from this area . . . down the hallway with Terry, who was in the jailer's office?"

"That same white man."

"That same white man and you, is that correct?"

"Yes."

"All right, when Mr. Alligood came back what then happened?"

"He came and stood beside me and I asked him could I use his ink pen and then . . . I used it and gave it back to him."

"You used the ink pen and gave it back to him?"

"Yes."

"And then what did you do? Speak up, please."

"I hung up the phone and then I went back to my cell."

"Went back to your cell?"

"Yes."

But Billy Woolard would later testify that he had left the jail before Clarence Alligood returned Terry Bell to his cell. He would say that "Joan Little was still on the phone" and that "Bell was still sitting there" when he "walked out and left" just after the jailer returned from assisting the unidentified woman. "I got up to go home and get to bed," he would state. "I told him [Alligood] I'd go out there tomorrow and get some vegetables." His testimony directly contradicted Joan Little's, but it did not establish that she was ever alone in the jailer's office. According to Woolard, both Joan Little and Terry Bell had been there when he went out, and he had no way of knowing which of the prisoners Clarence Alligood had secured first.

Terry Bell, the young trusty, was the only other person who might have testified about what had happened during this call. On the day of the killing Bell told investigators that he had been the first prisoner Alligood put back into close confinement. Joan Little had been "left alone at this time," the investigative report of Bell's comments would say, "and she was still on the telephone." Bell was the only person, therefore, who could have established that Joan Little had an opportunity to get the ice pick from the desk drawer without being seen.

But Terry Bell would never appear at the trial.

The investigation of the jailer's death would eventually reveal that Joan Little's call at about 10:30 p.m. on August 26 had been placed to the phone of Anna Eubanks, the mother of friends she and Julius had recently met and the woman to whom she had written on August 10 saying she would "be home real soon." The investigators who questioned Mrs. Eubanks reported that Joan Little had told her "she would see her on Friday and would call her again on Thursday," and that she had been very concerned about Julius Rodgers. Mrs. Eubanks also told them that she had advised Joan "not to do anything foolish," and that Joan had told her "she was getting very tired of the jail."

In formulating his case, the district attorney would place heavy emphasis on this information. Joan Little's conversation with Anna Eubanks seemed to provide a rational explanation for the events that had followed several hours later. Concerned about her boyfriend and "very tired of the jail," she might have decided to take the ice pick back to her cell and wait for an opportunity to stab the jailer and escape. What she had told Mrs. Eubanks loomed as a confession of intent, a prophecy she had been quick to fulfill.

This too was essential evidence—perhaps of premeditation—that the jury would never see or hear. Testimony from the investigators would have been inadmissible hearsay, and Anna Eubanks was not called as a witness. William Griffin interviewed her in the spring, more than six months after the killing, and found her to be hostile and uncooperative. By then her memory seemed to be thinning out, and she expressed reluctance to testify. Griffin felt that he could not rely on her to repeat the remarks she had made to the investigating officers and decided not to call her to the stand. During the trial Joan Little denied the substance of the report:

"Didn't you tell Mrs. Eubanks you were going to get out of jail?" Griffin asked.

"I told Mrs. Eubanks that there was court going on and

that I was hoping to go to court that week."

"Didn't you tell Mrs. Eubanks you were going to get out of jail and then didn't she reply to you, 'Don't do anything foolish'?"

"I don't remember Mrs. Eubanks saying anything like that."

"The reason you made the phone call was that you found out there wasn't any court and you weren't going to get any bond signed or allowed by that judge that was there the previous two weeks, wasn't it?"

"No, that's not true."

There were more questions, many of them aimless, groping. Griffin asked the defendant whether she had been upset because she did not get bond signed during the two weeks while court was actually in session. She replied that she "wasn't upset," and said that Rodgers and Bernholz had told her on the twenty-third that they were either coming to the jail or sending "some papers concerning the bond. . . ." But then Joan Little was compelled to admit that she had not heard anything more from either of them when she called Anna Eubanks on the following Monday.

"And that's why you made the phone call that night, to try to find out what was going on, didn't you?"

"No."

"Well, why did you make the phone call?"

"Mrs. Eubanks wrote a letter and I told her that I was going to call her and I told her that I would probably have some good news for her because I was thinking that I was going to court that week and that's what I was going to tell her on the phone."

By then the cross-examination was beginning to seem futile. Griffin had been unable to shake Joan Little's explanation of the phone call made sometime after 10:00 p.m. or her insistence that she had believed she would soon be free. He would make one further effort before shifting to another line of questions.

"And on Monday, was there any court session going on the following Monday, the twenty-seventh of August?"

"I think there was. I'm not sure."

"Well, you know that court was going on on Friday, don't you? You said you did?"

"From what the jailer said."

"How about on Monday, did you know that court was in session?"

"I don't understand what you're talking about."

"I'm trying to find out whether or not you knew on Monday that there was no court the twenty-sixth?"

"I didn't know it for sure but I can only say that the jailer said that there was court going on."

"Which jailer?"

"Clarence Alligood told me."

"When?"

"When I went to make the phone call. . . ."

Here again were hints of a crucial discrepancy. Joan Little had said, "I was thinking that I was going to court that week and that's what I was going to tell [Anna Eubanks] on the telephone." But then she had said she "didn't know for sure" that court was still in session, and that she had been told by Clarence Alligood that it was only as she "went to make the phone call" rather than before she asked permission to do so. On direct examination, she had said she "knew [she] was going to court that week," and that she knew "they had extended it . . . not for just that two weeks but for another third week" because of "what the attorney [Bernholz] had told" her. Before the trial the defense attorneys had suggested privately that Joan Little was simply "confused" about court procedures, even after talking to Roger Bernholz. If that were the case, however, if she believed after discussing her situation with the attorney that she would get a hearing in Beaufort County sometime that week, her testimony on cross-examination suggested that doubts had crept into her mind during the weekend and required the further difficult assumption that the jailer killed just a few hours later had reassured her for some reason that court was still going on when, in fact, it had adjourned the week before.

Was Joan Little certain on the night of August 26 that she would soon get a new day in court? Or had she begun to doubt her chances of getting out of jail? Had William Griffin posed the correct questions, only to hear the wrong answers? Roger Bernholz might have been able to clarify the matter, but on the witness stand he was never asked exactly what he had said to the defendant regarding the August court session in Beaufort County.

By 11:00 p.m. all prisoners in the Beaufort County jail had been returned to their cells. Terry Bell was in the juvenile section but had access to a narrow hall leading from the jail elevator to the main part of the jail. The hallway was secured by a locked door with a small window through which the entrance to the women's section could be seen across a corridor. Joan Little had been taken back to the women's area and locked inside her cellblock. At that time, according to her testimony, Clarence Alligood made the first of several sexual overtures toward her that night.

"I asked him to go to Terry Bell and ask him to send me some cigarettes and he said he would."

"All right," Paul went on, "when he came back what did he say to you, if anything?"

"He gave me the cigarettes that Terry had sent me and he told me that he would get me a pack of cigarettes if I didn't have any. I told him I didn't want him to get me any cigarettes and he said that he would get me some and I could pay him back later and he continued to stand there and he started talking to me telling me how nice I looked again, and that he want[ed] me, you know, to give him some pussy is what he said."

"All right, what did you say at that time?"

"I told him no, and I would really appreciate it if he left and he left."

.   .   .

Sometime after two o'clock that morning Washington police officer Johnny Rose wheeled his pale-blue patrol car into the driveway beside the Beaufort County Courthouse and drove to the back of the building. In the parking lot he could see the silhouette of a man standing in a shaft of light coming from an open door. On the seat beside Rose there was a brown paper bag filled with hot food—three sausage dogs, one ham-and-cheese sandwich, one cheeseburger, one barbecue sandwich, and a slice of potato pie—which he had picked up a few moments earlier as he was leaving the Chuckwagon restaurant after a coffee break. Because he had radioed ahead, he was expected at the jail.

Rose pulled to a halt and rolled down a window as the silhouette moved away from the building and came toward his car. Clarence Alligood took the sandwich bag and thanked the officer, then hurried back inside the courthouse. Rose drove on around the building, turned right on to Second Street, and continued his patrol. He would return to the jail less than two hours later, and by then the jailer would be dead.

Clarence Alligood went first to the jailer's office, where he sat alone and ate some of the food Rose had delivered. Investigators would find sandwich wrappings in a wastebasket the next morning. Within a short time he also went to the women's section of the jail and offered a sandwich to Joan Little. The brown paper bag containing wrappers and some of the food would be found inside the women's cellblock. She would testify that he had brought her a package of menthol cigarettes and that he had again mentioned something about "having sex" with her. "He said that he had brought the sandwiches and that he was going to talk to the dispatcher," she would recall, "and I took the sandwiches and he kept standing there and he said that—by that time I had changed into my gown and he was telling me that I looked real nice in my gown and that he was gonna, you know, wanted to have sex with me. . . . And I took the sandwiches and that time he left."

Sometime thereafter, shortly before three o'clock, Clarence Alligood did leave the jail and walk across the basement to the communications room, where Beverly King sat before a complex array of microphones, lights, and switches. It was not unusual for the night jailer to stop in for a chat during the watch, and until later Beverly King would think nothing of this visit. They talked briefly, and at some point Alligood asked whether all the deputies had checked in for the night. Later she would insist that his question was not out of the ordinary. She told him that all of the deputies had gone off active patrol except one, who was on his way home at that moment. A while later Alligood left the communications room and returned to the jail.

Except for Joan Little, Beverly King was probably the last person to see Clarence Alligood alive. Sometime during the next hour he went back to the women's section and let himself into the cellblock, where Joan Little, wearing her nightgown, was lying on the bunk in cell number one. She would later say that she thought another female prisoner was being admitted when she heard the door swing on its hinges, and that only when she got up did she realize the jailer was alone.

Clarence Alligood did not survive to explain why he went back to the women's section of the jail a third time that morning. He died there, leaving only one person to tell the story. Joan Little's personal account of the incident would not become known until she took the witness stand, but secondhand descriptions had been published before then by her attorneys and by journalists who interviewed members of the defense team. Most such accounts stigmatized the jailer as a would-be rapist and portrayed Joan Little as a victim of male chauvinism and racial aggression. Most were based, at least indirectly, on information first contained in a confidential scenario of the episode prepared by Jerry Paul for his own use in formulating the defense:*

He asked her if she was going to be nice to him, saying that he had been nice to her.
She said, "What do you mean?"
He then said, "I want you to have sex with me."
Joan said, "No, I am not."
He then started towards her, and said, "What's wrong, do you think that you are too good for me, I know you do it with others."
He backed her up to the back of the cell where the sink was. At this time he had all his clothes on. He went up to her and started to feel of her breasts. He said, "Don't be scared, I just want to have some fun, come on over to the bunk."
At this time he took off her nightgown. He pulled the nightgown up and took it off and dropped it on the floor. He then started to feel of her again between her legs and also her breasts. At this time his clothes were still on and at this time he began to take his clothes off. He stood in the door and took off his shoes first and put them in the hall.
She offered no resistance because no other person was in the cellblock and the other prisoners were locked up and no one could hear her. She had been to the magistrate's office before and knew where the other people were located.
Alligood stood up to take his clothes off. He took off his pants and underpants and unbuttoned his shirt but left it on. He then sat down on the bunk and told her to come over and suck his dick. He put his hand on her after playing with himself for a few seconds and he had a hard-on at this time. She said, "Hell no, I ain't going to do no shit like that," and reached down to pick up her gown.
He picked up [his] pants and when she stood back up and

*Punctuation, grammar, syntax, and spelling have been corrected for clarity where possible, but nothing has been omitted from the original statement.

looked he had the ice pick in his hand, and at that time he told her that regardless of "what you say or who you tell, they will not believe you, so you had better do what I say. David or Ellis neither one will believe you nor will Red."

The pants had been on the bed and as she saw the ice pick he reached over [to] grab her and pulled her to him. He was seated [and] had his hands on her and then pulled her over. He said, "You had better do what I say."

The ice pick was in his left hand, and his right hand was on her. She got on her knees as he pulled her down to where he was sitting. She began to suck his dick and did so for 4 or 5 minutes. She only put her mouth around it and did not move. As she was doing it the pick was partly on the bunk. She grabbed for it with her right hand. It fell on the floor between the bunk and the sink. He leaned over to get it and she lunged for it, got it, and turned and pushed him in the stomach. He was behind at first and she turned and pushed him and he went back towards the bunk. While [he was] reaching out for her she struck at him with the pick and every time he reached, she struck. She kept hitting out and aiming for his chest. He was on the bunk and he got up and got behind her and got his hands on her wrist. She had her feet on the bunk and was pushing back against him. She switched the pick to her left hand and began to strike behind her anywhere that she could. She struck all up and down his body. After [she hit] him in the [head] he turned her loose and fell to his knees. She got away from him and he fell across the bunk. She ran to the next cell and grabbed her pants, blouse, and pocketbook. When she came out of the cell, Alligood was next to the bench, just standing there. She went around him but was close to him. At that time he did not have the ice pick in his hand. She was running during this time. She slammed the door. The keys were in the door.

She had blood on her hands when she went to shut the door. She was putting her clothes on. She took the key from the green box and went out.

At about the same time, Clarence Alligood slumped to his left on the bunk in cell number one. Blood oozed from a small wound in his temple and trickled across his cheek onto the sheet. Snagged in the fingers of his left hand was the belt loop of his trousers. His right arm dangled over his body toward the floor, and the fingers of his right hand were curved lightly around the handle of the ice pick.

CHAPTER 5

OH MY GOD

It was around 4:00 a.m. when Officer Johnny Rose arrived back at the jail, and this time he came with a prisoner, a drunk woman he had arrested as she dug up flowers in someone else's yard. Rose was met by Police Sergeant Jerry Helms, who had answered his call for assistance when the woman began to scream and thrash around in the back seat of his patrol car. Together they marched the wobbly prisoner into the courthouse and down a short hallway. She was handcuffed, and at the jail door she became subdued.

Helms rang the door buzzer, while Rose gripped the woman's elbow to hold her steady. No answer. Helms pressed the buzzer again, and they waited. No response. Then he placed his finger on the button and depressed it for several seconds, and he could hear the bell ringing inside. The woman fidgeted and mumbled an epithet under her breath. Still no one came to let them in. They waited a few seconds longer, then Helms shrugged and pushed on the door. It opened without a sound.

Jerry Helms discovered the body five minutes later as he wandered about the jail looking for Clarence Alligood. Johnny Rose was at the booking counter trying to question the drunk woman, and Beverly King had come from the communications room to give assistance with the female prisoner. Helms had looked in a storage room and in the kitchen before noticing that the door to the women's section was open. He walked in, assuming no one was there, then hesitated and peered slowly around the corner through the bars. He saw a woman's underclothes hanging outside the cells, and then he saw what appeared to be a man's stockinged feet on the floor on top of a folded blanket in cell number one.

"Is that Alligood?" Helms said when Beverly King and Johnny Rose joined him a moment later.

"Well, I don't know, Jerry," Rose responded. "Let's go in and find out."

The cover on the control box on the wall beside the cellblock door was closed but not locked. Helms opened it and depressed one of the levers. The spring bolt inside the mechanical door dropped back, and the door popped open. Johnny Rose opened it wider and walked in, his heart beginning to pound.

Rose sensed the awful discovery they were about to make, and his thoughts became jumbled in the excitement. He noticed a pair of shoes on the floor outside the cells, men's shoes, unlaced. Then he looked into cell number one and saw Clarence Alligood with blood on his head and on his right thigh. This first clear view of the jailer would later cloud Rose's recollection of the scene inside the cell, and at the trial he would not remember seeing the jailer's pants, the blankets on the floor and on the bunk, the nightgown on the floor, or the ice pick. But he would recall touching Alligood's neck to search for a pulse, and not finding it.

Helms stood in the cell doorway. More experienced than Rose and more alert, he noted "a small splotch of blood" on the dead man's hip, blood on the side of his head and on his forehead, and a pair of men's glasses on the floor near the toilet. He saw that the jailer's shirt was unbuttoned, and that he was wearing an undershirt. He also saw that the jailer's green pants were hanging from his left hand, as if he might have been trying to grasp them up, and that the fingers of his right hand were curled around the handle of a thin, pointed instrument. It looked like an ice pick.

Helms rushed from the cellblock a moment later, after telling Rose not to touch anything, and made two quick calls from the jailer's office. He alerted the Beaufort

County Rescue Squad first, then dialed the home of Chief Deputy Ottis Davis. While he was on the phone with Davis, he asked Beverly King for the name of any female who had been in jail that night, and then he ordered Johnny Rose to take the drunk woman home and to go back on patrol, to begin looking for Joan Little. Beverly King began calling the other deputies from a telephone in the communications room, and she also contacted several Washington policemen, including Danny Respass, a photographer and fingerprint specialist. Helms, meanwhile, returned to the women's section and paced back and forth in front of the cellblock. Finally, he walked outside, just as the rescue squad truck arrived.

Ed Mercer and Charles "Mike" Alligood had been rousted from bed to answer the call, and they had no idea what to expect when they got to the courthouse. "Send the rescue squad to the jail!" was all Helms had said before slamming down the phone. But additional information would have made no difference to them. Mike Alligood was not related to Clarence Alligood and had never even heard of him, and there was nothing either he or Ed Mercer could have done for the jailer anyway.

The three men rushed into cell number one. Mercer immediately leaned over the bunk to check the body for signs of life, then straightened up and shrugged. Mike Alligood stepped forward and placed his fingertips lightly at a point along the man's neck, but he could feel no pulse. Both men took a step back, out of the cell, and for the first time noticed that the corpse on the bunk was disrobed from the waist down except for the socks on the feet. Then they moved on out of the cellblock, and one of them suggested to Helms that the medical examiner should be called.

Within minutes the deputies began to arrive. Ottis Davis and Willis Peachey were the first to get there, and others soon followed. One by one, they walked into the women's section, gazed in awkward disbelief at the body, then went back outside. All of them wanted something to do, and none of them could think of anything. No one gave any orders until Ottis Davis finally told everyone to clear out of the cellblock and to make sure nothing there was disturbed. Davis was thinking first about the injured jailer, not about the investigation. He hoped desperately that the man could be revived. He paced the jail corridor, then walked outside to wait alone in the parking lot until the medical examiner arrived. For the moment, no one had taken clear command at the scene of the crime.

Dr. Harry Carpenter had no reason to assume there was a medical emergency at the jail, and he had not rushed to get there. Carpenter had been awake when the call came from the hospital, and he had dinstinctly heard the nurse say that "a jailer had been stabbed to death." But when he drove into the parking lot, Ottis Davis dashed out and flung open his car door. The jailer was seriously hurt, Davis shouted, and he had to come at once. "Oh my god!" Carpenter murmured, leaping out of the car to follow the stout chief deputy at a dead run. "Oh my god."

But when he got inside the cell, Carpenter knew there was nothing he could do, nothing he could have done. He went over the body quickly, detecting no heartbeat or respiration, observing that the man's eyelids were fixed and that his eyes were dilated. He stood up, turned to Ottis Davis, and told him there was no hope of reviving Clarence Alligood, no hope whatsoever.

The keys to the jail were missing. The deputies had searched the halls, the lounge, behind the desk, and under the counter in the jailer's office, and the keys could not be found anywhere. The escapee had taken them—cleverly, it seemed, because the sheriff's department had been thrown into chaos. But Joan Little could not have known that there was no extra set of keys, and that it would be days, or weeks, before new ones could be ordered from the manufacturer.

For the first time, attention shifted to the prisoners still behind bars. The four men confined on the other side of the

jail had no way to escape if fire broke out in the building.
Willis Peachey decided to check on them. He went upstairs, let himself into the elevator, and rode back downstairs to the basement. The door opened onto a narrow
corridor that led to the men's cellblock and the juvenile
section. Without keys, he could not get into the men's section, but he saw through a small opening in the door that
everything was secure. Farther on he found the juvenile
section accessible, woke up Terry Bell, and told him what
had happened. The boy seemed stunned and his mouth
sagged open.

"Terry, get ahold of yourself," Peachey said.

Bell did not reply.

"Terry, did you hear anything?" Peachey asked.

Still Bell did not respond. He did not speak or move for
several minutes. When he did, he said he had heard nothing. Peachey left him there and rode the elevator back
upstairs. Someone told him a machinist had been called to
open the men's cells with a blowtorch.

The police photographer had arrived and was taking
pictures of the corpse and the jail cell. Danny Respass had
brought two cameras, but only one with a flash attachment,
which failed to operate. Because he had no other way to
illuminate the dim cell, the few photos he took were not of
good quality. They showed the body from various angles,
and the hand holding the ice pick, but there were no pictures of the interior of the cell where the sink and toilet
were located, of cell number two, where a number of books
and magazines were found, or of other areas, including the
jailer's office. There would later be criticism, even from
inside the sheriff's department, about the failure to obtain
more on-scene photographs. But Chief Deputy Ottis Davis
was in his office with the door closed while Respass was in
the cellblock, and no one had been assigned to take charge
of the investigation or to direct the photographer's work.

As soon as Respass had finished, Harry Carpenter began
a more thorough examination of the body. Using a borrowed flashlight, he studied the scalp wound about an inch

above the ear and the small punctures on the leg and in the chest. Only the scalp wound was still bleeding, sending a dark stream languidly across the man's cheek into a widening stain on the sheet beneath his head. Carpenter checked for signs of the time of death, and then made an estimate: The man had been dead less than one hour and might have died only moments before Rose and Helms had entered the jail at about 4:00 a.m.

Carpenter then took time to think about the circumstances in the cellblock. The condition of the body and its implications were obvious and deeply troubling, and during the examination he had discovered something he considered extraordinary and provocative. On the inside of the left thigh there was a pool of cloudy liquid, which he estimated to be about two cubic centimeters in volume, and from the end of the man's penis to the pool there was a connecting thread of the same substance. But in the faint light inside cell number one, he could not observe the liquid clearly. He had no way to preserve a sample of it until he could get to a laboratory and no equipment to test it on the scene. He could only make an assumption about what it was and why it was there.

Chief Deputy Ottis "Red" Davis had come by his nickname honestly, though after twenty-three years with the sheriff's department his short-cropped hair was not the sparkling color it had once been. Paunchy and red-faced, he smoked an odorous pipe, chewed the stumps of smelly cigars, and had instincts shaped by years of small-town law enforcement and courthouse politics. He was the Democratic candidate for county sheriff, having already won the party primary in May, and would be elected unopposed in November. From the beginning he sought to handle the jailer's death as a local matter, and he was reluctant to acknowledge that it might have wider implications even after reporters from all over the world had swarmed into Beaufort County to write about it. "What's so important about this case?" he would ask, snatching his cigar out of his mouth as if to punctuate a question he thought could not really be answered.

Instead of deploying his deputies at once, Davis closed himself in his office and went to the telephone to begin the search for Joan Little himself. He started with the assumptions that she would try to contact Julius Rodgers, or that she might already be with him, and that she had been helped in her escape by an accomplice from the outside. The circumstances suggested seduction and homicide to him, not self-defense. An all-points bulletin had already been dispatched saying that Joan Little was wanted in connection with the death of the jailer.

Davis first roused Jennings Freeman, a bondsman who was Clarence Alligood's friend as well as Davis's brother-in-law and next-door neighbor. Did Freeman know where to locate Julius Rodgers? Freeman said he thought Rodgers was in Chapel Hill.

Then Davis began to contact informants, asking whether they knew anything about Rodgers and Joan Little. While he was making one of these calls, Harry Carpenter stepped into the office and stood nearby, close enough to overhear what Davis was saying. Dr. Carpenter had come in to make certain that Davis understood his view of the situation. The jailer's pants might have been removed after he was dead to confuse the investigation, but Carpenter thought that the liquid on his thigh could not have been induced after he died. He was certain that he had observed seminal fluid on the jailer's leg, and he assumed that it was the residue of an ejaculation caused by sexual excitation just prior to death. Clarence Alligood might have gone to the cell by invitation or to force himself on the prisoner, Carpenter thought, but either way there was more to this killing than murder and escape. Many people were to make the same assumption as this case progressed. It was to become such a compelling point that experienced medical experts who insisted the presence of seminal fluid on the body did not indicate recent sexual activity would often simply be ignored.

Carpenter was relieved when he thought he had found out that Davis was aware of these complexities. As he came into the office, he got the impression that Davis was speaking to someone who knew where Joan Little was, and that he was "telling this person that he needed to get in touch with her because it was clear that it was important to hear her side of the story, to hear her point of view. . . ." Even later Carpenter would recall that Davis's attitude had been positive and sympathetic. "He was aware of the implications and distressed about them. He kept saying over and over, 'I really thought this man was a fine jailer,' and so on, as if he'd just discovered he might not have been a fine jailer. . . . I think he understood the implications. . . . I think he was honestly and earnestly trying to convey his feeling that she had a story, favorable to her, to tell."

But Carpenter had misjudged Ottis Davis, who saw only a dead jailer and an inmate on the run. "Bullshit!" Davis would roar, explaining his intentions that morning. "I called some informants to try to locate Joan Little—that's all!"

Around 6:30 a.m. Dr. Carpenter returned to the cellblock to supervise the removal of the body. It would be taken first to the Beaufort County Hospital, and from there to the Pitt Memorial Hospital in Greenville, where a regional pathologist, Dr. Charles Gilbert, would perform the autopsy.

The investigation in the cellblock seemed complete. Willis Peachey had written some notes and had sketched a rough diagram locating the body and various artifacts in the cell—bloodstained toilet tissues, an open jar of Vaseline, and a package of Salem cigarettes with two Marlboros inside. He had also gathered some of the loose items scattered about—paperback books, crossword-puzzle magazines, a Bible, and some women's clothing. He and Respass had discussed whether to collect the jailer's personal belongings from cell number one, as well as what to do with the ice pick. Respass thought no usable fingerprints could be taken from either the scarred wooden grip or the corroded shaft, and finally he had lifted it out of the hand of the corpse and turned it over to Peachey, who had shoved it into his back pocket. Respass had finished taking pictures and had made impressions of several red smears on the bars and on the mechanical door, which he hoped would yield a positive identification of the jailer's assailant. But no one had thought to have him dust for fingerprints anywhere outside the cellblock, and so it would be impossible to prove that Joan Little had ever touched the middle drawer of the smooth metal desk where the ice pick was always kept.

Now, with Carpenter looking on, the body was raised slowly and leaned against the wall to determine whether the scalp wound might have caused a bloodstain over the bunk. The height of the stain corresponded to the place where the jailer's head would have rested if he had slumped against the wall before toppling over. Outside the cellblock, Ed Mercer and Mike Alligood wrestled to get an unwieldy stretcher into place, and Gordon Edwards, a television newsman who had just arrived, aimed his motion-picture camera toward the cell door. Then the body was lifted onto the stretcher and draped with a sheet, and the jailer's property—including his pants and underwear, his glasses and his shoes—was gathered and placed between his legs. A moment later Mercer and Mike Alligood wheeled the shrouded corpse down the corridor and outside into the drizzling rain that had just begun to fall.

CHAPTER 6

BRUTAL MURDER

The morning grew sultry, but there were no further developments in the case. Police all over the state had been alerted, and deputies were now aimlessly combing Beaufort County. Ottis Davis sat in his office by the telephone, stymied. Around nine o'clock Ellis Tetterton came in. "Are they through in there?" he asked, gesturing over his shoulder toward the jail. "Yeah," Davis muttered. "Clean it up." A few minutes later the keys were found under a bush outside.

The family of the slain jailer had been informed of his death by one of the female deputies, and shortly after nine o'clock several of his sons arrived. Davis asked them if they really wished to hear everything, and they said they did. "I told the Alligood family," he would later recall, "that the man was naked from the waist down."

The official investigation did not really begin until eleven o'clock, when two agents from the North Carolina State Bureau of Investigation got to the jail. William Slaughter and Terry Newell had been told nothing except that the county sheriff was in the hospital and his chief deputy was in charge. They would soon learn that the case had already spun out of control.

The intent of the 1937 legislation establishing North Carolina's SBI was not to set up a state police force, and the law did not confer original jurisdiction on the agency to investigate crimes of violence except in emergencies declared by the governor. In theory, the SBI served an advisory function, intervening only to augment local law enforcement with technology and specially trained investigators. In fact, its agents were frequently called in at once and deferred to by local officers, who were usually unskilled in case analysis and uninterested in the drudgery of crime detection. But this convenient interface did not always work smoothly, especially when local lawmen failed to realize they needed help.

Thinking Joan Little would soon be captured by his own deputies, Ottis Davis did not seek assistance from the SBI that morning. His lack of initiative would later be cited by defense attorneys as evidence of a plan to silence the fugitive and cover up the circumstances of the jailer's death. Davis would say it simply had not occurred to him to involve the state agency. SBI District Director Warren Campbell had seen the statewide alert, however, and about ten o'clock he telephoned Beaufort County and spoke to Davis. Less than an hour later, Slaughter and Newell were sitting in the sheriff's office. Slaughter, who would become the agent in charge, had never handled an investigation in Beaufort County and knew only a few of the deputies there. Burly and crew-cut, he had received investigative training in the military before joining the SBI a few years earlier and was one of its youngest agents. He had tried to avoid this assignment, vaguely anticipating difficulties with the local authorities in an investigation of the killing of one of their own men. Newell, a crime-lab technician, would leave soon after discovering that there was nothing for him to do at the jail.

Davis told the agents the investigation was well in hand. The medical examiner was already preparing his report, he said, and evidence had been collected from the cell and stored in a locker in the squad room next to his office. He also informed them of the first big break in the case—the discovery that a telephone call had been made from the jail at about the time the jailer was thought to have been stabbed.

Danny Respass had inadvertently uncovered this information by talking to the night operators about Joan Little's long-distance call around 10:30 the preceding evening. From one of the two operators on duty during the late evening and early morning hours he learned that another call had been made from the jail between 3:00 and 3:30 a.m., a station-to-station collect call to a number in Chapel Hill placed by a woman who had "identified herself as Joan Little." Slaughter's report, filed later after the investigation led to clues that Joan Little had told someone on the telephone she was soon going to get out of jail, would state "that at approximately 3:23 a.m. suspect Little made a long-distance call to the residence of Anna Eubanks. . . ."

Willis Peachey, the rookie in the Sheriff's Department although he had had prior police experience in a small town near Washington, arrived some time after eleven o'clock and went to the squad room to turn the evidence over to the SBI. Peachey and Danny Respass had randomly collected a few items from the women's cells early that morning, and later Peachey had checked the cellblock once more but had removed nothing else. Now he expected to be finished with the case once the materials in his locker had been turned over to the state agents. Peachey had little interest in investigative police work, and hoped he would not be drawn further into this investigation. He looked forward to transferring soon to the North Carolina State Highway Patrol, where the emphasis was on law enforcement rather than on crime detection. While the officers were all together, however, Ottis Davis suggested that Peachey continue to assist Slaughter and Newell and then walked out of the room. From then on, Willis Peachey was the local officer in charge of the investigation. It was an assignment he would soon regret.

Once he had glanced through the magazines and looked at the ice pick, Slaughter asked to see the pictures Danny Respass had taken—which were hanging up to dry in the photo lab—and then he asked to see where Clarence Alligood had died. He knew as soon as the jailer showed them through the doorway to the women's section that the case was turning sour. The area was not cordoned off, and the cellblock was spotlessly clean. Every trace of evidence had disappeared. Peachey was startled. He had checked the cellblock two hours earlier and it had not been disturbed. But now the mattress in cell number one was bare of sheets and blankets, the floor and the wall had been washed, the stainless-steel toilet and sink had been scrubbed and shined dry, the blood spots on the floor and the stain on the wall were gone, and the bloodstained toilet tissues, the jar of Vaseline, and the package of cigarettes had been disposed of. In his subsequent report Slaughter could say only that "the crime scene search had been conducted by the Washington Police Department and the Beaufort County Sheriff's Department."

All during the long afternoon the rambling search for Joan Little went on. Without specific orders, the deputies patrolled casually, checking places where they thought she might be. The Pic-Wic was kept under surveillance, and several houses were searched, but she could not be found. Later reports would seem to exaggerate the intensity and sophistication of the hunt. One magazine article would say that it had been conducted "with riot weapons and helicopters," and literature distributed by the defense would claim that police had "searched the shack [where Joan Little was hiding] with their shotguns at the ready." Helicopters were not brought in and officers denied using shotguns or riot weapons, but there was nevertheless a plodding effort to find the missing woman that overreached the bounds of law as well as good law enforcement. Willis Peachey said he had gone into one house in a black neighborhood with his pistol drawn, and none of the searches was conducted with a warrant.

Slaughter and Peachey soon went to interview Joan Little's mother, after learning she had called to say she had just heard about the jailer's death on the radio. But they discovered she had actually learned of her daughter's escape "early in the morning" when she had talked to her by telephone. According to the SBI report, Mrs. Williams had been told "not to talk but to listen," and that Joan "had gotten help, and . . . was going to leave town." She also told the officers that Joan had warned her "not to call the sheriff, and if they came after her, she would kill herself."

In spite of this warning, Jessie Williams decided to cooperate with the authorities, at least in part because she was informed that her daughter might be declared an outlaw. It was no idle threat. Outlaw declarations were legal in North Carolina, the only state that still deemed it reasonable to encourage this form of vigilantism.* Slaughter told Mrs. Williams that Joan "could be shot if she did not surrender herself to law-enforcement officers or any civilian," and she gave him the names of people her daughter might try to contact—Julius Rodgers and Anna Eubanks—and told him the telephone call that morning had come from the home of Raymond Cobb, her nephew.

But Jessie Williams did not say anything that day about an attempted rape, an omission that would later seem puzzling. How could she have remained silent, especially after hearing that an outlaw declaration might be forthcoming? Within a short time Mrs. Williams would disclose to newsmen that her daughter had complained to her about conditions inside the jail earlier in August, but she said nothing about this to the investigators either. Later developments in the case would eventually lead Slaughter and Peachey to speculate that Joan Little had not yet contrived her story when she talked to her mother or that they were not on good terms and did not share confidences, which might have explained why Jessie Williams appeared to know nothing about the reasons later to be given for the escape.

---

*The hundred-year-old state outlaw statute eliminated all criminal and civil sanctions if a hunted fugitive was wounded or killed by a private citizen. It was to be declared unconstitutional by a federal court two years later in an unrelated case. Joan Little was never declared an outlaw.

Progress in the investigation soon dimmed the former assumption, however, and at the trial the latter assumption
would be demolished.

"And you told your mother that you had escaped from
the jail and not to try to find you, isn't that what you told
your mother?" William Griffin asked on cross-examination.

"Not in those words," Joan Little answered.

"Isn't that what you told your mother?"

"Not in those words, Mr. Griffin."

"What words?"

"I told her that the jailer had came in and tried to force
me to have sex with him, and that I wasn't sure whether
he was hurt or not and that I was gonna try to find somebody to help me and not to send anybody looking for me
and if the policemen came after me that I was gonna kill
myself."

Peachey and Slaughter also interviewed Mr. and Mrs.
Raymond Cobb during the afternoon of August 27,
speaking first to Mrs. Cobb around 3:30 p.m. and then
to her husband several hours later. Both of them
seemed to know more than Jessie Williams about what
had happened.

> . . . Subject [Mrs. Cobb] advised that suspect Little came to
> her house sometime around 3:30 a.m., to 4:00 a.m. That sus-
> pect knocked on the door and her husband let her in. That
> suspect told them that she had killed a man.
>
> Subject's husband asked who, and suspect Little replied,
> "the jailer." Suspect stated that the jailer tried to make her
> have sex with him; that he made her take her clothes off and
> when he started to take his clothes off, she stabbed him.
>
> Subject advised that her husband told suspect that she
> could not stay in their house, that he did not want any
> trouble with the law. Suspect made a telephone call to her
> mother prior to leaving their home, and that she did not
> know where suspect Little went after that. . . .
>
> Reporting Agent was distracted from this interview, and
> did not clearly overhear the statement that Mrs. Cobb made.

*Deputy Peachey advised that he understood Mrs. Cobb to say
that suspect Little stated that the jailer attempted to have sex
with her. That he made her take off her clothes. That when
he was taking off his clothes, she ran and got the ice pick.
When the jailer got close to her, she stabbed him.*

Raymond Cobb was unable to give them much additional information. He said he had not heard the conversation between Joan Little and his wife, but he did tell the
officers he had heard Joan say "that she had killed the jailer
and escaped." Even before the trial the defense attorneys
would begin to maintain that Joan Little had not known the
jailer was dying when she ran out of the cellblock, and she
would testify she had last seen him standing up with a "silly
grin" on his face. But on the day of the killing the investigation turned up evidence suggesting she knew Clarence
Alligood was dead even before she fled, contributing to the
officer's suspicion that escape had been her intention all
along.

The Cobbs were never called as witnesses because they
had no firsthand knowledge, but their comments became
very influential during the investigation. Several passages
in Mrs. Cobb's interview seemed particularly significant.
She told the officers that Joan Little had said she stabbed
the jailer "when he started to take his clothes off. . . . That
when he was taking off his clothes, she ran and got the ice
pick." Until the trial the prosecution had no other information with which to form a supposition about what had happened in the cell, and these clues raised questions that
seemed to require answers in court.* The defense would
soon claim that Joan Little had acted purely in self-defense,
but the investigation had revealed that she first said she
stabbed the man while he was fumbling with his trousers,

---

*Joan Little was never interrogated by any sheriff's deputy or SBI agent, and
she never volunteered to give a statement to the authorities explaining the
jailer's death. A great deal of information would be released by the defense and
would sometimes be taken as authoritative by the press, but the defendant never
publicly discussed the significant details of the case with anyone.

suggesting that she already had the ice pick in her cellblock and even that she used it with some forethought. A prosecution theory soon began to fit together, with the slivers of information from Mrs. Cobb as essential turns in the maze: A lone female inmate, desperate to get out of jail and join her lover, perhaps desperate to reclaim a lost love, had lured Clarence Alligood back to her cell, first asking for cigarettes and later sharing his sandwiches. Then, when he returned for the third time that night, encouraged to believe that she wished to satisfy her sexual appetite after nearly three months in jail, Joan Little had attacked him with the ice pick taken from the desk drawer earlier during her call to Chapel Hill. She had gauged her moves well, they speculated, waiting until the jailer was half-unclad and vulnerable, and as he tugged defenselessly at his trousers she had plunged the pick into his body again and again and again.

Until the trial, nothing happened to make it seem that this was not a plausible interpretation of the case or to change the district attorney's mind about continuing the prosecution. Clarence Alligood had been stabbed eleven times, an indication that his assailant had meant to injure him critically, and there was evidence that he might have been struck down at a moment when he was unlikely to have been able to defend himself. At the trial, however, the defendant would testify that she had grappled with the jailer only after he had removed his trousers, and because of the hearsay rule there would be no way for the prosecution to use the information received the day of the killing from the first person Joan Little spoke to after fleeing from the jail.

The killing was news statewide, although the first reports were sketchy and incomplete. The public was informed that a jailer had died in the line of duty, but none of the controversial details were disclosed. It was revealed that the dead man had been found inside a woman's cell, but not that the body had been found half-clad. Only a handful of people—those who had been in the cellblock—knew the full story.

There might have been a more intense reaction in Beaufort County if the slain man had been a prominent citizen, but Clarence Alligood was not a banker or a merchant or a civic leader, not a force in the community. He owned a small plot of farmland but earned his livelihood executing public responsibilities few people knew or cared anything about. The jail was a place for drunks and thugs, not respectable citizens. Those who had no reason ever to go near the jail could not help being vaguely suspicious of those who did, even if to work there. Within the courthouse, even within the sheriff's department, jailers occupied the lowest station, the position of least respect. In a remote way Clarence Alligood and Joan Little seemed to share the same dark niche in society, an unfamiliar context in which his death somehow did not seem extraordinary.

A few people reacted with perfunctory outrage, however, and one of them was sixty-three-year-old Ashley Futrell, the owner-editor of the local newspaper, the Washington *Daily News*. A gray-haired conservative politician and former state senator, Futrell often presumed to speak for the community from his editorial page but less often dared to be its conscience. His paper went into most homes in the area, black and white, but staunchly reflected the views of the area's conservative white elite. During this case Futrell would frequently implore black and white citizens to work together to solve the local racial tensions it engendered. A year after the trial, however, his paper would insensitively run a picture of a white deputy pulling a drowned black man out of the river by a cord tied to the ankle of the corpse.

Early on the morning of the killing, Ottis Davis called Futrell, and the two men met later in Davis's office for a private interview. Futrell learned from Davis that Joan Little was thought to have stabbed Clarence Alligood as part of an escape plot, and that there was a strong possibil-

ity she had been helped by an accomplice. Davis also told
him about the telephone calls she had made from the jail,
and said he thought Alligood had been killed after permitting the prisoner to contact her friends in Chapel Hill.
There was even a suggestion that the 3:30 a.m. call had
been some sort of signal. Futrell asked if there was anything else he should know. "There are a lot of things," he
would later recall Davis's reply, "but I wouldn't know how
to give them news value."

JAILER FOUND SLAIN, the headline read that afternoon in
the *Daily News.* There was a subheadline, WOMAN ES-
CAPEE SOUGHT, and there were pictures of the jailer's
office and the cell (after it had been cleaned), as well as a
picture of Ottis Davis captioned "Deputy Sheriff Davis
Heads Investigation," and frontal and profile police photos
of Joan Little taken when she had been arrested in January
for the break-ins. The story had been written by a staff
reporter, Peter Galuszka, entirely from Futrell's notes. No
effort was made to check Davis's information, and no one
else at the jail was questioned. The rescue-squad volunteers were not contacted, nor was the medical examiner
called even to verify the presumed cause of death. As soon
as he returned to the office, Futrell went to his own type-
writer to compose an editorial about the killing for publication the following day, when he would be out of town.

Dr. Harry Carpenter was astonished when he read the
Daily News that evening, and by the next day he was "very
pumped up" about the grossly inaccurate reports in the
morning papers and on radio and television. None of the
crucial information about the condition of the body had
been disclosed, and the ice pick was being called "the murder weapon." Carpenter sensed urgently that a shroud was
falling over the investigation to protect the jailer's reputation and permit Joan Little to be hunted down as a wanton
killer. "They're blowing this case," he told a fellow doctor,
knowing that his colleague was Peter Galuszka's father. A
short time later, as he had expected, he got a call from the

young reporter. "I thought we were betrayed by the press," Dr. Carpenter would say later, "and we were betrayed first locally [because] I waited twenty-four hours and then I personally conveyed the facts to them." Patiently, he gave Galuszka a detailed description of the circumstances in the cell and the condition of the body, and then he waited anxiously to see whether "the facts" would finally appear in print.

Peter Galuszka had the most explosive story of his short newspaper career, and he put through a long-distance call at once to get permission to run it. Ashley Futrell was in Durham to enroll his son at Duke University when the call came, and he had to be paged on a public-address system. Galuszka had told the operator it was an emergency, and later Futrell would recall that hearing his name come over the loudspeaker "scared me to death." He went to the phone shaken and upset, and listened as Galuszka excitedly reviewed what he had just learned. Then Futrell advised his dismayed reporter that the information was "very sensitive morally, legally, and journalistically" and told him not to print a word of it.

Galuszka was "gung ho," Futrell would later say. "I was reluctant to go with it. I realized the implications. I was real worried about what we had to do. It put a completely new focus on the case—against our own people, black and white. I wasn't wavering on doing it, but I was afraid of the reaction. Some radical could have put blacks against whites." He also realized, even as he was talking to Galuszka, that if this story ever got out "they would rub our noses in it all over the country." The implications had shaped his decision. "I believe a part of the role of a local editor is to defend his community when it is attacked," he would say, "even when the attack is only implied."

That day's edition of the Washington *Daily News* went to press later in the afternoon, just as Ashley Futrell was leaving to return home from Durham. No new developments were reported in the hunt for the escaped prisoner, and nothing was said about the information Peter Galuszka had received from Harry Carpenter. But the editorial Futrell had written the day before ran on schedule, even though there had been time to order it stricken from the paper. Beaufort County would wait almost a week for the whole story to break, but a day after the killing Joan Little would seem to be convicted in a blunt commentary that had enormous implications of its own:

BRUTAL MURDER

The murder of Clarence G. [sic] Alligood, age 62, Beaufort County night jailer, is one of the most brutal to happen in this county.

At this very moment, we look at what happened, we look at his family and loved ones, and what is there to say? Here was a man who gave his life in the line of duty. Here was a good man who never made the headlines in life, but in death there must be an appreciation for him and what he did that he never lived to realize.

We look so often at the death of a law enforcement officer, and within a day the story belongs to history. We express great sympathy at the time, but all too soon the story fades away.

Clarence Alligood gave his best to his job. He gave his life in the performance of his duties. What more can any man give?

It is with deeper sympathy than words can express that we feel a part of this story. There will be other Clarence Alligoods who give their lives and there will be other stories of a similar nature. But this one is here at home, and it represents a brutal chapter of a continuing story.

He was a good man.

Even a year later, after this editorial had often been cited as proof that hot blood was pumping through a lynch-minded town following the jailer's death, Futrell did not seem to understand the part he had played in foiling his own prediction. The story had not faded away, and by then all the dreadful implications he had feared were reverberating through his community. "Why?" he would ask, though a partial answer had been available to him all along. On the wall of his cluttered office there was a framed copy of a statement of principles adopted by the North Carolina Press Association in 1955, the same year he had come to the

Washington *Daily News.* "I'm very conscious of these principles," he would say. In part, they read: "A good editor . . . has a special responsibility to defend the weak, to prod the public conscience, to speak out against the injustices of which a majority can sometimes be guilty."

PART IV

AUGUST 1974
—
MARCH 1975

CHAPTER 7

SHE WAS A SISTER

For nearly a week Joan Little was able to hide in a small house only six blocks from the Beaufort County jail while the search for her thinned out over the eastern part of the state and then broke up. By the weekend most lawmen were ready to assume that she had eluded their dragnet and was long gone. But the getaway did not actually occur until five days after her escape, and then only because the first fragile coalition formed to help her had already begun to disintegrate.

It was difficult for black people in Beaufort County to be complacent when they heard about the killing, difficult for them to believe that any jailer found dead inside a woman's cell could really have been a "good man." In the black neighborhoods social class and economic status did not so sharply divide people, and it was not uncommon for even the most respectable of black citizens to know someone with a firsthand understanding of conditions inside the jail. Many blacks were aware that men guarded women day and night, and that men had ready access to the cells occupied by women. Female prisoners in the Beaufort County jail were, quite literally, put at the mercy of their custodians. As the potential for violence was high, so was the potential for abuse. Not all female prisoners were black, but it might have seemed to blacks that black women were the most likely of all to be abused. The disclosures soon to come about the circumstances of the jailer's death would outrage blacks more than whites, but surprise them far less.

An undercurrent of resistance quickly sprang up, moving on rumors that there was more to the story than had been disclosed. Joan Little had few friends outside the enclave called "Dodge City," but an old man named Willie "Pop" Barnes gave her refuge and agreed to contact someone who could help her. Few people wanted to become personally involved, but there were many who hoped she would be able to get out of the area safely. Reliable police informants fell mysteriously silent, and officers found it impossible to tap the flood of gossip surging through all the black neighborhoods about where she was hiding. On Wednesday and Thursday black teenagers went from house to house collecting money they said would be used to get Joan Little out of North Carolina. "It was a chance for black people to do something for one of their own," said a black woman who gave money that week. "The young people picked up on it right away. They weren't looking at her morals—whether she was good or bad. She was a sister. She was in need. She needed help."

Help arrived on Friday evening, when Jerry Paul drove his battered bronze Cadillac into town. A local member of the Southern Christian Leadership Conference named Margie Wright had summoned him, and he arrived with Golden Frinks, the North Carolina field secretary of the SCLC, whose release from prison Paul had arranged earlier that day.* They went to a motel on the outskirts of town, where Margie Wright was waiting with Jessie Williams. Much later Paul would tell the jury that the Joan Little case had been divinely inspired, and Frinks would soon say to a reporter that "God has chosen this girl, with all her little shortcomings, to be the savior of black women who are incarcerated." But it was really men such as these, activists and opportunists sensitive to dramatic issues lying just beneath the surface of the case, who would make Joan Little's name a household word around the world. "I recog-

---

*Arrested and jailed numerous times in connection with civil-rights demonstrations, Frinks had served a short sentence in connection with his conviction several years earlier for leading an unlawful march.

nized the potential," Paul would say privately, "as soon as
I heard about it."

Jerry Paul was an unhappy conundrum, a hard man to
know. Inside him there seemed to rage perpetual painful
conflicts between the past and the present, embodiments
of a personal schism that had severed one period of his life
from another and set him adrift to find a place for himself
without benchmarks or signposts to guide the way. Paul
was, in a sense, two different people: the one, a brawny
youth with little understanding of the world around him;
the other, an adult sagging beneath the weight of worldly
woes not of his own making.

In many ways, Jerry Paul had spent his whole life searching for an identity. He never knew his real parents, or
where he had been born. Adopted as an infant, he grew up
in comfortable circumstances only a mile or two from the
house where Joan Little's mother raised her family. Paul's
father was a successful merchant, a hardware dealer. His
mother was socially active, a member of church societies
and garden clubs. As a youth he was strapping and strong,
a good-natured, likable boy who looked suitably uncomfortable on Sundays when he acted as an usher at the First
Methodist Church. But as a teenager he began to grow
slovenly and rebellious, defying his parents and teachers
and the tight social conventions of his peers, defying almost
everyone except his high school football coach, a man he
would respect and in some ways try to emulate for years to
come.

Paul often claimed to have profound insights about
human nature and the people around him, especially those
on the other side of the Joan Little case, but he lived his
own life as a trite sports metaphor. Though apparently
converted to a philosophy of nonviolence some time during law school, he invariably spoke of himself and of his
efforts as a lawyer in terms of football, a violent game. The
Joan Little defense team had a quarterback, halfbacks, and
linemen. He was the player-coach.

Coaching had been Paul's first real ambition. He distin-

guished himself very early on the football field and found
there an identity and a camaraderie he had not known
before. A disinterested student, he excelled in contact
sports, including wrestling, but it was as a football lineman
that he attained a certain notoriety among the students at
Washington High School. He became a tough kid, swagger-
ing and usually jovial, but somehow slightly malevolent,
not one to date the head cheerleader or lead a pep rally.

A sense of dislocation and alienation began slowly to
overtake Jerry Paul while he was in high school, setting
into motion a pattern of rejection and retaliation that
would eventually sever most of his earlier personal ties,
even with his family and best friends. "You know," he said
years later, recalling a chance encounter with his closest
companion from the football team, "I didn't have anything
to say to him." When his parents died in 1974, his father first
and his mother barely a month later, Paul would feud over
household possessions with the other relatives of the man
and woman he had hardly spoken to in years. His father's
quickening alcoholism while he was in high school may
have contributed to Paul's disaffection; it did make him
wary of intoxicating beverages and cause him to limit his
own drinking to an occasional glass of wine. But there was
more to the changes which came over him than a reaction
to his environment. Jerry Paul was searching for something, and he would not find it in Washington, North Carolina.

After a year of prep school in Georgia to boost his academic average, Paul enrolled in East Carolina College in
Greenville, North Carolina, on an athletic scholarship. His
parents had hoped that he would attend a major university
and pursue a career in medicine or law; they were so dis-
pleased, according to Paul, that they refused to help him
move his belongings to the campus. Paul went to East
Carolina for one reason: to play football.

As a freshman he was a good lineman, tenacious and
tough, an asset to a strong football program. Then injuries
began to sideline him. Finally, late in the season, a blow to

his shoulder ended his formal football career for good. He would continue at East Carolina for three more years, but as a trainer and assistant coach, not as a player. His interest in the game began to diminish, as did his ambition to coach in high school or college. More than his body had been injured; in a sense, so had his identity.

Paul got married as a sophomore to a young woman from a socially prominent family in Tarboro, another eastern North Carolina town. When he graduated from college, he and his wife already had two children, but Paul had nowhere to go and nothing to do. Despite being unable to play the game, he had spent most of his time at East Carolina working in the football program instead of preparing himself for a career. His parents offered to support him if he got into law school, and Paul applied to the University of North Carolina at Chapel Hill. Later he would say he had done so just to give himself "time to think." But the next few years proved to be more than a period of transition for him. They changed his whole life.

At the beginning, in 1966, law school was an uneasy experience for Paul. The academic habitat in Chapel Hill was different from anything he had faced before, and so was the social life. Few of his former classmates were there, and none of his friends from the football team. He felt isolated and alone, as though he were among strangers with whom he could not communicate. "Here I was, just an old country boy watching this go on," he would remember much later. "Not only were they strange to me; I was strange to them." Disagreements with other students ensued, and then a fistfight during an intramural football game on a grassy field behind the law school. After the altercation, Paul's own teammates drove him out of the game, a reaction he could not understand. "I interpreted their disapproval as cultural discrimination," he would say, recalling the incident vividly. What he had done was revive his old high school identity, only to find that in his new surroundings deference, restraint, and a flair for barbed words were more respected than physical prowess.

Jerry Paul could almost mark the moment when his life took new direction. Very soon after starting law school he began to veer away from most of the other students in his class, to adopt unconventional causes, to flirt with unpopular or extreme political ideals. At first he wanted only to accentuate the differences between himself and the others, to shape a new identity out of intellectual rebellion. Later he would become consumed by the ideals themselves. There was, Paul would recall, a visiting professor who had "radical" political opinions, who "believed in integration and civil rights." Paul discerned that "many students despised him" for his beliefs, and he was therefore drawn to the man and to his ideas. He had soon gravitated into a circle of students deeply committed to reform, and in some ways to revolution. In the following year he met and was influenced by another faculty member, a professor of constitutional and labor law who was active in the civil-rights movement and in the American Civil Liberties Union. Through these people Paul got to know others with similar views and gradually became more interested in the causes they espoused. From them, he would later say, he learned that "at some point in life you have to ask yourself what the real issues are and deal with them." Civil-rights activism followed, along with volunteer work in Eugene McCarthy's 1968 presidential campaign, while Paul studied to arm himself with the skills he would need to practice law. His perception of the "real issues" was steadily being shaped, and he was working hard to learn to "deal with them." But the profound change in his outlook had occurred during his first year in law school. On a spring day in Chapel Hill, Jerry Paul would remember later, he had been sitting in a criminal-law class when suddenly, for the first time in his life, he felt "radicalized." He had, at last, found an identity.

There was an irony in Paul's appearance in Washington almost eight years later, a few days after Joan Little's escape. He had grown up there, in a fine house on a sloping manicured lawn. But much had happened since then, and both Paul and his hometown were different. He had never really left eastern North Carolina. After law school he had returned to Greenville, only twenty-one miles from Washington, to set up a law practice. In the late 1960s, civil-rights discontent had reached even into this region, and demonstrations held in Greenville and elsewhere were tense and sometimes bloody. Paul soon joined the marchers and began to defend them when they were arrested, quickly gaining a reputation among people who often found it difficult to secure counsel as a white man willing to stand up for their rights in the streets as well as in court. During this period he met and began to represent Golden Frinks of the SCLC, as well as other local activists, but he also lost the opportunity to establish a solid law practice for himself in Greenville. His years there were stormy, but financially unsuccessful. Eventually he had to leave, taking his family back to Chapel Hill where he could earn a living and they would not feel estranged from the community around them. Even in 1974, though, he still had black friends throughout eastern North Carolina, and the mention of his name in black communities would still often invoke a reverence reserved for no other white man.

Paul had set up his new law office in Durham, in the more urban Piedmont region of the state, and there he had become known as a radical lawyer who represented not only Frinks and the SCLC but also the North Carolina Black Panther Party and its leader, Winston-Salem activist Larry Little. His reputation soon extended across the state, built on his representation of blacks and his involvement in civil-rights activities. His trial tactics were often successful, always flamboyant and controversial. He became a rogue, a maverick who frustrated prosecutors and made judges shudder at the sight of his bulky frame coming through the courtroom door. Other attorneys accused him of dilatory tactics and weak legal skills, of filing excessive numbers of motions and waging verbose arguments on unimportant points, but such criticism did not dissuade Paul or make him change his methods. Disorderly and unkempt, he practiced law much as he had played football—on defense, scratching and kicking at the line of scrimmage to hold the opposing team out of the end zone. He would defend Joan Little the same way. He had been preparing for years, and he was ready when he heard about the young black woman in Beaufort County who had killed a white jailer and escaped.

There was a power struggle from the beginning, a conflict between two generations of reform and protest, between Margie Wright, the young black feminist, and Golden Frinks, the veteran field secretary. Wright insisted on speaking to Paul privately, and in another motel room they made plans for Joan Little's flight to safety and decided not to involve Frinks in the case.

But Frinks saw potential in the situation at least as clearly as Jerry Paul did, though in a different way, and he was determined not to be shut out. For twenty years he had been leading desegregation demonstrations and serving time for civil disobedience, and his first impulse, now as always, was to march. Golden Frinks was a sad anachronism, a black Don Quixote who had continued to tilt uselessly at yesterday's windmills. For years he had been losing respect and support, alienating even many black people who were embarrassed by his opportunistic sense of injustice, his stale belief that any protest was progress, and his willingness to collect money for any cause. Now he learned from Jessie Williams that even she did not know where Joan was hiding and that she wanted her daughter to surrender as soon as possible. Frinks assured her that he would do everything he could to help, and when Paul and Margie Wright returned he announced that he was taking charge of the situation. With Mrs. Williams nodding her approval, he told them he would issue a call for Joan to give herself up and would begin at once to raise funds for her defense.

Joan Little was spirited out of Beaufort County the next

night, before Golden Frinks could find out where she was hiding. She crouched on the floor in the back of Paul's car, then slumped on the back seat, as they took a circuitous route to Chapel Hill and arrived just before dawn on Sunday. Paul's neighbor, a physician named Arthur Finn, accompanied them on the trip and agreed to let her stay at his home until further plans could be made. Described by another doctor as "a man who is a little less satisfied than most with the way things are, so much so that he seems to go out and look for causes to sponsor," Finn had willingly helped get Joan Little out of eastern North Carolina. Later he would become active in the defense effort, but he would insist as a witness at the murder trial that he did not know she was a fugitive. "My understanding was that she was in the process of giving herself up," he explained to the prosecutor who was cross-examining him.*

A surrender was in progress, but it was still several days away when they got back to Chapel Hill on Sunday morning. After a few hours of sleep, Jerry Paul initiated the first phase of his still rudimentary defense strategy. He began calling friends and acquaintances who were involved in civil-rights work and activist politics, inviting them to meet Joan Little at a reception at his home on Monday evening. The list of interested people quickly grew, and a second meeting had to be set up for later Monday night in Durham.

On Sunday evening Paul went to Arthur Finn's house, where he and Finn went over the details of the incident with Joan Little for the first time. Until that night, after he had issued his first call for public support, Paul had not

---

*At the time, North Carolina law prohibited prosecution for harboring a fugitive unless the fugitive was subsequently convicted of the crime for which he had been sought. Two years later the law was changed to permit prosecution irrespective of the disposition of the fugitive's case, primarily as a result of the circumstances of Joan Little's flight from Beaufort County to Chapel Hill. "The philosophy," said Burley Mitchell, a spokesman for the North Carolina Association of District Attorneys, which had recommended the change to the state legislature, "is that no citizen should have the right to substitute his judgment for that of a jury or court after a person has been charged with a felony."

discussed the jailer's death with his new client. The strategy had been implemented even before he had tried to
satisfy himself about the circumstances of the killing. Dr.
Finn would testify at the trial that Joan Little was unable
to speak of the experience during their flight out of Beaufort County and that she first explained what had happened when the three of them talked on Sunday night.
"The whole statement was emotional," he would recall. "It
seemed clear to me it was the truth."

"Objection!"

"You're invading the province of the jury," Judge Hobgood would tell the doctor impatiently. "You can't give a
medical opinion about the truth of a statement."

On cross-examination, Finn would admit that he had no
background or special expertise in psychiatry, and that he
was not professionally qualified to "pass on the mental state
of a patient."

Monday was Labor Day, and the defense effort burgeoned.
Over the weekend Golden Frinks had set up headquarters
in a motel room in Washington and had learned what he
could about the case. On Monday he called a press conference and announced the formation of the Fairness to Joan
Little Committee, telling reporters that the SCLC had arranged for a statewide radio hook-up to broadcast his appeal for her surrender and that a "highly placed" state
official had assured him she would not be harmed if she
gave herself up. "We're after the truth, no matter whom
it hurts," he said. "If Joan's guilty, we'll go from there. If
she says she's not guilty, we'll defend her."

Paul was at work on Monday morning arranging for an
appointment with the director of the State Bureau of Investigation, Charles Dunn, at Dunn's office in Raleigh. During a private meeting later that day he engineered Joan
Little's surrender and obtained valuable information about
the investigation, information he would later exploit to
good advantage. After several hours of negotiation Dunn

consented to Paul's terms. Joan Little would be guaranteed safe confinement and would not be returned to Beaufort County. She would also be permitted to give herself up voluntarily at SBI headquarters, and she would be allowed to make a statement to reporters before surrendering. "Dunn is a politician . . . and was as happy as we were to have the press there," Paul would later say. "That's why I chose him, because I knew he would give us leeway with the press." The first media event had been scheduled with the help of a high-ranking state official, himself a former newspaperman, and Jerry Paul's calculated defense gamble was successfully under way.

Joan Little made only brief and tearful appearances at Paul's house and at the meeting in Durham later that night, but these gatherings served an important purpose: They brought together a nucleus of energetic people, almost all of whom would become active in some way in the defense. Many of them would participate in the work of the Joann Little Defense Fund, a tax-exempt organization soon founded to raise the money needed for the elaborate defense effort Jerry Paul had begun to conceive. Several would join as members of the Fund's executive committee, and Dr. Arthur Finn would become the committee chairman. This group alone would raise well over $100,000 in contributions from all over the world.

The surrender was set for 3:00 p.m. Tuesday.

Calls had gone out early from Paul's law office telling newsmen to be at SBI headquarters that afternoon, while preparations were made for Joan Little to meet reporters for the first time. Golden Frinks had been in Chapel Hill and Durham on Monday night, but by Tuesday morning he was back in Washington, where he called a press conference to disclose the plans himself and to take credit for arranging the surrender. With Jessie Williams at his side, Frinks appeared before the newsmen in regalia they had come to associate with the SCLC leader—a jump suit, low-top boots, a medallion and chain, and a leather shoulder bag.

The afternoon sky was darkening as about a dozen reporters and television cameramen gathered on the sidewalk outside SBI headquarters in Raleigh. There was a light sprinkle, and after the rain had stopped, Paul's car pulled to the curb and Joan Little stepped out to face the waiting newsmen for the first time. "It looked like she had been to the beauty parlor," one reporter would recall. "She was nicely dressed and her hair was nicely done."

Standing in the background while Joan Little answered questions in a barely audible whisper was another young black woman, Karen Galloway, a recent graduate of Duke University Law School who had just learned she had passed the bar examination and would be admitted to practice law in North Carolina. Karen Galloway was from Raleigh, the daughter of a schoolteacher and a postal employee, and she had known Jerry Paul since his days as a lawyer in Greenville while she was attending college there. A bright, jovial woman with a flashing, friendly smile, she was to become the only woman and the only black person included on the Joan Little defense team. She considered herself "politicized" but not radical and "not the type of person to jump on anybody's bandwagon." She had joined Paul's firm only a few days earlier, and because of her inexperience she would play a limited role at the trial. But she would become a prominent figure in the defense movement, traveling and speaking frequently as Paul's defense "co-counsel," a cosmetic role she would play willingly because of the contribution she could make to the overall defense effort by doing so. In private, however, Paul referred to her as his "assistant," not as his associate. "The appearance is that Karen and I are co-counsel," he would explain before the trial, "and . . . it was our purpose to give the appearance of co-counsel because that looked better and certainly made it easier for us to raise funds with those groups that can relate better to her—the black groups and the women's groups. They felt better if she's co-counsel."

Joan Little was arrested in Charles Dunn's office after the brief news conference on the sidewalk. A ritual had been worked out the day before, and it was executed after Paul and Dunn exchanged a few remarks. Special Agent William Slaughter stood by to read the required Miranda warning: "You have the right to remain silent. . . ." Then a female agent stepped forward and took the prisoner into custody.

In another room, alone and out of sight, Chief Deputy Ottis Davis and Deputy Willis Peachey waited impatiently. Late on Monday, Davis had been informed of the impending surrender and told to obtain an order committing Joan Little to the state's prison for women in Raleigh. Davis and Peachey had arrived at the SBI headquarters well before 3:00 p.m. on Tuesday, but, to their surprise, they had been asked to wait elsewhere while the surrender took place. This exclusion, demanded by Paul as part of his arrangements with Charles Dunn, mystified and dejected both lawmen. "I have plenty of questions as to what was said in that room," Davis would complain. "I should have been there. I represented the forty thousand people in Beaufort County."

After the arrest Davis was shown into Dunn's office, where he handed the order to Paul. There was no conversation. No one was permitted to ask Joan Little any questions. A few moments later she was escorted to a Wake County sheriff's car and driven away to prison. Jerry Paul and Karen Galloway left shortly through the front door. By then all the reporters were gone, but Paul was already making plans to call them back again.

CHAPTER 8

TRUE BILL

On Wednesday the story broke: REPORT SAYS JAILER FOUND PARTLY NUDE.

Several days before the surrender Ottis Davis had been asked to comment on rumors about unusual conditions inside the cell when the jailer's body was found. "It'll all come out after she's apprehended at the proper time and place," Davis had said. "I ain't trying to hide a thing in the world. I've just been advised by court officials that I can't say too much or I'd ruin the case."

Then on Wednesday a reporter telephoned Dr. Harry Carpenter about the medical examiner's report. Golden Frinks was making strong accusations. Chief Deputy Davis had said there was "more" to the case. The Washington *Daily News,* still sitting on Carpenter's information even after Ashley Futrell had checked it with Davis, nevertheless had alluded to undisclosed "further details."* Would he care to comment? Carpenter was still willing to talk, but by then he had submitted his written report to the chief state medical examiner in Chapel Hill. Instead of making

---

*On September 2, however, a cryptic clue to the real circumstances in the cell had appeared deep in the *Daily News* story about the charges of jail harassment made by Golden Frinks and Jessie Williams. "County Medical Examiner Dr. Harry Carpenter disclosed last week that jailer Alligood was found clad only in a 'T' shirt in Little's cellblock bunk," Peter Galuszka's story had said in a runover column on page 12. Futrell would not recall having printed this belated reference to Carpenter's information when he discussed the role of the *Daily News* in the case nearly a year later. Because he did not routinely edit the paper's news copy, it was unlikely he even knew about the long-overlooked disclosure before it was published.

a statement, he referred the reporter to the office of Dr. R. Page Hudson at Memorial Hospital.

Hudson was, in fact, preparing to release the report at the moment the newsman called him later that same morning. His staff doctors had become alarmed over the weekend because news accounts continued to say nothing about the circumstances Carpenter had described when he submitted the results of his examination to their office. Earlier in the week they had called Jerry Paul to the hospital to discuss the information received from the local medical examiner, information which had so far been withheld from the press and the defense attorneys. Paul had arrived for their conference with Dr. Arthur Finn, and both had been shown a copy of Carpenter's brief report:

> *The deceased jailer was found near the foot of the jail cell cot, feet on floor slumped over with left side of face down. His shoes were in the corridor, socks on feet but otherwise naked from the waist down with open yellow plaid shirt and undershirt on. The left arm was under the body and clutching his pants which were touching the cell floor. His right hand contained an ice pick. There was blood on the sheet, cell floor, corridor, and possibly the outside cell block door. Body heat was present, no rigor and dependent livor of the left side of the face and neck. Beneath his buttocks was a decorated partially torn woman's kerchief. On the floor was a night gown and on the cell door was a brassiere and night jacket. His watch was running and showed the correct time. There were multiple puncture wounds of the body including one of the right parietal scalp, seven chest wounds, one left quadrant wound and two in the right lateral thigh. The chest wounds corresponded with similar blood stained holes in his undershirt. Extending from the penis to his thigh skin was a string of what appeared to be seminal fluid.*

Once Paul had been informed privately of the contents of Carpenter's report, Hudson and the other doctors decided to release it with more than ordinary fanfare. Their concern seemed to shift from protecting the escapee to publicizing their role in developing evidence her attorneys could use, and they were soon planning to showcase the work of the medical examiner's office at a press conference at the hospital. "We were interested in projecting the image of the system as an agency to gather information of potential use to both the prosecution and the defense," one of the staff pathologists would explain later. But then a joint news conference with the defense attorneys was proposed by Paul, and that seemed an even better way to dramatize the contribution their office had made. What Hudson and the others did not know was that Jerry Paul had already begun to formulate his own publicity plans—plans that were not concerned with reflecting credit on the medical examiner system.

But the proposed timing of the disclosure was thrown off by the inquiring reporter. Hudson released Carpenter's report on Wednesday, in time for an Associated Press story to reach a few afternoon papers that day. "A preliminary [sic] medical examiner's report has confirmed," the AP story said, "that the body of a Beaufort County jailer was partially naked when found in a jail cell after a woman prisoner escaped last week." The next morning, the Raleigh *News & Observer* informed eastern North Carolina that not all the facts about the incident at the Beaufort County jail had yet been reported:

CHAPEL HILL—A preliminary [sic] medical examiner's report released Wednesday confirmed that the body of a Beaufort County jailer was partially clothed when he was found in a jail cell after a female prisoner escaped last week.

The report, prepared by Beaufort County Medical Examiner Dr. Harry Carpenter, said the jailer, Clarence G. [sic] Alligood, 62, was clothed only in his shirt and undershirt and was nude from the waist down. . . .

Civil rights activist Golden Frinks, who helped negotiate [Joan Little's] surrender, said Miss Little claimed that Alligood attempted to rape her. He said the jailer had threatened her with an ice pick and she denied that she killed Alligood. . . .

Frinks has charged that Alligood was alive when Miss Little fled the jail, and he suggested that [the] jailer committed suicide.

State authorities said Wednesday that suicide is still a possibility as a cause of death.

"As far as I'm concerned, it has not been ruled out," Dr. R. Page Hudson, state medical examiner, said.

Dr. Linda Norton, assistant chief medical examiner, said in a separate interview that suicide is possible, but "it is not the most likely possibility." She said she based that opinion on the nature and number of the wounds.

During the previous evening the wire service teletypes of the Associated Press and United Press International had been clacking out similar stories to their subscribers all over the state. "The body of a Beaufort County jailer was partially nude when found in a jail cell last week after a woman prisoner escaped," the AP reported. "The body of a Beaufort County jailer was partially clothed when he was found stabbed to death in a jail cell from which a female prisoner escaped last week," said UPI. Moments later, with the flip of a switch, the news leaped over to the national wire, and the whole country began to learn that something had been going on down in a backwater of the South, something involving a black woman and a white man and an ice pick and sex.

By law, it had not been Harry Carpenter's responsibility to commence an investigation into the death of Clarence Alligood, nor had he been required to play detective or forensic pathologist at the scene of the killing. His report was not meant to be an exhaustive survey of the cell area, and it was not surprising that it did not mention every detail about the body and the circumstances in the cell-block.

It was evident from the police photos, for example, that a blanket had been tied to the corner of the bars in front of the small cell, partially obscuring the view into that area from outside the cellblock bars. Under the dead man's buttocks on the bunk there was a rumpled second blanket. Beneath his feet there was still another blanket, partially unfolded. Below his right hand, which held the ice pick, were his pants and his underwear. At the head of the bunk, near the toilet, a pair of black-rimmed glasses lay on the floor surrounded by several large spots which Carpenter and the investigating officers would later assume were drops of blood.

Neither the photos taken by Danny Respass nor the report filed by Carpenter indicated that there was a bloodstain on the wall over the bunk or a stream of blood running down the wall to a pool on the floor beneath the bed, but the motion-picture film shot by Gordon Edwards showed such a stain, and at the trial there would be a controversy about whether it had been there before the arrival of the medical examiner (suggesting that the jailer had leaned against the wall before slumping over on the bunk) or whether the stain had been made while the body was being removed from the cell.

It was also impossible to establish from the photos whether there were bloodstained pieces of toilet tissue in the sink or in the toilet in cell number one, and Carpenter's report made no mention of them. Willis Peachey had observed the bloody pieces of paper and had made reference to them in his diagram of the cell. But, like the package of cigarettes which Peachey included in his drawing, the tissues had disappeared during the clean-up later that morning. An open jar of Vaseline said by the investigating officers to have been found on the sink in cell number one was not shown in the photos or mentioned in Carpenter's report. The diagram prepared by Peachey indicated the location of the jar where he had noticed it when he first entered the cell. Like the cigarettes and the tissues, it was gone within a short time and never reappeared. Some time later even Peachey's original diagram would be discarded, and he would have to sketch another from memory just before the trial, nearly a year later.

By coincidence the autopsy report from Dr. Charles Gilbert arrived in Page Hudson's office on Friday, the day of the news conference. It contained no surprises. Cause of death: "Cardiac tamponade secondary to a penetrating injury to the left ventricle." Clarence Alligood had been stabbed in the heart. After receiving the wound, the sac around the heart had gradually filled with blood, slowly squeezing it to a stop. Several doctors, including Gilbert, would later testify that Alligood might have remained conscious from two to ten minutes after the fatal blow was struck. All of the medical experts would agree that he did not die instantly, that he probably was able to move around for at least several minutes after being stabbed, and that a period of unconsciousness preceded death.

Otherwise, neither of the medical reports contained much information of value in determining what might have happened between Clarence Alligood and Joan Little or where the legal responsibility for his death should lie. The jailer's body organs had all been intact and functional. He had not been under the influence of alcohol or drugs. He had been stabbed seven times in the chest, twice in the thigh, once in the head, and once in the lower abdomen. Lawyers might have assumed that five stab wounds close to the heart were significant, but the doctors reported them with statistical objectivity. The pathology report indicated that one of the chest wounds had pierced the aorta, causing "severe" internal bleeding and eventually death.

But misunderstandings about the importance of these reports would arise almost immediately because of loose press interpretations and would persist because medical testimony would be incompetently handled at the trial. It would be widely assumed that Dr. Carpenter had seen seminal fluid (the Associated Press would state that the liquid on the jailer's thigh had "contained spermatozoa") and that Dr. Gilbert had confirmed Carpenter's observation during the autopsy. "The [medical examiner's] report . . . said there was seminal fluid on his thigh," the *News &*

Observer would declare. "An autopsy later confirmed that the fluid contained spermatozoa. . . ." In fact Carpenter had only reported seeing "what appeared to be seminal fluid," and Gilbert had clearly indicated that he was unable to confirm the medical examiner's visual observation pathologically. Gilbert's report stated in two places that "material resembling seminal fluid was not present on the thighs," but said elsewhere that "smears were made from fluid in the anterior urethra" and that those "smears were teening [sic] with spermatozoa." There was no apparent pathological connection between what Carpenter had seen on the man's thigh and what Gilbert had extracted from the end of his penis nearly twelve hours later, but these unrelated aspects of the two reports would be thrown into a heap by careless newsmen, who for months relentlessly reported "clear evidence of sexual activity" without medical data to support the assertion.

The lawyers would do no better. None of the doctors was interviewed by the prosecution before the trial, and so the district attorney had only a vague idea what Carpenter and Gilbert might say when he needlessly called them to the witness stand. Almost inadvertently, Carpenter was permitted to make the assumption that what he had seen was seminal fluid, and he testified that he thought the pool of liquid on the man's thigh was indicative of recent sexual activity. In the same way, Gilbert was allowed to state that the presence of sperm in the urethral fluid indicated the jailer "had ejaculated prior to death" because "the ejaculatory mechanism" had to be stimulated in order for sperm to appear there.

These opinions would seem unsound and indefensible to the forensic pathologists in the state medical examiner's office, all of whom were experts in analyzing the biology of death. One of them would later say that some of the medical evidence imparted to the jury during this trial was "absolutely ridiculous." The prosecution could have called any of these doctors and introduced both medical reports along with expert testimony to establish that a post-mortem purge of seminal fluid did not indicate recent sexual activity. According to these physicians, there were at least three pathological explanations for the presence of spermatozoa in the urethra that had nothing to do with overt sexual stimulation at the time of death.* But William Griffin had gotten the impression that Page Hudson was sympathetic to the defense and never even asked him for a medical opinion of the evidence.

The defense attorneys thoroughly interviewed both Carpenter and Gilbert before the trial, however, and so they were prepared for effective cross-examination when these doctors appeared. Dr. Hudson was eventually called by the defense and he did testify that the presence of seminal fluid should not be considered an indication of recent sexual activity. But the attorneys moved away from the subject when Hudson spoke up, and his comment seemed to have no impact on the jury.

The press conference—held on Friday in a small church on the edge of the University of North Carolina campus—was jammed with reporters from all over the state. Overnight, the Joan Little case had become big news.

Dr. Neil Hoffman arrived with a stack of press releases

---

*Pathologists and experts in human sexuality indicated that pre-coital fluid secreted by male organs during casual sexual excitation contains spermatozoa that may be deposited along the urethral canal whether or not direct stimulation and ejaculation occurs, and that body liquids expelled by urination may also transport spermatozoa to the urethra. Gilbert's report stated that "the urinary bladder contained approximately 15 cc. of urine," and he would testify on cross examination by the defense that this small amount of urine in the bladder indicated that Alligood "had been to the bathroom recently. . . ." Hypothetically, it was also possible that the advance of rigor mortis had forced seminal fluid bearing spermatozoa into the urethral canal prior to Gilbert's autopsy. Gradwohl's *Legal Medicine*, a standard text used by medical examiners in North Carolina, stated that "when the walls of the seminal vesicles are affected" by the onset of rigor mortis "seminal fluid might be discharged from the penis." Dr. Carpenter had detected no rigor mortis when he examined the body at the jail, and so this did not account for the substance he saw on the jailer's leg. But Dr. Gilbert's autopsy was performed hours later, long after rigor mortis had set in.

he had prepared to explain the role of the state medical examiner's office. Because Page Hudson was out of town, Hoffman would stand in as the staff's representative. He was surprised to learn that Jerry Paul would not participate in the news conference, but that Karen Galloway would. He was also surprised to see various political activists circulating among the reporters, including people he would later identify as members of the North Carolina Alliance Against Racist and Political Repression, an affiliate of the radical organization headed by Angela Davis, a friend of Jerry Paul's and an avowed communist. Through the National Alliance Against Racist and Political Repression, Davis would herself eventually become a prominent force in the political movement that welled up around the case. Her appearances at rallies with Joan Little in the spring would spark rumors of a power struggle between the Alliance and the defense attorneys and would give rise to reports of communist influences on the defense team.

While Hoffman was passing out his news release, the press conference began. He took a seat beside Karen Galloway at a small table and sat in surprised and embarrassed disbelief as she launched an attack on local officials in Beaufort County for the way they had handled the case. Later he would recall hearing Galloway say that a "terrible thing had been done" to Joan Little, and that she had "clearly acted in self-defense." Galloway also announced that an effort would be made to move the trial out of the eastern part of North Carolina by challenging the constitutionality of a state law restricting changes of venue beyond adjoining jurisdictions. "The Washington *Daily News* and law enforcement agencies in Beaufort County have tried to inflame public reaction against Joan Little by releasing only part of the facts in the case," she told the reporters, sounding themes that the defense attorneys would often repeat during the coming months.

Then it was Hoffman's turn to speak, and he realized that almost anything he said would appear to support the accusations Karen Galloway had just made. The first few questions were easy. "The release of seminal fluid quite commonly occurs at the time of death," he told the reporters, "and it is not necessarily related to the cause of death or to the status of the individual at the time of death." But then someone asked about the jailer's pants. Karen Galloway had asserted that they were missing, and the newsmen wanted to know why. Thrown off balance because he had not expected to be questioned about the clothing (neither the medical reports nor his own statement had mentioned the whereabouts of the jailer's personal effects), Hoffman hesitated, then gave a vague response. "I told them it was routine policy that the clothing should be preserved and transported with the body," he would recall later. "They drew their own conclusions."

Press accounts of this news conference would contribute to an enduring suspicion that evidence was being withheld from the defense attorneys, an issue they kept alive by periodically accusing the authorities of failing to cooperate with them. One newspaper speculated the next morning that the Medical Examiner's office was launching an all-out effort to locate the trousers, implying that they were actually missing and might have been destroyed. The mystery seemed to deepen when Charles Dunn and Ottis Davis were both unable to place the trousers, though Davis said he thought they had been turned over to the SBI after the autopsy. None of the reporters contacted the officers directly involved in the investigation or the two doctors who had submitted medical reports.

In fact the jailer's clothing had been collected by the local medical examiner, placed on the stretcher in a container, and transported with the body in accordance with the policy stressed by Hoffman. Gilbert had later given the clothing to William Slaughter after the autopsy, as Davis had suspected, and all of it had been returned to the Beaufort County jail. The shirt and undershirt were taken to the SBI laboratory for analysis, but the trousers did not seem important. For months they hung in a locker in the squad room of the sheriff's department.

Later Neil Hoffman would reflect unhappily on the press conference. His insistence that the pool of liquid on the dead man's thigh was not indicative of recent sexual activity had been largely ignored, and his speculation about the preservation of evidence had cast a shadow over the investigation by local authorities. "I hadn't meant to be there to align the medical examiner's office with either side in the case," he would say. "I didn't want to make anyone look good or bad except the medical examiner system."

But Hoffman and the state medical examiner's office, like the press, had been manipulated. "Because they expressed a desire to say that their office was neutral and that they were not an agency of the state, I perceived I could get them to a press conference under the guise of saying that," Jerry Paul would explain. "That really swung things in our favor, because then I had the medical examiner saying something was fishy." In the climate of opinion created by the reluctance of the Beaufort County Sheriff's Department to disclose these "fishy" details and the failure of the *Daily News* to report them fully, it was easy to believe that a conspiracy might have been afoot to further suppress vital evidence. Heightening the drama, Karen Galloway announced that the defense had filed a motion earlier on Friday for a protective order to compel production of the trousers. But the interest of the defense attorneys in preserving this evidence, while certainly genuine, seemed as belated as it was intense. Neither Paul nor Galloway had asked either William Slaughter or Willis Peachey about the pants when they were together for the surrender earlier in the week, and they had waited four days after learning that Charles Dunn did not know where the trousers were before filing a simple motion to insure against their loss or destruction. Instead of going to the courts at once, they had spent the week maneuvering for the attention of the press, an allocation of time and energy reflecting basic priorities in the defense strategy that would endure for the remainder of the case.

Following the surrender, Golden Frinks recast his Fairness to Joan Little Committee as the Free Joan Little Committee, and with the help of local activists and Jessie Williams he organized a short parade through Washington and a rally on the steps of the Beaufort County Courthouse in the name of his new defense organization and the Southern Christian Leadership Conference. The *Daily News* gave prominent advance publicity to the march, which took place on Sunday, September 8, and the local police cooperated by handling traffic at each intersection and by assigning only plainclothes officers to monitor the demonstrators. About 350 people participated, singing hymns, hearing speeches, and offering silent prayers.

Jerry Paul was invited, but declined to attend. On Friday the formation of the Joann Little Defense Fund had been announced, and the contest for control of the case was already apparent. The outcome was inevitable. Golden Frinks had Joan Little's mother, but Jerry Paul had Joan Little.

The next day the September term of criminal court opened in Beaufort County and a grand jury of eighteen people— fourteen whites and four blacks, nine men and nine women—was selected and impaneled. Before being shown to a closed hearing room, the jurors were instructed by two judges to consider the bills of indictment that would be presented and to decide only whether there was sufficient evidence to send each case to trial, not whether the accused was guilty.

It was mid-afternoon when this grand jury reached the bill of indictment naming Joan Little. District Attorney William Griffin had submitted it believing he had a strong case, and he expected the return of a "true bill." Later he would be criticized by the defense attorneys for bringing the indictment, and especially for going to the grand jury on first-degree murder, but at the time Joan Little had not spoken out with her version of the incident and the known facts suggested to Griffin that this might indeed turn out to be a premeditated killing. There were indications that Joan Little had been unhappy in jail, frustrated by her inability to arrange bail. There were eleven stab wounds, five clustered around the heart, suggesting that Clarence Alligood's assailant had intended to strike him repeatedly in a vital part of the body and had managed to do so with deadly accuracy. And there was the report of an SBI interview with Anna Eubanks, which raised suspicions that Joan Little had been planning an escape. "All I knew at the time," Griffin would later recall, "was that the man was dead—even though his pants were off, he was full of holes—that she had fled, and that she had told somebody in Chapel Hill she was going to get out of jail. That looked like a case of first-degree murder."*

William Griffin had submitted this bill of indictment with no premonitions about the difficulties that lay ahead of him. He hoped to dispose of the matter in his usual way, quickly and without fanfare, by submitting the facts to a jury and accepting its verdict without comment or criticism. Griffin knew that Jerry Paul would be the opposing counsel and expected complications as a result, but unlike Ashley Futrell he did not perceive the implications of the case for the community or for himself. In the coming months his decision to bring Joan Little to trial for first-degree murder would gain him the public scorn of the defense attorneys as well as the private condemnation of her supporters all over the country and the world. Repeated attacks on his integrity and his handling of the case would be translated into press criticism and public skepticism, distractions that would eventually have a debilitating effect on his trial preparations and on the vigor of his efforts in the courtroom. His prosecutorial tendency to emphasize those as-

*Unlike the defense attorneys, Griffin had not yet received copies of the medical reports.

pects of the case which suggested guilt more than innocence would often be interpreted as benign bigotry; his
reluctance to deal with reporters would be regarded by
some of them as an indication he had something to hide.
After the jury had rendered an acquittal and the furor over
the case had died down, he would look back on the trial
with only bitter regard for the press and a lingering certainty that Joan Little was guilty, "guilty as hell."

Griffin was born and raised in the eastern North Carolina
town of Williamston, a community not unlike Washington,
but located in Martin County about twenty miles away. His
family had lived in the area for generations, and owned
property and business interests there. He was an only child.
People in Williamston remembered him as a young man
who "always knew where he was going," though for a while
Griffin himself had not seemed to know. Drifting from
college at the University of North Carolina to law school at
Rutgers University in New Jersey "for a change of sce-
nery," he had come back to Martin County without clear
plans about what he intended to do with his life. A chance
to become an assistant United States attorney slipped away
when the Republicans swept into office in 1968, and then
some political friends urged him to run for district attorney
in the Second Judicial District, which included Martin,
Beaufort, and three other coastal counties. Until the suggestion was made, he had not thought about becoming a
local prosecutor.

Griffin had chosen law as a profession mainly because it
seemed certain to afford him a degree of personal independence and a comfortable income. He had vaguely anticipated a career in business, and had had a passing interest in admiralty law, but now he settled quickly into the
routine of rural criminal prosecution. Married and soon to
be the father of two boys, he built a house in Williamston
and set up his office there in an old building across from the
county's white stucco courthouse. The work was strenuous.
At the outset he had only one assistant, who was stationed
in Beaufort County where the caseload was heaviest. But

the job was low-key and he was largely his own man. Although he appeared in court in each of the five counties on a rotating basis, there were afternoons when he could take time off to go fishing and he was always home in the evenings to tend his garden and be with his family. He soon became a lay-leader in the Presbyterian Church, a settled member of the community.

The new district attorney had no firmly preconceived ideas about criminal justice, but with experience William Griffin was to gain a certain parochial faith in the judicial process of which he was a part. He believed, as many prosecutors do, in trial by ambush rather than in extensive pre-trial discovery procedures. He felt that such procedures, which forced early disclosure of the state's case, tended to encourage opposing lawyers to frame a defense around the state's evidence. Still, he had an abiding faith in the ability of jurors to fathom the facts and arrive at a just conclusion based on adversary presentations made in court. "Our system of dealing with criminals is based upon the premise that a jury is to pass upon the guilt or innocence of a defendant relying entirely upon the facts and evidence they hear in the courtroom," he had written to the editor of the Washington *Daily News* early in 1974, "and that their decision on the facts is final." His inclination was to lay out the evidence in open court, not to substitute his own judgment for the jury's when the facts were unclear. His intention was to handle all cases, even one that had assumed worldwide gravity, in exactly the same manner. Throughout the coming months he would profess a willingness to plea-bargain with Joan Little's attorneys—to negotiate a reduction in the charges in exchange for a guilty plea—but he would refuse to consider unilaterally dropping the case unless all suspicions about Joan Little's guilt could be resolved. The best way to prosecute fairly, he would say, "is to throw all the facts up for the jury and let them make a decision."

By September 1974, William Griffin had become an established, experienced prosecutor. In the courtroom he relied on precision and diligence rather than flamboyance and ringing oratory. He remained personally aloof, seldom giving selective attention to one defendant, seldom becoming subjectively concerned about the merits of a particular verdict. "You can't win them all," he told a reporter, referring to a case he had lost, despite resounding evidence of guilt, because the jury had felt sorry for the defendant. Even when pre-trial publicity heaped ridicule on his efforts to prosecute Joan Little and made him something of a villain, he would continue to say that he was more interested in the maintenance of the judicial system than he was in the disposition of this one case. He had no special stake in the murder prosecution of Joan Little—he had never met the dead man and he could not recall having been involved in the defendant's prior scrapes with the law. He had personal self-regard and confidence in his abilities but little of the egoism that might have marked him as an acutely ambitious man. "William is just a little bit lazy," sighed a harried official in Beaufort County; and a graduate student from Michigan who interviewed him after the trial would say as he was leaving, "You know, you're not such a bad guy after all."

In North Carolina, unlike many states, grand juries operate autonomously, without the interference or influence of the district attorney. A foreman, selected by the grand jurors themselves, coordinates their activities, calls witnesses, and orchestrates the submission of testimony and evidence. The function of the grand jury is to act as a buffer between the citizen and the state, to prevent capricious prosecution. An indictment is handed down, if at all, because the grand jurors feel there is sufficient evidence to warrant a trial of the facts. But the district attorney makes no appearance before them and has no opportunity to argue his side of the case.

The foreman of this grand jury was a craftsman named Phil Weston, and he was the first to look over the bill of indictment naming Joan Little. At the time, William Griffin was on the other side of the building conducting a trial in the Superior Courtroom. Listed on the indictment form as possible witnesses were Ottis Davis, Willis Peachey, Jerry Helms, William Slaughter, and Dr. Harry Carpenter.* All these names had been copied by Griffin's secretary directly from the murder warrant issued for Joan Little. Weston asked a bailiff which of these men was available, and Willis Peachey was summoned and was the first to testify, showing the jurors the books taken from the cellblock and the pictures of the body. Then William Slaughter was called. "We wanted the man who knew the most about the case," Weston would explain later at a pre-trial hearing. "We wanted the SBI man." Slaughter arrived with a copy of Harry Carpenter's report and read it aloud as the grand jurors listened. Then he was asked one question and excused.

Two witnesses had been heard—the minimum required in a capital case—and a vote was taken. The results were unanimous. Phil Weston placed a check mark in a box on the indictment form beside the words "True Bill," and the grand jury moved on to its next case.

Joan Little had been indicted for first-degree murder.

*The indictment form was later the subject of controversy because, at some point, Dr. Carpenter's name was crossed off with a heavy ink line. Carpenter had received a subpoena, however, and was prepared to report to the courthouse if he was called to testify.

CHAPTER 9

THE SELLING OF JOAN LITTLE

Among other things, the Sixth Amendment to the United States Constitution assures every criminal defendant a "speedy" trial. In theory it is considered a bedrock principle of criminal justice, a fundamental response to the notion that justice delayed is justice denied. But set against the ideal of the Sixth Amendment is the courthouse reality that often there is justice delayed or no justice at all. Dockets in most jurisdictions are seriously backlogged, and in some places the courts are near collapse under an ever-expanding case load. There are too few judges and courtrooms. There are too many defendants, and perhaps too many lawyers. Delay has become a commonplace trial tactic, especially for the defense, a way to gain more time to prepare or to bargain a plea, more time for evidence to be misplaced or destroyed, more time for the memory of witnesses to fade and falter.

At Joan Little's surrender Jerry Paul had told reporters that his "only option" was to "attempt to obtain a fair and speedy trial in . . . court," but within the week he was to initiate a series of procedural maneuvers that would delay the trial for months. In Beaufort County, Paul sought a change of venue to an unspecified location outside eastern North Carolina, in effect asking for relief the court could not give without invalidating a state law prohibiting the transfer of a trial beyond a county adjoining the county in which the case had arisen. Although Joan Little had not been declared an indigent, Paul sought funds in another motion to pay what were described as "legal expenses," including $2,500 to hire a "sociological survey team" to determine which county in the state "would afford the defendant a fair and impartial trial." Already Paul had signaled the direction in which he would attempt to move the case. He would argue that a fair trial was impossible because of the sociology of the place where the killing had occurred. He would say that Joan Little could not get a fair trial in Beaufort County because of who she was, not what she had done.*

In Wake County Superior Court in Raleigh, Paul soon filed a motion to have his client released from Women's Prison pending trial. Here too was a precursor of the coming marathon defense effort. Paul argued that pre-trial appellate procedures in the case might require more than a year to complete. After reading the medical examiner's report and the autopsy report, Judge James H. Pou Bailey set bail at $100,000. It was a figure suggested to the judge in chambers by Paul himself.

On October 9 the motion for a change of venue was denied, but a special venire of jurors drawn from another county was ordered to hear the case. The defense appealed and asked for a stay beyond November 18, when the trial was set to begin. The motion for a stay was denied, and so Paul submitted a motion for a continuance to the trial judge, Henry McKinnon. "Counsel are of the opinion," Paul's written motion said, "that the defense will not be fully prepared to proceed to trial on 18 November 1974." After conferring with resident judges and with District

*Written motions filed by the defense generally referred also to adverse pre-trial publicity and other traditional and more obvious influences on the impartiality of the forum; and at hearings on the original motion for a change of venue, evidence of adverse publicity was submitted. In later arguments, however, the defense would base its entire presentation on sociological evidence of prejudice against blacks and women in eastern North Carolina.

Attorney Griffin, McKinnon granted the continuance. The trial was indefinitely postponed, and the order for a special venire was permitted to expire.

Within a month the SBI concluded its investigation into the death of Clarence Alligood. William Slaughter had interviewed several people who might have been involved in Joan Little's escape, and had found no evidence of aid by an accomplice. Julius Rodgers had been located in Chapel Hill: "Subject [Rodgers] stated that he has not heard from Joanne and that he does not want to hear from Joanne. That he does not want to get involved in this thing. Subject advised that he has never heard anything about Joanne being mistreated in the Beaufort County Jail."

In Washington, Slaughter had interviewed the jail staff, including the radio dispatcher, Beverly King, and the other jailers. King informed him "that around 3:00 a.m., Mr. Alligood asked her if all the deputies had gone in for the night," and that "she advised him that they had." She said she had heard no "noise or commotion" in the jail that morning, and "that Mr. Alligood had always been very nice to her and had never made any advances toward her."

Ellis Tetterton told Slaughter he had known Joan Little four years and that she had been in the Beaufort County jail several times. According to Slaughter's report, Tetterton said "she had never given him any trouble. That she would worry you about making phone calls. That he [Tetterton] never heard her use any bad language. That she never appeared to be seductive." Tetterton was also asked for information about the slain jailer. He told the officer "that he did not know anything against Mr. Alligood. That he appeared to know his job and demonstrated that he was a most cautious and competent jailer. He could not imagine why he went back and unlocked her cell."

David Watson was questioned at length by both Slaughter and Willis Peachey. He told them that when he went off duty the drawer containing the ice pick was "pushed all the way together." According to Slaughter's report:

Subject [Watson] advised that he noticed nothing unusual about the way Mr. Alligood acted or behaved that night. Subject advised that he never had had any trouble with suspect Little. That as far as he knew she was a good prisoner. That he had allowed her to make several phone calls during his shift and that he had occasionally denied her phone calls, because he was too busy to take care of it right that minute. That she did not walk around undressed. That most of the night she wore a nightgown, however, she kept a blanket around her. That when he went into her cell area, he would always knock first. That she never attempted to seduce him, never used profane language. That there was no change in her attitude. That there was no indication about her trying to get out. Subject advised that Mr. Alligood had never talked about sex around him and had never mentioned anything about his sexual habits or his desire for suspect Little.

Interviews were also conducted with several inmates and former inmates of the jail. Romona Markarian, a white woman arrested on August 23, 1974, for driving under the influence of alcohol and assault on a police officer, told Slaughter that Joan Little was a "very nice and considerate person." She said she and Joan had talked about "how she had gotten a bad deal from the court; also, that the food was bad and they did not give you clean sheets." Romona Markarian would later testify for the defense at the trial.

Another former female inmate advised Slaughter that Joan Little "never made any complaint about being mistreated. That [she] talked about her boyfriend and getting out of jail." Another said that Joan "appeared well treated while she was in the Beaufort County Jail." Yet another said "that suspect Little acted like she liked Mr. Alligood a lot," and that "Mr. Alligood brought them food every night. . . ."

On September 9 the SBI launched a separate investigation into the conduct of jailers and inmates inside the Beaufort County jail. Reports were filed on interviews with sixty-seven former female prisoners who had been confined there during the preceding year. Sixty-three of the women said they had not been abused while they were in jail, although one claimed to have been propositioned by a bondsman and another said she had been mistreated by a highway patrolman.

Among the four who did complain were two young black women who had accompanied Joan Little from Chapel Hill to Washington for her trial in June 1974 and had somehow wound up behind bars themselves. They told investigators that a young white male had propositioned them while they were detained in Beaufort County, and that he had exposed himself to them. Another young woman, who was in jail at the same time and who knew the boy, said that he had propositioned all of them in the juvenile section, but that she did not see him expose himself. In follow-up interviews by the SBI, both of Joan Little's friends confirmed that they had been accosted by an inmate, not a jailer, and one "stated that [he] was trying to avoid the jailor while in the act."

Two other women, both adults, informed the officers that they had been annoyed by Clarence Alligood while they were in the Beaufort County jail. One said he had asked her "on several occasions if she was ready for sex since she had been in the jail so long and that she told him to go on and leave her alone, and that he always would." The other, a trusty, reported "that a lot of nights Mr. Alligood would come by and wake her up and get sandwiches for her and [that] sometimes [he] would try to feel her breasts and that she always told him she didn't play that mess and he would not persist and that she never saw him mess with anyone else or heard anyone else talk about same." Both these women said they had already been contacted by the defense when the SBI questioned them. Both later testified for the defense at the trial.

Not very much additional information was obtained. Handwriting samples were analyzed at the SBI laboratory along with samples of the script in the puzzle books. All were thought to be Joan Little's writing. The examination of Alligood's bloody shirt and undershirt proved inconclusive, and these items were returned to Slaughter. By mid-October most of the routine reports had been filed and the investigation had shriveled to a close. But no one had questioned Harry Carpenter, Charles Gilbert, Roger Bernholz, Willie Barnes, Margie Wright, Arthur Finn, or others involved in the case, including Joan Little herself. No one had attempted to lift fingerprints from the desk in the jailer's office, from the handle or shaft of the ice pick, from the shoes found outside the cell, or from the eyeglasses lying on the floor at the head of the bunk. No one had tried to find out who had cleaned up the cellblock or exactly what had been done with the paraphernalia that had disappeared from cell number one. And no one had obtained the toll records of long-distance calls made from Beaufort County on August 27, 1974. The investigation was finished, but it was far from complete.

By late autumn the case had stalled.

The Joann Little Defense Fund was operating out of a musty room in the modest second-floor offices of Jerry Paul's four-man law firm, but it was not much more than a meager bank account and several boxes of index cards. The board of directors had been expanded to include not only Arthur Finn and Joan Little but a sociology professor at the University of North Carolina, a law student at North Carolina Central University in Durham, an undergraduate student, and a teenage auto mechanic who eventually became treasurer of the organization. There was no staff. Paul's secretary could handle all the work in her spare time.

Contributions had been trickling in from all parts of North Carolina—from individuals, church groups, and civic clubs—but not in amounts sufficient even to meet office expenses. No money had been collected toward the $100,000 bail Paul had suggested to Judge Bailey, nor were there funds to hire the additional investigators and consulting criminologists he wanted even though local private detectives had already been retained and a team of amateur investigators had been put to work. To make matters worse, illness and other distractions had caused Paul to neglect his paying clients and his law firm was now operating in the red. No meaningful work had been done on the Joan Little case in weeks. The defense was at a standstill.

In December, however, things began to change. Feminists and civil-rights activists in other parts of the country had begun to hear about the case and, like Paul, they had seen its "potential." Several major newspapers suddenly became interested in the story, and on December 1 *The New York Times* published a brief and poorly researched account of the killing and the surrender, accompanied by a picture of Jerry Paul and Joan Little. Other papers soon followed with their own features, some of which relied on the *Times* article and compounded its inaccuracy. Without consulting any of the medical authorities, the *Times* reported that "the medical examiner reported clear evidence of recent sexual activity by the jailer," and observed also that "the case . . . has become a cause célèbre among women's and civil rights groups but has attracted only slight national attention."

In Montgomery, Alabama, a peripatetic attorney and financier named Morris Dees saw the *New York Times* story and reacted to it immediately. Dees, a natty thirty-eight-year-old millionaire described as "a genius at fund-raising," had conceived the Southern Poverty Law Center in 1970 along with another Montgomery attorney, Joe Levin, as a "new approach to the implementation of civil-rights legislation." Under their guidance, the SPLC had been set up as a charitable foundation, a unique philanthropic law firm with civil-rights spokesman and Georgia state legislator Julian Bond as its titular head. Dees and

Levin had begun a number of individual and class-action lawsuits in various parts of the country—in New York, Michigan, and California, as well as in Georgia, Alabama, and North Carolina—most of which were instituted in the name of defendants who could not afford to pay for the sophisticated services the SPLC brought to bear on their cases. In its first five years, therefore, the fund-raising efforts of the SPLC had expanded along with its legal activities. By 1975 the foundation's executive director had a staff of six administrators plus three secretaries, while only two lawyers besides Dees and Levin were actually engaged in pursuing litigation for the poor.

Morris Dees had grown especially intense in his opposition to the death penalty since creating the Southern Poverty Law Center, and had managed to become involved in a number of capital-punishment cases around the country. In December, Dees was in eastern North Carolina to work on the appeal of three black men convicted of raping a white woman and sentenced to die in the state's gas chamber. In his briefcase he was carrying the *Times* clipping, and he soon got in touch with Jerry Paul and arranged to discuss the situation with him. They met at Paul's home and went over the matter in detail. Dees offered the resources of the Southern Poverty Law Center, proposing a massive fund-raising effort that would attract nationwide attention and generate the money Paul said he needed to defend Joan Little. In exchange, Dees wanted to participate in the trial. Paul seized the opportunity at once, and Morris Dees became the first attorney from outside Paul's firm to join the defense team.

As the alliance between Morris Dees and Jerry Paul was taking shape, the relationship between Paul and Golden Frinks was rapidly deteriorating. For years Paul had been a friend and legal counsel to Frinks, but the Joan Little case had quickly driven a wedge between them, a wedge whittled in the struggle for control of the political movement and the fund-raising activities that were now becoming essential aspects of the defense strategy. Frinks had been mounting his own effort to raise defense money throughout eastern North Carolina, but his Free Joan Little Committee had been no match for the Joann Little Defense Fund even in Beaufort County, where many blacks had seemed to become ambivalent about the case following the surrender and Paul's emergence as the leading defense counsel. Eventually Frinks would go to Paul and suggest joining forces, and later he would claim that Paul had offered him a percentage of all money contributed to the defense for the purpose of organizing protest rallies. But Paul seemed to have reasons for wanting to discourage any such activities. Despite the fact that he had spent years defending blacks and speaking out on their behalf, Paul was scornful of the political sophistication of black leaders, including Frinks, in the eastern part of the state. He also felt that Frinks's insistence on staging loosely organized street demonstrations was old-fashioned and inefficient, a tactical throwback to the days of civil disobedience that would not generate 'sufficient revenues and that might arouse antipathy for Joan Little and her supporters among some people who would eventually sit on the jury.*

Whether or not Paul and Frinks ever reached an agreement to share defense money, Paul took drastic steps at about the same time to prevent any further interference from Frinks in the case. He went to the authorities and accused the SCLC leader of collecting money in the name of the Joann Little Defense Fund but appropriating it for his own use, and through District Attorney William Griffin

---

*The Joann Little Defense Fund would raise most of its money through donations at benefits and cocktail parties, collections at carefully controlled indoor rallies, and direct-mail solicitation. The JLDF received funds from many sources, including the Southern Poverty Law Center, its largest single contributor. Like the SPLC, its money-raising activities were concentrated in metropolitan areas outside North Carolina. A few outdoor marches and rallies would be staged before and during the trial, but usually without the participation of the defendant or her attorneys, who were careful to keep a distance between themselves and their chanting, banner-carrying supporters.

he requested an SBI investigation into Frinks's financial transactions. The SBI probe began on December 9 and lasted several weeks. It was dropped at the end of the month when Paul showed no interest in having the matter pursued further. By then Frinks was no longer his primary concern. The case was beginning to gather force, and Paul had other things on his mind.

Earlier in the month Morris Dees had flown home to Montgomery, where a sign at the airport welcomed travelers to "The Heart of Dixie." Relying on notes from his meeting with Paul and the *New York Times* article, Dees drafted a three-page solicitation letter and sent it to a clearinghouse in Chicago for duplication and distribution through computerized and scientifically organized mailing lists. Copies of the letter were deployed to all parts of the country before the end of December, but most went to the Northeast and the Far West, to individuals who subscribed to certain magazines, belonged to certain organizations, or contributed to certain political candidates and causes. In 1972 Dees had successfully used the same method to raise money for George McGovern's presidential campaign, and his faith in this technique and in this case was so keen that he ordered two million copies of the letter despite the fact that the SPLC had listed only 70,000 "supporting members" on its roster as of July 1974.

It was, as Dees had promised Paul, a massive campaign. Eventually the SPLC would invest more than $200,000 in fund-raising for the defense, according to Center officials, and would raise almost twice that amount in donations. At least $171,000 would be contributed directly by the SPLC to the Joann Little Defense Fund in Durham, $100,000 would be obligated for the defendant's bail, and $30,000 would be itemized as lawyer's expenses. But such figures told only part of the story. During fiscal 1975, the period in which the Joan Little solicitation occurred, supporting membership in the SPLC jumped from 70,000 to 150,000. The Center's financial statement for the year indicated that $2,429,588 in "public support" contributions had been received. Total expenses for the year ran to $1,420,552, including $476,199 which went for "fund raising." At the beginning of fiscal 1975 the Center had had an "Unrestricted Fund" account of $483,537, with an additional $58,437 in its "Land, Building and Equipment Fund." At the beginning of fiscal 1976, the "Unrestricted Fund" had swollen to $916,451, and the "Land, Building and Use Fund" amounted to $108,209, including the value of the new offices purchased by the Center just before the start of the Joan Little trial.

The Southern Poverty Law Center had established a practice of building large reserve funds before 1975 and of spending a high percentage of its income on fund-raising activities. In its first three years of operation, the Center raised a total of $1,764,290, of which 67 percent went to fund-raising or into reserve. In 1974 the Center spent $271,-174 on fund-raising, and ended the period with a reserve of $308,437. During that year, according to a report in the Charlotte *Observer*, the Southern Poverty Law Center had "spent only 17.4 percent of its income defending poor people."

The SPLC's solid fiscal situation, as well as its success in raising money and public support for the Joan Little defense, resulted largely from the Center's tax-exempt status and the favorable postage rates accorded to it as a "nonprofit" organization. Federal law does not control how such "charities" expend their funds, and contributions to them are tax deductible to the contributor as long as the organization continues to be "operated exclusively for religious, charitable, scientific, testing for public safety, literary, or educational purposes, or for the prevention of cruelty to children or animals. . . ." According to its Articles of Incorporation, the SPLC was formed "to educate the economically and educationally deprived" and to "help mobilize resources . . . in a concerted effort to attack injustices," as well as "to stimulate . . . equal justice for the poor" and to "receive and administer funds for the aforesaid purposes." After the trial, officials of the SPLC would insist that the subscriptions received in response to Dees's letter were general contributions to the Center rather than to the Joan Little defense, but the letter mentioned no other SPLC project and, along with a reminder that "Your tax-deductible contribution of $15, $20, anything you can spare, is urgently needed now," specifically asked recipients to "join me now and stand beside Joanne in her hour of trial and need." Similar though perhaps more general appeals are often used by national organizations involved in voluntary litigation, including the American Civil Liberties Union and the National Association for the Advancement of Colored People. But the Center's fund-raising methods aggravated William Griffin, who would later disdain the SPLC effort with an allusion to the application of advertising techniques in conventional political campaigns. He would call it "the selling of Joan Little."

The solicitation did rest on techniques more prevalent in advertising than in legal advocacy. The case was called "one of the most shocking and outrageous examples of injustice against women on record." Readers were informed that Joan Little had been in jail "awaiting action on her appeal of a questionable breaking and entering conviction," but nothing was said about her confession or about the testimony of her brother. "Women who have stayed in that jail have said that Alligood and others made advances on them," the letter said, although no evidence was ever produced to show that other jailers had molested prisoners or that other officers had mistreated inmates inside the jail. "The state medical examiner was prepared to support Joanne's story from his observations of the evidence, but he was not allowed to testify before the grand jury that indicted her," readers learned, although the state medical examiner had never viewed the evidence and the local medical examiner's report had been read at the grand-jury hearing. "Joanne is to be tried in Beaufort County [where] pitifully few black people of either sex are called to serve on juries," Dees wrote. Yet one half of the grand jurors had been women, and one quarter of them had been black.

It was an unabashed publicity release, designed not so much to inform as to arouse interest and sympathy, and the purpose was accomplished. A wide range of controversies had been evoked in one simple but dynamic context, and emotions were stimulated across a broad band of social concerns. Jerry Paul had first perceived the potential in these issues, but it was Morris Dees who first articulated them. Civil rights, women's rights, prison and jail reform, even the "very right of a woman to defend herself against sexual attack" were "at stake." But the core of the campaign lay in the letter's first sentence: "Joanne Little may be put to death because she defended herself against the jail guard who tried to rape her." This was the palpable injustice. "Our first goal is to save Joanne's life," the letter said, infusing all the issues with even larger meaning and moment. The specter of the gas chamber now hung on the horizon. The Joan Little case became the Joan Little movement, and the Joan Little movement became a matter of life and death.

The response was swift and overwhelming. Money poured in to the Southern Poverty Law Center during January and February, and as news of the case spread there was also a surge in donations to the Joann Little Defense Fund as well. Spontaneous fund drives sprang up in major cities, many sponsored by NOW, the National Organization for Women. The 185,000-member American Association of University Women declared its intention to work with the SPLC and issued a statement expressing "concern for any lack of equal justice before the law such as may be the case of the Beaufort County incident." A few independent Joan Little defense funds sprouted in diverse locations—on Long Island, in the Midwest, in California. Donations and letters of support came to the Defense Fund from all parts of the country—from Alpha Kappa Alpha sorority in Seattle; the Bay Area Women Against Rape in California; the National Association of Black Social Workers in Atlanta; the

National Association of Black Women Attorneys in Washington, D.C.; the Chicago Committee to Free Inez Garcia; the State Civil Rights Commission of Indianapolis; the Hawaii Women's Political Caucus; inmates at Attica Prison; the University of Massachusetts Joanne Little Support Committee; the Ad Hoc Committee for the Defense of Joan Little of Muncie, Indiana; Lesbians for Liberation, Albany, New York; various Rape Crisis Centers; the Rhode Island Feminist Theatre; the Playboy Foundation; a motorcycle club in Chicago; the Student Union, University of Saskatchewan, Canada; and an organization in Dallas called W.A.S.P. Contributions came from other organizations in Illinois, Pennsylvania, Virginia, Michigan, South Carolina, and Maryland; and from churches and civic groups in North Carolina. There were a few individual contributors from Beaufort County, and close to the time of the trial a check came from the Elite Club of Washington, North Carolina.

By mid-February, Jerry Paul told a reporter at the time, more than $130,000 had been collected for the defense. That figure may have been grossly exaggerated,* but by then money was surging in both from the Southern Poverty Law Center and from direct contributions to the Joann Little Defense Fund. Paul could now afford to begin recruiting the people he wanted. He flew to New York, Washington, D.C., and California to discuss the case with those whose help he was seeking, and at his Durham office he began to receive inquiries from others who were interested in joining the defense effort. In Alexandria, Virginia, Paul spoke to a friend, attorney Marvin Miller, and persuaded him to begin work on pre-trial motions. Miller was offered a fee of $5,000, which would later be increased

*None of the defense attorneys was ever certain exactly how much money was collected by the Joann Little Defense Fund in Durham, which never retained an experienced treasurer to handle its finances and keep accurate records. At a press conference more than a month after Paul made this estimate, the secretary of the Defense Fund would tell reporters that about $60,000 had been raised, and that only half that amount had come from the Southern Poverty Law Center.

substantially. On the same trip Paul encountered Patricia Chance, a former law student who said she wanted to work for the Defense Fund. She became a salaried employee.

In Durham, Paul met Courtney Mullin, a graduate student in social psychology at North Carolina State University who had some experience with computer science. She proposed to conduct attitude surveys in Beaufort County and in other areas of the state to support the defense motion for a change of venue. Although she wanted to embark on the project in connection with her work toward a graduate degree, Paul was able to finance her research, which came to be called the Fair Jury Project, and to pay her a salary that eventually reached several thousand dollars a month.

Others with assorted talents and different purposes soon began to gravitate toward the defense. Lawyer James Gillespie was added to Paul's firm as an associate, primarily to handle other work while Paul concentrated on the Joan Little case. Larry Little, the Black Panther leader, who was not related to the defendant, joined the Defense Fund to promote rallies and meetings outside the state. Richard Wolf, an astrologer and personal counselor, was hired to keep peace on the defense team during trial preparations. A friend of Courtney Mullin, who first brought him to Paul's attention, Wolf claimed to possess extrasensory powers of perception. At first Paul was not certain what role this unusual man would play on the defense team, but eventually Wolf was to be instrumental in resolving serious personality conflicts among those working on the case and in preparing Joan Little to face cross-examination.

By the end of February Morris Dees was ready to post bond for Joan Little, and arrangements were made to secure a $100,000 certificate of deposit by using funds from the reserve account of the Southern Poverty Law Center. At the same time Jerry Paul filed a motion in Beaufort County Superior Court to have bail reinstated in the larceny case, which he had earlier taken to the North Carolina Court of Appeals on a writ of *certiorari.*

By then the impact of the SPLC letter was apparent and William Griffin had already grown bitter about what he considered the transparent duplicity of the defense attorneys. He had acquiesced in the continuance granted in November (he would later say that the defense attorneys had led him to believe they were interested in plea bargaining in exchange for a confession), but now he felt they had used the additional time only to distort the facts and fabricate issues he believed would taint the objectivity of the prospective jurors. Griffin had earlier filed a motion to prohibit Joan Little and her lawyers from giving press interviews, making statements, or discussing the case in public in any way that might "make a fair and impartial trial impossible," but it got no response.* Now he submitted a strong objection to the motion to renew bail, hoping to force the defense to trial by keeping their client in jail. At a hearing on February 24, however, Superior Court Judge Elbert Peel ignored Griffin's argument and set bail again at $15,000. The next day Paul gathered a group of eight volunteers in Chapel Hill—many of whom had met Joan Little at Paul's house before she surrendered—and drove them to Washington, where they all signed bonds for the defendant. On February 27, she was released and whisked into seclusion, first to a motel in Durham, then to a hospital in Washington, D.C., then to a hideaway in Virginia. She would not be seen or heard from again for more than a month, but her disappearance would do nothing to check the spread of her fame or the growing interest in her case.

---

*No gag order was ever issued, but a later trial order by Judge McKinnon did refer to various sections of the state bar's Code of Professional Responsibility, saying they would "be enforced by such sanctions as are available by law." One such section stipulated that a lawyer "shall not make or participate in making an extra-judicial statement" which disclosed information not already available elsewhere or not necessary to aid an investigation or to warn of dangers to the public. After the trial, two attorneys involved in the case—one on the defense and one on the prosecution—would be cited by the bar's Ethics Committee for violations of this rule before and during Joan Little's trial.

PART V

MARCH 1975 — JULY 1975

CHAPTER 10

A VICTORY
FOR THE PEOPLE

By mid-March the Joan Little case was international news. Stories about it had appeared in newspapers and magazines all over the world, and foreign papers were beginning to give it continuing attention. The Beaufort County Courthouse was already receiving requests for press credentials from correspondents and reporters who anticipated covering the trial, which was set to begin April 14. County officials were busy formulating plans to accommodate the media and the crowds of spectators that were expected to be in Beaufort County for the courtroom showdown. Then, at a pre-trial conference, the defense attorneys moved for another continuance, claiming that local officials in twenty-three eastern counties were obstructing their efforts to examine jury lists "for the purpose of showing discrimination in the jury-selection system" and alleging again that evidence was being withheld by the authorities. The motion also stated that the defendant would "not be medically able to go to trial on April 14, 1975."

Soon after her release from prison, Joan Little had been taken from Durham to Washington, D.C., where she had been examined by two doctors and hospitalized for several days. "The medical history and examination revealed that Ms. Little had signs and symptoms which could be attributed to the dysfunction of more than one organ system," one of the physicians had written to Karen Galloway on March 7. A few days later Joan Little had been admitted to a private clinic under the name "Mrs. JoAnn McDonald."*

Along with the motion for a continuance, affidavits from the doctors attending Joan Little were submitted which stated that she "could not be required to continue consultations with her attorneys to prepare for the scheduled trial date of April 14" and that she could "not withstand continuation of the consultations with her attorneys to aid in the preparation of her defense." The motion written by the lawyers argued, in addition, that her condition had degenerated because she "did not receive any medication" for a thyroid condition while she was incarcerated in the Beaufort County jail and in Women's Prison. A few days later Joan Little herself would seem to refute this assertion when she told a reporter she had voluntarily stopped taking thyroid medicine several years earlier because she "didn't like it." By then, in any event, the continuance had been granted. The defense attorneys had asked that "this cause be continued for at least 60 days and that the term of court set for April 14, 1975, be used to hear pre-trial motions." Preliminary matters would be argued in mid-April, the judge said, but once more the trial would be delayed indefinitely.

The attorneys met again on March 27, this time to examine the state's evidence in accordance with discovery arrangements ordered by Judge McKinnon during the earlier pre-trial conference in response to several defense motions. Strictly interpreting the judge's orders, William Griffin objected repeatedly when Morris Dees tried to question Willis Peachey while the meeting was in progress. "We're not here for an interrogation! We're here to review the evidence!" Griffin exploded at one point. "Are you

*For anonymity, she had assumed the surname of her bodyguard, Russell McDonald. A landscape architect and former Black Panther, McDonald had been hired by Jerry Paul on the day of the release. He quickly became one of Joan Little's trusted confidants and remained her close companion until the end of the trial.

trying to hide something?" Dees shot back. The meeting soon broke up with everyone in a spoiled mood. Feelings were hardening on both sides. The defense attorneys would continue to claim that information was being withheld from them. The prosecution would begin to insist that all the evidence against Joan Little had been divulged before the trial began.

Interest in the case dwindled temporarily when it was learned that only pre-trial motions would be heard on April 14, but rumors of the growing rifts among Joan Little's supporters kept her name in the news. Golden Frinks soon announced a new round of rallies and demonstrations in eastern North Carolina and said he planned to put up a tent city in Washington to house the thousands of people he thought would gather there. "Even if they go to Raleigh," he told a reporter, referring to a new defense motion for a change of venue, "this is where we'll stay. This is where the crime was committed. This is where we'll take a stand."

The strife between Golden Frinks and Jerry Paul was drawing to a climax. Their dispute finally broke into the open when Paul released a letter to Frinks formally ending his representation of the SCLC leader. Frinks responded by joining with Joan Little's mother in a lawsuit in federal court to block the further expenditure of money collected by the Defense Fund. Their complaint alleged that Jessie Williams had been informed of "a scheme to defraud the courts" and accused both Paul and Karen Galloway of deception by "falsely proclaiming Joan Little to be ill" in order to delay the trial. Paul denied the allegations immediately, but took them seriously enough to have Joan Little telephone a reporter from Virginia to explain: "When I told my mother I was going into the hospital, I told her I was really doing okay. She gets worried real quick."

On March 28 Frinks made good his intention to begin raising a tent city in the shadow of the courthouse. He set up a wall tent and several pup tents on a vacant lot about four blocks away, telling a small crowd of curious onlookers that this would be the "nerve center" of his defense campaign. Then he christened the area Resurrection City Number Three and predicted that fifteen hundred people would be quartered in forty-seven tents on the site. But no more tents were ever erected, and no one ever stayed in the ones already there.

On April 4, however, Frinks did stage another rally in Washington to coincide with the seventh anniversary of the assassination of Martin Luther King, Jr. A band of marchers, led by Ralph David Abernathy, the president of the national SCLC, went from the tent city to the courthouse and, after speeches and photographs, disbanded peacefully. Two months earlier Abernathy had flown to North Carolina for a ten-minute meeting with Joan Little at Women's Prison, then had declared his belief that she was innocent and pledged his own efforts to win her acquittal. "I'm a nonviolent minister," he had told an airport press conference, "but I'm here in this white racist state to give the white man hell. When Joan Little comes to trial, I'm going to bring reporters from all over the world to North Carolina. I'm going to bring them from Red China, and I'm going to bring them from Russia to see democracy in action. The only people who are getting justice in North Carolina are the white folks." But his rhetoric at the rally in early April, after Frinks and Paul had splintered their relationship, was more subdued. From the courthouse steps he called for the dismissal of all charges against Joan Little and said, "We're tired of the abuse of black womanhood by white males."

On the prior evening—barely two weeks after the defense had been granted a continuance due to her poor health—Joan Little had appeared in Winston-Salem to denounce Golden Frinks and the SCLC march scheduled for the next day. At a press conference she told newsmen, "Mr. Frinks is not doing anything in support of the legal [Joann Little Defense] fund. The funds he is raising under my name, really, I never see any of the funds." At a rally in a Baptist Church sponsored by the Black Panther Party, she announced that Larry Little had become the state coordi-

nator for her defense and referred to Frinks as "Golden
Freaks." In Washington, Frinks responded by telling re-
porters that words had been put into Joan Little's mouth.
"I know Sister Joan didn't say those things in Winston-
Salem," he commented. "Someone has brainwashed her."

For two more weeks Frinks clung to his intention to have
some influence in the defense effort, but on the first day of
the pre-trial hearings Larry Little staged a demonstration
in Washington that effectively ended the SCLC leader's
involvement. Little brought two buses filled with black
college students to the Beaufort County Courthouse. They
sat quietly in the courtroom during the morning session as
the hearings got under way, then filed outside and formed
up in front of the building at the start of the lunch recess.
"One, two, three, Joan must be set free!" the students
chanted as they marched up the courthouse steps and
massed on the promenade Frinks and Ralph Abernathy
had recently occupied. Then, in unison, they began to
shout, "Down with Golden Frinks! Up with Joan Little!
Down with Golden Frinks! Up with Joan Little!"

Several sheriff's deputies watched impassively from a
distance as Larry Little, standing below the demonstrators
on the sidewalk, exhorted them to louder and louder
chants. Signs and banners were unfurled: POWER TO THE
ICE PICK and FREE JOAN LITTLE. Seemingly dismayed,
Frinks hovered at the edge of the crowd of reporters who
had gathered to watch. Suddenly, Larry Little whirled and
pointed a finger in his direction. "Look at him!" Little
shouted venomously. "He don't have any support!"

It was true, and at last Frinks had to admit it. The next
day reporters were summoned to a news conference in the
lot among the empty tents. "We will not have any more
active participation in the Joan Little case, but we will
continue to support her morally," Frinks announced softly,
glancing around at his forlorn Resurrection City. "I can't
stay here," he told one reporter, stuffing his hands deep
into the pockets of his jump suit. "They're beating me to
death." A few days later Frinks and Jessie Williams

dropped their federal court suit against the Defense Fund, after Karen Galloway filed a dismissal motion saying the suit represented "a vicious, greedy, unconscionable effort by plaintiffs and their lawyer to exploit a tragic situation for their own financial gain."

If the Joan Little case was ever to attain lasting legal significance, as Jerry Paul and some of the other defense attorneys had already claimed it would, the hearings that began on April 14 were crucial. Only the defendant's culpability, only the factual question whether the jailer's death had been murder or self-defense, would be contested before the jury. The social and political issues raised by the defense, questions of racism and sexism, questions of black power and women's rights, had to be debated here in the motions filed by the defense lawyers for Judge McKinnon's consideration. This would be their chance to sortie against the system, to expose any constitutional or procedural defects which might have deprived the defendant of her fundamental rights. McKinnon's decisions, not the jury's verdict, would then form the basis for any appeal to a higher court, where judge-made law might eventually be handed down that would affect not only this case but any similar ones to follow. These pre-trial hearings, rather than the trial, would afford the defense its only real opportunity to effect profound and wide-reaching changes in the basics of criminal justice. The importance of so-called landmark cases does not arise from their facts or from the jury's view of guilt or innocence but from the lasting impact they have on the mechanics of jurisprudence.

The defense arrived for the hearings with a platoon of young attorneys—some of whom would not appear again —and with eighteen motions attacking most facets of the case. They were to spend three tense weeks debating fine points of law in a nearly empty courtroom before a jury of dozing reporters, but few of their motions were original or even artfully drafted and none was effectively presented.

The key issues were "racism and sexism," Jerry Paul
stressed repeatedly, but he and the others had little success
putting these concerns into context. Days went by as they
insisted that the state's system of selecting jurors from tax
and voter-registration rolls was inherently discriminatory
to minorities and women. Their argument seemed to have
merit, if only because blacks and women were proportion-
ately under-represented on both source lists, but in the end
they failed to demonstrate conclusively that juries in Beaufort County had been intentionally unbalanced at the time
Joan Little was indicted. In general, representation on
Beaufort County grand juries had conformed proportion-
ately to representation on the source lists, even though the
source lists did not accurately reflect the proportions of
women and blacks in the community. Earlier United States
Supreme Court opinions had determined that similar sys-
tems in other states were not unconstitutionally prejudicial
to defendants. The county's disorganized method of keeping records and purging juror lists prompted Judge McKinnon to suggest that improvements could be made, but he
denied the defense request to dismiss the indictment. "The
things that came out today," Paul nevertheless told reporters, "are the things that landmark decisions are made of."

After more than two grueling weeks, during which tem-
pers occasionally flared and hyperbolic rhetoric rang out
sporadically from both sides of the courtroom,* only one
motion remained. The defense had asked for a change of
venue "to Wake County or another county free from bias
and prejudice and able to accommodate the defendant's
trial. . . ." The defense motion cited traditional grounds for
moving the venue, including "excessive and prejudicial
pre-trial publicity in Beaufort and surrounding counties"

*Jerry Paul declared himself and the other defense attorneys to be "new
abolitionists," then told Judge McKinnon that he had worked on civil-rights cases
for years only to learn that "when you argue for racial justice, you lose." William
Griffin accused the defense of "sandbagging" the court and said the pre-trial
hearings had "been a trial of Beaufort County by innuendo, assertion and pseudo-
science."

and "prosecutorial misconduct," but in court the defense attorneys based their plea almost solely on the notion that a fair trial was impossible anywhere in eastern North Carolina because of the "high level of [racial] prejudice" there. Unlike the other defense arguments, which were conventional except in scope, this one was remarkable in its striking premise. Neither demonstrable injustices nor the anticipated numerical balance of the jury between men and women or blacks and whites was specifically attacked. Instead the defense asserted that nowhere in the eastern part of the state could twelve people be found who were capable of laying aside prejudice and acting as impartial jurors. This broad indictment, based largely on research sponsored and paid for by the Joann Little Defense Fund, was leveled at men as well as women, blacks as well as whites. Everyone in a twenty-three-county area was swept into a heap and accused of a vague and immutable bias against Joan Little.

The target of the attack was a rather distinct and homogeneous region of the state, a coastal plain where flat marshlands rose gently from the sea and stretched two hundred miles inland before the roll of the hilly Piedmont began around Raleigh. It was a rural area where stands of angular pines alternated with dusty tobacco fields along twisting, two-lane roads; where some people lived comfortably and few lived well, but many lingered in the bleak breach of poverty, in fallen-down houses and forlorn house trailers; where the hopeful often sought relief from their worldly circumstances in the fundamentals of Old Testament religion and George Wallace politics. The defense attorneys feared, and would attempt to prove, that the old ways of thinking were still predominant here, that Joan Little would be judged according to an implacable code, judged by history rather than by law. They asserted that the trial should be moved out of this area not merely because she had killed a local jailer and might be deemed deserving of some punishment for striking out at an authoritarian figure but also because there was a prevailing prejudice against her due to her race and sex. If they won on this argument, the trial would be transferred to an urban area, probably Raleigh, a place very different in tradition and spirit from Beaufort County, a place where they believed jurors more sympathetic to this defendant could be found. If they lost but won on subsequent appeal, it might mean that neither Joan Little nor any other black woman could be tried before a jury composed of eastern North Carolinians. When the arguments on this last motion began, it was still possible for the Joan Little case to become a landmark.

For three days the defense attorneys introduced evidence intended to support their sweeping argument, mainly the statistical results of a $30,000 survey conducted by Courtney Mullin's Fair Jury Project based on the hypothesis that "levels of prejudice against Joan Little . . . would cause people in eastern counties to be unable to give her a fair trial and that the trial should be held in another county where . . . levels of prejudice were lower." It was not argued that impartial jurors could be found elsewhere; it was argued that "levels of prejudice" were lower in other parts of the state and that a "fair" trial would be more likely somewhere else. An effort was made to distinguish between the social perceptions of people in the east and people in the Piedmont, and to demonstrate that whites were more likely to dominate blacks and that men were more likely to dominate women even on proportionately balanced juries in the east.

The prosecution objected to this generalized, sociological interpretation of the bare language of the Sixth Amendment, which assures criminal defendants a quick trial "by an impartial jury." They pointed out that the issue should not be whether prospective jurors were prejudiced but whether they were capable of laying aside their prejudices and judging the facts dispassionately. These objections appeared to be well taken, and the defense seemed to be getting nowhere. Several times during their arguments Judge McKinnon openly expressed doubts about the force and relevance of their theories and their supporting evi-

dence, which consisted largely of uncorroborated sociological data. On Friday, May 1, however, the hearings took a
sharp and unexpected turn. McKinnon abruptly called the
attorneys into chambers for a long conference. Several
hours passed, during which the defendant and her bodyguard arrived and were shown into the judge's conference
room. The clerk of court came out a while later and got a
Bible from her desk. More time passed, until about noon,
when McKinnon briskly reappeared and announced that
the trial would be moved to Raleigh as the defense had
requested. He made his decision known without explanation, a wry smile on his face, saying only that it was "not
the result of a finding that a fair trial could not be had in"
eastern North Carolina.

William Griffin seemed to accept the apparent setback
stoically. He left the courtroom quickly when the hearings
adjourned a few moments later. The defense attorneys met
with reporters and immediately claimed a conquest.
"We've shown there is a high level of racism in this area
that must be dealt with in order to get a fair trial for black
defendants," Jerry Paul declared on the courthouse steps.
"I don't know if McKinnon understands all the ramifications of his decision, but he could see that there's prejudice
in eastern North Carolina." At a televised news conference
that afternoon Karen Galloway said the case had already
become a "landmark," and Paul called the decision "a victory for the people, like the victories in Cambodia and
Vietnam."

But things were not as the defense attorneys wanted
them to seem, or as the complacent newsmen were willing
to report. The site of the trial had been shifted not because
of innovative arguments on the change-of-venue motion
but because of the laborious attack on the jury-selection
system during the first week of the hearings. Henry McKinnon had come to Beaufort County already prepared to
consider moving the trial to Raleigh. Several weeks earlier
he had asked for a memorandum of law from the North
Carolina attorney general's office detailing his options

under the state's archaic and restrictive change-of-venue statute. McKinnon might not have anticipated the unorthodox defense arguments—racism and sexism were not mentioned in the written motion they had filed—but he was concerned about the impact of pre-trial publicity and about courthouse security in the event there were disturbances at the time of the trial. Golden Frinks had predicted that he could bring a horde of demonstrators to the occasion, and the influence of the Black Panther Party in the defense movement made violence seem all the more likely. It was evident, too, that this trial was going to be complex and expensive. Few if any of the sparsely populated counties in the east could afford to stage proceedings that would cost thousands of dollars and place extraordinary demands on the time and energy of the courthouse staff.

With these considerations in mind, McKinnon had let the defense attorneys make their oral arguments, then had called all the lawyers into chambers for a private meeting. The first motion, to quash the indictment because of a defective Beaufort County grand jury, had taken seven court days to hear. In Wake County, which used essentially the same selection method and exactly the same source lists, the issue could take twice that long to resolve, and from there ninety-eight other counties in the state could be attacked one by one. So McKinnon proposed to give them something and to take something away. If the defense attorneys believed that Joan Little could get a fairer trial in Wake County, then the venue would be changed in accordance with their motion. But the state also believed she could be given a fair trial in Wake County, and no further challenge to the jury-selection system would be entertained. The decision they made became clear a few days later when the judge's written order disclosed that "the waiver of any right to challenge the jury pool or the jury list in Wake County is freely, understandingly and voluntarily made by the defendant in her own person and by her counsel."

In spite of what the defense attorneys had said, therefore, McKinnon's decision was not really a "victory for the people" or an indication that they had "shown a high level of racism in [the east] that must be dealt with in order to get a fair trial for black defendants." It was not a triumph won in open court for the benefit of all women and all minorities; it was a political compromise suiting the purpose of judicial expediency at least as much as the interest of the defense in having this particular case tried somewhere outside eastern North Carolina. The move was "in the best interest of justice for both the state and the defendant," Henry McKinnon had told a reporter shortly after the close of the hearings. But settling the matter at the trial-court level ensured that the judge's disposition would apply only to this case, not to any other black or woman defendant. Instead of winning a landmark decision, as they claimed, the defense lawyers had secured a limited ruling that was certain to have only ephemeral, and possibly negative, impact on the criminal-justice system.

They had, however, achieved their primary objective. "I wanted a change of venue to Wake County and I got it," Paul said shortly after the hearings ended. "We're ready to go to trial as soon as possible." But when the trial opened in Raleigh two months later his attitude seemed to have changed. He tried at once to renege on the deal he had made with McKinnon by moving to quash the indictment because the jury pool in Wake County did not "include a fair representation of blacks, women, and youth."

His casual motion stunned the unsuspecting trial judge.

"You can't make a defendant relinquish one constitutional right in order to get another one," Paul said, although procedurally such an objection should have been raised in Beaufort County before the compact was accepted.

"Why did you do it down there?" the judge asked.

"To get the trial moved," Paul replied.

The motion was denied.

.   .   .

Except in a historical sense, Beaufort County was finished
with the Joan Little case. Though the defense had argued
that feelings against the defendant were swelling over in
the county, few people there seemed distressed by the
judge's decision to move the trial. Animosity among whites
seemed to run higher against the defense attorneys than
against Joan Little, especially against Jerry Paul, a local boy
who had returned, it was felt, to smear his hometown with
false charges of racism and sexism. Many people believed
that Joan Little might deserve a measure of retribution for
her part in the jailer's death, but months had passed since
the killing and most of them would now be content to see
justice meted out elsewhere. Farmers in the area were
already preoccupied with spring planting, and townspeo-
ple had begun to grow fearful that gangs of demonstrators
might rampage through their community. Local attorneys
had let it be known during the hearings that they would
not mind if the venue was changed because they did not
want the courthouse tied up while the trial was going on,
and an official of the Chamber of Commerce had privately
contacted William Griffin and implored him to accept any
conditions to get the case moved out of the county.

But there were those with different views who thought
they had a personal stake in the case, those who could not
see the change of venue as a positive development. A local
lawyer and politician named John Wilkinson had been retained by the Alligood family to assist the district attorney,
and he began to reconsider his involvement in the case in
light of the costs and additional time involved in going to
Raleigh for the trial. Ashley Futrell responded to the rhetoric of the defense by deploring the ruling in his editorials
as an affront to the people of Beaufort County, despite
what Judge McKinnon had said at the close of the hearings.
Futrell and Wilkinson were political foes and not particularly good friends, but now they found themselves in sympathy and soon they met to commiserate. Two days after

the hearings had adjourned, they called William Griffin to a meeting in Wilkinson's office and insisted that McKinnon's order must be appealed.

John Wilkinson's appearance at the pre-trial hearings had infuriated the defense attorneys, and they filed strong objections to his participation as a "private prosecutor."* A native of the area who had known Jerry Paul as a youngster, Wilkinson traced his family with aristocratic pride back to a small farm in the eastern end of the county, where his forebears had settled in 1750 and where a high school had been named after his father. Cherubic in appearance, Wilkinson was a blustering, belligerent eccentric who practiced law out of an office decorated with photographs and salutations from prominent conservative politicians such as Ronald Reagan and Senator Jesse Helms. A man of property and wealth, a member of the Board of Trustees of the University of North Carolina at Chapel Hill, and once a Republican candidate for the United States Senate, Wilkinson was a doctrinaire reactionary with a suspicious view of history and human nature. He was anathema to the defense attorneys, an incarnation of everything they saw themselves pitted against. For his part, Wilkinson was no happier with the defense team than they were with him, and throughout the hearings he had tormented them with biting criticism and quick disdain. Unlike William Griffin, Wilkinson was willing to talk to reporters, and Griffin would later say that the private prosecutor was "driven by the publicity aspects of the case." Ironically, Wilkinson himself had twice represented Joan Little and

*Once justified almost everywhere as a way to relieve the burden on overworked prosecutors, the hiring of private attorneys to assist in criminal cases has recently lost popularity and in some states has been banned altogether. In North Carolina, however, the State Supreme Court ruled in 1972 that modern reforms in criminal justice, including the maintenance of a permanent prosecutorial staff in each judicial district, "did not . . . prohibit the practice of employing private counsel to assist the solicitor." It remained true, therefore, that in North Carolina criminal defendants were not guaranteed equal treatment under the law, that the vigor of prosecution could depend on who had been the victim rather than on established public policies regarding law enforcement.

had been her brother's court-appointed counsel at the breaking-and-entering trial in June 1974. He was the lawyer to whom she had first confessed her part in the thefts. The defense attorneys had argued to McKinnon that Wilkinson could not prosecute his former client without compromising himself in a conflict of interest, but the judge had not made any final decision and so, for the time being, the special prosecutor remained an influence in the case.*

William Griffin did not want to challenge the change of venue and he did not intend to when he arrived for the meeting in John Wilkinson's office. He was not certain the ruling could even be taken up through ordinary appellate channels, and he was less distressed than the private prosecutor about having to try the case in Raleigh instead of Washington. Griffin's faith in the jury system compelled him to reject the defense argument that racism and sexism would play a part in the verdict, in Beaufort County or elsewhere, and he had already begun to think that a more sophisticated jury might be better able to grasp the technicalities of the case. Unlike Wilkinson and Futrell, moreover, Griffin recognized that there was little community sentiment for keeping the trial there and understood McKinnon's reasons for moving the case. He and the judge had discussed the possibility of a change of venue in private before the ruling was announced, and McKinnon had asked whether the district attorney would acquiesce in a decision to transfer the trial to Raleigh. Griffin had told the judge he would be willing to go anywhere as long as they could "get it over with."

But at the meeting Griffin was persuaded to change his

---

*The Ethics Committee of the North Carolina State Bar would later rule that Wilkinson's participation raised no conflict of interest because he had not represented Joan Little in any matter related to this case or to her incarceration at the time of the jailer's death. At the start of the murder trial, in a final effort to have Wilkinson removed and before the Ethics Committee ruling, the defense would put both Joan Little and her mother on the witness stand to testify that they had discussed the case with him and tried to hire him before the breaking-and-entering trial. Wilkinson then took the stand to deny that he had ever discussed the facts of the case with either of them.

mind. Wilkinson had learned that Jerry Paul was claiming credit for the change-of-venue memorandum written before the hearings by the attorney general's office ("We prepared it on our own stationery," Paul had told Greensboro *Daily News* reporter Bob Burchette, who later mentioned the comment to Wilkinson), and Ashley Futrell had discovered after making several phone calls to Raleigh that the memo had been produced by Joan Byers, an assistant attorney general who knew several members of the defense team and who had gone to law school with Karen Galloway. Byers denied that anyone connected with the defense had influenced her conclusions, but while writing the opinion she had discussed legal authorities on the change-of-venue question with at least one defense lawyer. Futrell and Wilkinson were convinced that they had exposed a plot to subvert the prosecution at the expense of the people in Beaufort County, perhaps in an effort to ensure an acquittal and avoid further bad publicity for the state. They insisted to Griffin that the defense would win by a gross default unless some action could be taken right away. Griffin did not say anything about his conversation with McKinnon or his own desire to get the case behind him. The implications of Paul's boast to Burchette and of what Ashley Futrell had learned could not be explained or ignored. "When they told me about the memorandum, I no longer had any choice," he would say later. "I had to do something."

On May 9 a motion was filed with the North Carolina Supreme Court to prevent the change of venue, even though virtually everyone was satisfied with McKinnon's decision except the private prosecutor and the editor of the Washington *Daily News*. The effort accomplished nothing, except to give the defense another crack at Beaufort County and another chance to obscure the real basis for the ruling. Jerry Paul reiterated in his answer a few days later that the change of venue was necessary "in order to assure the defendant a fair and impartial trial," and the State Supreme Court responded with a cursory

ruling, signed by the chief justice, denying the prosecution's motion in order "to avoid further delay in the
trial. . . ."

After the Supreme Court's prickly rebuff, suspicions
about political intrigue in the state capital and signs of
slackening support from court officials began to drain William Griffin's resolve to continue with the case. Mounting
adverse publicity had already taken its toll—hate mail was
arriving at his office daily—and now it seemed that he was
being isolated, that his efforts were being undercut even by
those whose support he had thought he could rely on. How
far had the corrosive effects of external pressures cut into
the judicial system? The trial would begin six weeks later
in Wake County, and by then Griffin would suspect that a
conspiracy of political consensus against the prosecution of
Joan Little had reached deep into the judiciary, even to the
chief judge on the state's highest court.

CHAPTER 11

YOU AIN'T GOT NO CASE

In May, Henry McKinnon withdrew as the trial judge. Fatigued and troubled after the pre-trial hearings, he informed court officials that he was concerned about his health and the health of his wife, and that he wished to be reassigned. McKinnon had already spent six strained months on this case, and he was tired of it. His request was acknowledged, and the search for a new trial judge began at once.

A few days after the hearings ended, Jerry Paul ran into Roger Bernholz in the Orange County Courthouse near Chapel Hill and spoke to him briefly about appearing at the trial as a witness for the defense. Their conversation struck Bernholz as odd and disconcerting. He was first asked what he knew about the circumstances of the killing and what he had said to Joan Little during their two telephone conversations, but instead of concentrating on his recollections in detail Paul began to emphasize the social and political importance of the case and to encourage him to remember things that would be beneficial to the defendant.

Paul's manner surprised Roger Bernholz and left him with an uncomfortable feeling about Joan Little's chief defense counsel. "I was disturbed that his approach would be anything other than trying to find out as accurately as possible what had really happened," he would say later. "Jerry did not ask me to say anything that wasn't true, but he did come as close to that as you probably can. . . . I sensed that he was playing on his conception of my own political and social thoughts, and that is what he stressed to me, that this was an important case in that way, and that it would be helpful, very helpful, if I could recall the encouraging things that I said to Joan about getting her out on bond."

But Paul had misread Bernholz, at least as far as his idea of the importance of the Joan Little defense was concerned. "I didn't view this case . . . as involving the same social and legal questions as were played up in the national press," Bernholz would explain. "I didn't think it was a racial case, that it had very significant racial overtones. I did not think it had very significant sexist overtones—that is, having to do with the treatment of women prisoners as opposed to men prisoners. I had gotten the impression that Joan Little was being, if anything, afforded special considerations rather than being mistreated. . . . My personal feeling was that the social and legal issues which were raised in this case were manufactured by the defense. . . . The issues were just trumped up."

A few weeks after talking to Paul in the Orange County Courthouse, however, Roger Bernholz would give important testimony that seemed to corroborate Joan Little's statements about their telephone calls and about what they had discussed on August 23, just a few days before the jailer's death and her escape. His appearance at the murder trial would be brief but significant, cementing the defense contention that she had no motive for murder. Bernholz might have been an important witness for the prosecution rather than the defense, but after briefly trying to identify the Chapel Hill attorney who had called Joan Little (Bessie Cherry, the clerk of court, could not remember his name), William Griffin had abandoned the inquiry. Even the defense attorneys were not aware just how seriously they had jeopardized their own case by calling him. Bernholz would later say that no effort had been made to determine whether his recollections directly corroborated Joan Little's version of their conversations.

. . .

On Saturday, June 7, the defense attorneys gathered at a motel in Raleigh to discuss courtroom strategy. Morris Dees, sitting at the head of the conference table, produced an agenda he had prepared, but Jerry Paul—smoking cigarettes and drinking endless cups of hot tea—was clearly in command. They had met to coordinate their activities and to assign specific tasks prior to the trial. Dees was to organize the evidence and contact all "non-expert" witnesses. James Rowan, of Paul's firm, would be responsible for diagrams of the jail and for creating an "Alligood dummy" to illustrate the locations of the jailer's wounds. (The prosecution considered a similar idea, but neither side used a mannequin at the trial.) Rowan and James Gillespie would undertake all legal research and prepare legal memoranda. Karen Galloway would analyze the information in Joan Little's medical, juvenile, and prison records, which the district attorney had obtained with an *ex parte* order and which the defense did not want introduced at the trial. Paul and Galloway would "mutually decide the best way to prepare Joan Little to testify."

Jerry Paul had spent four hours the night before discussing the case with Joan Little, and he had already begun to think that her testimony would be the keystone of his courtroom presentation. But several of the other defense lawyers thought she would make a bad witness and were troubled by the prospect that she might have to take the stand. "They'll detail her to death," Marvin Miller speculated. "She'll have to say 'yes, sir' and 'no, sir' to those bastards." Morris Dees began to urge the others to consider working for a dismissal rather than an acquittal, a strategy to avoid any chance that the defendant would have to testify, and he asked whether there were plans to have Joan Little take a lie-detector test, a preliminary gauge of her credibility. Attorneys on both sides had discussed this matter on several occasions, and William Griffin had offered to dismiss the case if a polygraph test showed that she was "not culpable" in the death of Clarence Alligood. Griffin never expected his proposition to be accepted, as he would explain to Dees later in June when the subject came up again, because he thought the defense attorneys feared that any fair test would implicate their client. For the time being, at least, Griffin was right. Paul seemed irritated with Dees and showed no interest in arranging a polygraph examination. "She's not ready to take a lie-detector test," he snapped. "She wouldn't pass it next week."

That closed the discussion, but before the meeting was over, as if to buttress his view that the defense should maneuver for a dismissal, Morris Dees reminded everyone that "the whole point of this case is to get Joan Little off."

William Griffin went about his normal duties and made no special preparations for the trial in Raleigh until a week before it was to begin. In June he was back in Beaufort County Superior Court to prosecute several black men accused of murdering a middle-aged white woman. The victim had been tied up and then shot during a bank robbery in a small town twenty miles east of Washington. Griffin tried the case alone, facing five defense attorneys at once, but this trial was no dress rehearsal for the one to come later in Wake County. At times the courtroom was half filled with spectators and friends of the slain woman, but the only reporter present was from the local paper. The issues were different in this case, as were the circumstances and the people involved. It attracted no public attention outside the immediate area. Yet this trial did have an impact on the Joan Little case. Expected to last only a few days, it consumed almost a month and severely limited the amount of time Griffin might have had to prepare for the proceedings that would begin in July.

. . .

Early in June, Morris Dees filed a one-million-dollar class-action civil suit in federal court in the eastern district of North Carolina against the sheriff and the former sheriff of Beaufort County, the executor of the estate of Clarence Alligood, the county commissioners, and their "agents, servants, employees and successors," which included everyone who worked for the county. The complaint had been prepared in the SPLC offices in Alabama and was signed by both Dees and Paul, but there had been disagreement between them about when and even whether to institute such a suit. Having had success with federal class actions before, Dees was anxious to get this case before a federal judge as soon as possible. Paul insisted privately, however, that neither he nor Joan Little had any desire to sue the Alligood family or Beaufort County officials. But Paul had not been able to gain dominance over Dees, the chief source of defense money, and in this instance he was simply unable to prevent the volatile SPLC attorney from going ahead in federal court even against the wishes of others on the defense team. Afterwards, Paul hotly criticized Dees for acting impetuously, suggesting he had made a strategic blunder that might let the state bargain for a voluntary dismissal of the civil complaint in exchange for dropping the criminal charges. Paul also claimed that the suit had been filed in Joan Little's name but without her prior knowledge or consent.

It soon became apparent that the defense had indeed committed a tactical blunder, one more serious than even Paul had anticipated. John Wilkinson, who had been retained by the county and several county officials as well as the Alligood family, began preparations in connection with the civil case to depose Joan Little under oath before the start of the criminal trial. Dees hurriedly filed a "Motion to Stay Taking Depositions and Other Discovery," in effect asking the court to call time-out in the civil case. The federal suit had been brought not "to waive [Joan Little's] right of [sic] self-incrimination or to have her deposition taken to be used against her in [the] pending criminal case," the motion said, but solely for the purpose of preventing "the distribution . . . of the assets of the estate of Clarence Alligood." A "Summary" of the class action prepared by the Southern Poverty Law Center stated, however, that the suit "asks the federal court to establish and implement constitutional standards of care and supervision of female inmates in the Beaufort County jail," and said also that Joan Little was seeking damages because she had been "deprived of her constitutional rights . . ." and because of emotional and physical injuries she had sustained. On the other hand, Jerry Paul told reporters, "We're not really after money. It's more for the purpose of deterrence, to remind other jailers that to violate someone's civil rights is to run the risk of money damages." Neither the original complaint, the "Summary," nor the statements of Joan Little's attorneys mentioned anything about preventing the distribution of the assets of the dead jailer's estate, which had been valued at $28,754.

The "Motion to Stay" failed to persuade United States District Court Judge John Larkin, the man who had ordered public schools in Beaufort County desegregated more than a decade earlier. In July he appointed a "special master" to preside at the deposition, but by then it was too late to schedule a hearing before the criminal trial and the prosecution was deprived of the valuable advantage of knowing beforehand what Joan Little would say when she took the witness stand. After the murder trial, the far-reaching civil suit was simply allowed to wither and die. The Southern Poverty Law Center had sued to have the courts "set constitutionally acceptable standards for the incarceration, care and supervision of women inmates" in the jail where Joan Little had been housed, but once she was free no further action would be taken to correct the conditions stipulated in the complaint. The complaint itself had, nevertheless, represented a milestone in the murder case. It contained the first formal description of the incident involving the defendant and the dead jailer, the first defense version submitted to any court, and it differed from anything previously said about the case:

> ... *On August 27, 1974, at approximately 4:00 a.m., [sic]*
> *[Joan Little] was sexually attacked in her cell by the night*
> *jailer of the Beaufort County Sheriff's Department, Clarence*
> *G. [sic] Alligood. Jailer Alligood used an ice pick and physi-*
> *cal force to cause plaintiff to remove her clothes and to have*
> *unnatural sexual relations with him. During the brutal at-*
> *tack, which was perpetrated against the will of the plaintiff,*
> *she obtained the ice pick and killed Jailer Alligood in self-*
> *defense.*

Until the civil complaint appeared, nothing had been said about "unnatural sexual relations" between Clarence Alligood and Joan Little. Now, barely six weeks before the trial, the defense explanation of the events that had led to the jailer's death underwent a startling transformation. Her degradation seemed to assume new proportions, as it had nearly six months earlier when the SPLC solicitation letter first appeared. "The obvious motivation is to spur interest in the case and get the donations rolling in again," John Wilkinson told a reporter soon after he had read the complaint. "This will enhance the image of Joan Little as a martyr and spur the collections." The suit did throw more confusion into an already confused situation, and after several weeks in limbo the case emerged again as front-page news. "It is the first time the unnatural sexual activity charge has been made in public," one state newspaper said, "and could raise a question concerning the 62-year-old Alligood engaging in both an unnatural sex act and attempted rape on the same occasion." To explain these belated disclosures, Jerry Paul would say that Joan Little had been so traumatized by the jailer's attack and embarrassed by the act he had forced her to perform that only in early June had she finally been able to reveal "the full story." On the witness stand, however, she would testify that she had told Raymond Cobb on the night of her escape that the jailer had tried "to make me have oral sex with him."

These new revelations came as no real surprise to the prosecutors. William Griffin and Jerry Paul had already discussed the possibility that the jailer had been engaged in "unnatural sexual relations" with Joan Little when he was killed. Paul told Griffin in March that she could not yet cope with her disturbing recollections of the incident and that she would not be ready to take a polygraph examination until she could do so. Griffin had long suspected that more than rape might be involved. Until just before the trial he believed that Alligood could not have moved once he was wounded, leading to the mistaken premise that he must have been stabbed while he was in a sitting position and that he then slumped over and died.

Some of the investigating officers shared the same opinion, but for a different reason. They thought Alligood must have suspected that Joan Little was suffering from a female disorder while she was in the Beaufort County jail. Willis Peachey had explained the theory to Morris Dees, who believed that Peachey "knows a lot he's not telling" and recorded their conversation in his notes under the heading "JAL's vaginal condition." Peachey told him that Alligood "was there" when Joan Little had been taken to be examined by a physician, and that "Alligood [was] not screwing JAL because he knew of vaginal disease."

Joan Little had seen a doctor at least twice while she was in jail, on June 7 and again on June 10. Each time she had been accompanied to the Beaufort County Hospital by a different female deputy. But the reason she needed treatment was never firmly established. William Griffin learned from the deputies that both hospital trips had been required because of some unspecified female disorder, but Griffin made no effort to get the confidential medical records pertaining to these examinations and did not pursue the matter further. The defense attorneys tried unsuccessfully during the spring to obtain these records from a local doctor, who was reluctant to release them without a court

order, and then briefly discussed what Peachey had told
Dees during the trial strategy meeting in Raleigh in early
June. Before then, Morris Dees had also spoken to the other
jailers, and what they told him cast doubts on Peachey's
speculation. Ellis Tetterton remembered that Joan Little
"had some prescribed medicine" but he did not know what
it was and had paid no attention to the reasons for her
hospital visits. David Watson, whom Dees described in his
notes as "very honest, sincere, fair, thinks Alligood wrong,
likes JAL," told him that she was taking medicine, which
was kept in the jail office, but that he did not "remember
what it was." Dees found nothing to indicate that Clarence
Alligood knew more about her alleged "vaginal condition"
than the other jailers, and what he learned from Tetterton
and Watson made Peachey's assumptions appear to be
wrong, unless she had informed the night jailer personally.

Nevertheless, Peachey and some of the other investigating officers continued to believe that Joan Little's story of
rape and self-defense was implausible. They felt that Clarence Alligood would not have tried to engage in sexual
intercourse with a woman he knew or even suspected of
having some sort of vaginal disorder, and after it became
known in June that the defendant would say she had been
forced to have "unnatural sexual relations" with the jailer,
many of them thought the story had been concocted by the
defense because of what Dees and the others had learned
from the medical examiner's report and from various officials at the jail.

Superior Court Judge Hamilton Hobgood had spent the
month of May at his home in Louisburg, North Carolina,
north of Raleigh, recuperating from eye surgery. It was
there that he learned of Henry McKinnon's withdrawal
from the Joan Little case and first felt apprehension that he
might be asked to preside at the upcoming trial. Hobgood
had arranged an unusually light workload for the remain-

der of the summer in order to give himself plenty of time to recover from the operation, but he had been assigned by coincidence to the Wake County Courthouse beginning in July. He knew the convenience of his schedule would not escape the notice of those who would appoint McKinnon's successor, and he began to wonder whether, if asked, he would use his health as an excuse to turn down the case.

Hobgood's reputation as a jurist was excellent. A graduate of the University of North Carolina and of Wake Forest Law School, he had been appointed to the bench nineteen years earlier, after a successful law practice in Louisburg and several terms in the state legislature. At sixty-four, he looked ruddy and healthy, although he had suffered a serious heart attack in 1959, at the age of fifty. He was noted for hard work and a sharp mind, as well as for good humor and an even temper. Neat, orderly, and fastidious, he was a man of enormous self-confidence, a shrewd man who would not feel threatened by the ordeal of the long trial and who would know how to handle the diverse pressures of this case. He kept himself in good shape by playing golf avidly, and his only concession to the retirement age quickly overtaking him was a paunch, which conspired with a twinkle in his eyes to give him the advantage of being able to seem jolly even when he was not.

On June 9 his selection as the trial judge was announced. Neither the defense nor the prosecution had been consulted, and he would not have been the first choice of either side, but all of the attorneys seemed content with his selection. Jerry Paul had previously appeared before him to defend Golden Frinks and had won the case. William Griffin knew him only by reputation. Hobgood would tell an acquaintance some time later that he thought he had been selected because he would not declare a mistrial "if some lawyer acted up." Having recently presided at several lengthy and controversial criminal trials, he was a natural choice to hear the Joan Little case not only because of his respected legal abilities but because of his experience and temperament as well. If any judge could keep things under control and get the case over with as quickly as possible, it was he.

Morris Dees had already conducted an extensive investigation. During the spring he had interviewed Ottis Davis, the jailers, several of the deputies, the bondsman, and others in Beaufort County who knew Joan Little, including those who had helped her after the escape. In Chapel Hill, Dees had seen Roger Bernholz briefly and then had visited Anna Eubanks to obtain a copy of her telephone bill covering the period from August 19 to September 19, 1974.

In June, after the meeting in Raleigh where he was assigned to see all "non-expert" witnesses, Dees spent several more weeks in Beaufort County, again talking to Davis and others at the sheriff's department, including Beverly King. He also tried to contact a number of former inmates of the county jail, and eventually he located a young woman named Phyllis Ann Moore. SBI agents had questioned her during their investigation late in 1974, and the interview had been reported in one sentence: "Phyllis Ann Moore was incarcerated in the Beaufort County Jail July 13, 1974, for larceny and spent several days and nights and was treated very well in the jail." After talking to Dees, Phyllis Ann Moore became a witness for the defense and testified at the trial that Clarence Alligood had twice come into the women's section to ask Joan Little "if she missed her man."

Later in June, Dees turned his attention to the telephone calls made from the jail to the home of Anna Eubanks. In April, Mrs. Eubanks had told him that she received a call from Joan about 10:30 p.m. on August 26, and that she "talked about Julius," asking "where he was" and "why he hadn't called." According to Dees's notes, Joan "told Mrs. E she thought she 'was going to have a hearing and was getting out on bond,'" and that she was "trying to reach J.R. about bondsman (& atty.)." Mrs. Eubanks also told him that Joan "said she hoped she'd see us 'this weekend.'"

Two days later Dees learned from Ottis Davis that Joan was suspected of having called Anna Eubanks to tell her that she would "see them by Thursday," and that the investigators thought Mrs. Eubanks had warned her not to do "anything you'll be sorry for," which suggested to Davis that she had already been planning her escape. According to the SBI report: "Suspect Little told subject [Anna Eubanks] that she would see her on Friday and would call her again on Thursday. Subject advised that she told suspect Little not to do anything foolish."

Dees was also interested in the call made some time after three o'clock on August 27, which posed a threat to the defense case by indicating that Joan Little might have wanted to contact someone other than Anna Eubanks and by suggesting she had a second opportunity to get the ice pick out of the desk drawer in the jailer's office. The SBI had learned in September that Ervin Eubanks, Anna's son, had "talked with Joanne Little on Monday or Tuesday morning around 3:30 a.m." Peachey and Slaughter assumed that this merely confirmed what Danny Respass had already discovered when he interviewed the operator in Washington on the day of the escape.

But in June Dees visited John Cox, an official of the Chapel Hill Telephone Company, hoping to find a way to dispute the operator and prove that no such call had been made. In April, Ervin Eubanks had told him he could not remember exactly when Joan Little had telephoned early in the morning, but thought it "was about two weeks before the SBI talked to him."* Dees showed Cox a copy of the Eubanks telephone bill, which indicated that two collect calls had been placed from the Beaufort County jail to the Eubanks home, one on August 26 and another on August 27. Beside the record of the first call he had written

---

*The telephone bill sent to the Eubanks home tended to confirm what Ervin had told the SBI, however, not what he later told Dees. For the same reasons his mother did not appear at the trial, Ervin would not be called as a prosecution witness.

"11:00 p.m. to 8:00 a.m." and beside the record of the second call he had written "5:00 p.m. to 11:00 p.m." Dees asked Cox to verify these time periods by using a photocopy of a telephone-directory rate page which he had brought along in his briefcase. After checking the code information for each call, Cox said he concurred with Dees that the earlier one had been placed between 11:00 p.m. on August 26 and 8:00 a.m. on August 27, and that the later one had been placed after 5:00 p.m. on August 27.

As far as Dees was concerned, this meant that the prosecution could not prove an early-morning phone call had ever been made. One call had been placed on August 26 —the late-evening call that everyone knew about—and now a telephone-company official had said that the other must have been put through between 5:00 p.m. and 11:00 p.m. on August 27, hours after Joan Little had escaped. Later Cox would write to Dees reiterating his conclusions, and his letter would be used at the trial to refute prosecution testimony about the call that was supposed to have been made around 3:30 a.m. on August 27. Overlooked until too late was the fact that Anna Eubanks had talked to Joan Little between 10:00 and 10:30 p.m., half an hour before the first collect call could have been placed according to this interpretation.

The mystery of these telephone calls was never fully solved, but evidence and testimony about them were hotly disputed during the trial. Toll tickets recording the exact time of each call had been kept for six months in telephone-company files, but then routinely destroyed when no request to preserve them was made. A crucial, perhaps decisive bit of evidence was permitted to slip away through neglect, and the defense attorneys would later accuse William Griffin of failing to produce exculpatory information and of willfully permitting the tickets to be burned.

The only remaining written record of the calls was the Eubanks telephone bill. Once Joan Little had testified that she made only one call to the Eubanks home that night, the prosecution was permitted to introduce Washington tele-

phone operator Nancy Hollis as a rebuttal witness to interpret the coded information on the bill and to testify about
what had occurred while she was on duty the morning of
August 27, 1974. She told the jury there had actually been
two attempts to call Chapel Hill from the jail after midnight. The first, she remembered, had been a collect, person-to-person call, and had not been answered. The second, about "ten to fifteen minutes later," had been a
collect, station-to-station call to the same number. "The
party calling identified herself," she said, "as Joan Little."

This was damaging testimony, and would be one of the
few points the jury would stop to consider before acquit-
ting the defendant. Seeming to realize how significant her
appearance could be, Jerry Paul badgered the plump timid
woman relentlessly, trying to force her to say that the second call had been made after 5:00 p.m. on August 27. "Is
it not true," he asked, "that the phone bill shows that the
call was made at least twelve hours after you've testified
that it was made?"

"Well, yes . . . no, no, that's not right," she said. "Those
rates were in effect when I went on duty."

"When does the twenty-seventh start?"

"At midnight . . . midnight to midnight."

"I really don't know what you're talking about. The code
would be different."

"No, it wouldn't. I've tried to explain."

"The rate period starts on one day and ends on another.
. . . This period began at 5:00 p.m. on the twenty-sixth!"

"I don't follow you at all, Mr. Paul," Judge Hobgood
interrupted finally. By then most of the jurors were leaning
forward, listening to the exchange with quizzical expres-
sions on their faces. Relying on the letter from John Cox,
Paul wanted the operator to testify that the evening rate
began at 5:00 p.m. and ended at 11:00 p.m. the same day,
but she insisted that the evening rate began at 5:00 p.m. on
one day and ended at 8:00 a.m. the following day, while the
billing day changed at midnight. "The new day starts at 12
a.m.," she explained once more, "so the call was made

between 12:00 a.m. and 8:00 a.m. on the twenty-seventh."

"In essence, your testimony contradicts the phone bill!" Paul shouted.

"No, it doesn't," Nancy Hollis said again.

"Isn't it a fact," Paul asked furiously, flinging himself into his chair, "that of thirty-five telephone operators in Washington, you're the only one the District Attorney could get to come to Raleigh and tell a lie?"

Nancy Hollis blinked and then stiffened. "No," she replied softly but very firmly. "I haven't told a lie, Mr. Paul."

The prosecutors would make no effort to bolster this potentially important testimony, although they had earlier received a copy of Cox's letter to Dees and could have discovered for themselves certain discrepancies in his interpretation of the coded information on the telephone bill. In his summation Jerry Paul would tell the jury that Nancy Hollis, an employee of the Carolina Telephone & Telegraph Company, was unqualified to explain the separate billing procedures used by the Chapel Hill Telephone Company. In fact the Chapel Hill utility had no long-distance capability of its own and received charges for such calls from other companies, including CT&T, whose long-line equipment was used to complete the circuits. John Cox was actually unfamiliar with billing procedures used by the larger companies, and was less qualified than Nancy Hollis to describe times and rates for long-distance calls.

Cox's error—the same apparent mistake Dees had made and the same oversight employed by Paul to attack the operator on cross-examination—was to use the wrong rate schedule. Under the heading "Rate Periods for Calls to Points *Within* North Carolina" on the rate page Dees had supplied, there were two similar but not identical charts, one titled "Customer Dialed Calls" and the other titled "Operator Assisted Calls." The chart for determining the rate period for customer-dialed calls indicated that the "Evening Rate" from Monday to Friday was in effect from 5:00 p.m. until 11:00 p.m., and Cox had referred to this chart when Dees consulted him in June and when he wrote to

Dees in July. The other chart—the one ignored by Cox, Dees, and the defense and prosecution attorneys—indicated that the "Evening Rate" for operator-assisted calls during the week commenced at 5:00 p.m. and ended at 8:00 a.m. Of the calls about which Nancy Hollis testified, one had been placed person-to-person collect and the other station-to-station collect. All collect calls, as well as all person-to-person calls, required the assistance of an operator. Everyone had referred to the wrong chart. That was what Nancy Hollis had been trying to say on the witness stand when she was accused of lying.

The truth about these calls could never be sorted out, not only because the toll tickets had been destroyed but also because the Eubanks telephone bill was apparently defective. For the call made on "8/26 FROM WASHTN NC" the coded information was "4C," in which "4" meant "Collect Call" and "C" meant "Person to Person, Night." But the proper rate schedule indicated that there was no night rate for operator-assisted calls, only a "Day Rate" from 8:00 a.m. to 5:00 p.m. and an "Evening Rate" from 5:00 p.m. to 8:00 a.m. weekdays and all day Saturday and Sunday. If the date on the statement was correct, this was probably the call made to the Eubanks home shortly after Clarence Alligood came on duty on August 26, but neither the defense nor the prosecution asked Joan Little while she was on the witness stand whether she had placed the call person-to-person or station-to-station, or whether it had been put through collect.

The second call was more important and intriguing, but even less was known about it. Had Joan Little telephoned from the jail sometime during the morning, apparently at about the same time the jailer was killed? Or had the call been made later that day, perhaps by officers trying to locate Julius Rodgers? There was no apparent defect in the coded data; "4S," in which "4" meant "Collect Call" and "S" meant "Station to Station, Evening," was a legitimate rate and class for operator-assisted calls between points within North Carolina. The defense attorneys argued that this call must have been made after 5:00 p.m. on August 27, and referred to testimony by Willis Peachey that a call to the Eubanks home had been made from the jail on August 27 as part of the investigation. It was also possible, however, that the call had been placed between midnight and 8:00 a.m., and Nancy Hollis testified that a collect station call went through during that period from a person who identified herself as Joan Little.

Without toll tickets the evidence seemed muddled, but in fact it was more incomplete than contradictory. The Eubanks bill showed that only two operator-assisted calls had been placed from the jailer's phone, one on August 26 and one on August 27. Beaufort County telephone records showed, however, that yet another call had been placed from the jail to the Eubanks home on August 27, a customer-dialed call that lasted two minutes. At the trial the defense attorneys suggested that Willis Peachey must have been responsible for the August 27 call recorded on the Eubanks bill, an argument based on the speculative notion that he had placed a collect call in the line of duty from a jail phone and that someone at the Eubanks home had accepted the charges. The prosecution did not call Willis Peachey in rebuttal to clarify his testimony, nor were the jail telephone records introduced to corroborate his earlier statements, even though both sides had received copies of the Carolina Telephone & Telegraph Company bill for the jail several weeks before the trial began. The jury never learned, therefore, that two calls had been placed from the jail to the Eubanks home on August 27, one collect and the other customer-dialed. After the trial, Peachey would confirm that he had not reversed the charges when he placed his call.

Who, then, had initiated the only unexplained call from the jail, the collect call on August 27 to Chapel Hill, and exactly when had it gone through? Only a few people could have known: the members of the Eubanks family, who were never called to testify; the defendant, who denied making such a call; and the telephone operator, who testified that someone had put the call through between 3:00 and 3:30 a.m., someone who had "identified herself as Joan Little."

In June a former trusty at the Beaufort County jail confessed that he had been in the women's section on the night of August 27, 1974, and that he had helped Joan Little stage the killing to look like rape and self-defense.

Terry Bell, the frail felon who was a friend of all the jailers, had been telling other inmates at Polk Youth Center in Raleigh that he knew something about the case and that he had been involved in the incident. For months Bell had remained a forgotten figure in the investigation. His original statement had told the officers nothing they did not already know, and they had uncovered no evidence of an accomplice. No one suspected that he might have been a part of the killing, because they thought he had been confined to the juvenile section and the adjoining hallway on the night of Clarence Alligood's death. But once he got back to Beaufort County, where prison officials sent him for further interrogation, Bell broke down and gave William Griffin and Ottis Davis a statement laced with essential details about the crime scene and the condition of the body, details they felt he could not have known unless he had been there.

He had heard a noise around four o'clock in the morning, Bell told them, and he had left the juvenile section and gone to the door at the end of the corridor to investigate. Through the small window in the door he had been able to see Joan Little, fully clothed, standing at the entrance to the women's section across the hall. The jailer was nowhere around.

Curious, Bell had scaled the wall, using a protruding switchbox to reach and remove one of the punchboard ceiling panels, and then he had pulled himself into the crawl space above the false ceiling. Moving silently across the steam pipes and air-conditioning ducts, he had made his way to the other side of the jail, to the steel ceiling of the women's cellblock, where he had easily found the light fixture, pulled up the bulb, and peered down into cell number one. There he had seen Joan Little staring up at him, and on the floor beside her, his head and chest bloody, was Clarence Alligood.

"Help me," she had said, motioning for him to come down if he could, and he had moved to one side, away from the area over the cellblock, where he could remove another panel and drop to the floor. At first he had ignored her and had used wet toilet tissues to wipe blood from Alligood's face, but suddenly he had realized that the jailer was dead and he had noticed for the first time that she was watching him closely. "Help me," she had said again, telling him what she wanted done, and in shock he had taken off the man's trousers and underwear after hoisting his body onto the bunk. As he stepped back, she had pushed the corpse over on its side, and then she had leaned down to place the ice pick between the man's fingers. Abruptly aware of what was happening, Bell had scrambled out of the cellblock, up into the crawl space, across to the other side, and back into his own cell. She might have called after him, he could not be sure. Alone, in his own bunk, he had begun to cry, and finally he had fallen asleep.

Terry Bell's statement was astonishing, but William Griffin could not be certain he was telling the truth. Bell was asked to describe the cell, and in doing so he mentioned several items the officers had found there. Then he was asked how he had discovered the overhead route to the other side of the jail, and he explained that he had often used it to change light bulbs while he was a trusty. Finally, Griffin asked Bell how he could climb into the overhead without a ladder, and Bell showed him. With an SBI photographer taking pictures, he climbed the wall in the corridor outside the juvenile section, made his way without a sound across to the other side, and looked down at Griffin and Davis through the light fixture in cell number one.

Ottis Davis thought they had finally found a way to explain the circumstances of Clarence Alligood's death, but Griffin remained uneasy about Bell's story. He returned to his office and went over it several times more. Clearly, Bell knew a great deal about the jail scene—he had mentioned the toilet tissues, the jar of Vaseline, and the eyeglasses. Clearly, too, he was capable of doing what he said he had done. But there were nagging doubts, vague inconsistencies, and the extraordinary confession seemed incomprehensible. Bell had admitted that he "liked Mr. Alligood" and that he had not liked Joan Little. Had he contrived an elaborate lie out of some twisted respect for the jailer, or for some other reason, in order to make sure that she did not go unpunished for Alligood's death? Did he realize that he was implicating himself as an accomplice in first-degree murder? What, if anything, did Terry Bell really know about this killing?

William Griffin decided that Bell should undergo a polygraph examination at once.

On the morning of June 19 the defendant and three members of the defense team caught an early flight from Durham to Washington, D.C., and checked into a motel near the airport to wait for Marvin Miller. With Jerry Paul and Karen Galloway were Joan Little and Richard Wolf, who had by then become an integral member of Paul's staff. Wolf's advice had been relied on during the pre-trial hearings, when he had sat near the defense attorneys and interpreted for them the psychic impressions he received about the judge, the prosecutors, and the various witnesses. Now he was involved in preparations for the arduous process of jury selection, and in a project perhaps even more crucial to the outcome of the trial, the preparation of Joan Little to take the witness stand in her own defense.

Once they were settled in their motel room, Wolf lowered the blinds and took a seat across from Joan Little. They looked directly into each other's eyes, and Wolf began to speak very softly. "Okay, we're going to go into a deeper, more healthy state of mind, a deeper meditative state . . . very peaceful . . . very aware. . . . Imagine yourself on an elevator. . . ." Almost at once Joan Little's heavy eyelids began to flicker and fall.

Richard Wolf had been working with the defendant for weeks, making meditative tapes for her to play when she was alone, talking with her about feelings and emotions, casting star charts and interpreting her dreams, and often putting her into a hypnotic sleep. He called his technique of psychic preparation and instruction "programming," and he had found Joan Little to be a pliant subject. By June 19 this routine had become familiar to both of them. He was "taking her down" in order to "program her at the deepest subconscious levels." He was using techniques often employed by doctors, dentists, and psychologists who delve into the subconscious in an effort to modify behavioral and emotional responses experienced by the conscious mind. "I put her into what might be called a trance," he would explain privately before the trial. "I program her that she will have absolutely no [reactions], that she will register absolutely nothing, that she will see things exactly as they happen, no more and no less, that she will become more relaxed with every question. . . . The instructions I gave her were not to respond to any question that was asked by another person. . . ."

Later that morning, after Joan Little had been "programmed" by hypnosis, Marvin Miller drove Paul, Galloway, and the defendant to the office of Lloyd Furr in McLean, Virginia. Richard Wolf stayed behind. A private detective and a trained polygraph examiner, Furr had helped Miller on cases before, and now he had been retained to subject Joan Little to a secret polygraph test. Only two weeks earlier Paul had told Morris Dees that his client was "not ready" and "wouldn't pass" a lie-detector examination. Now he would find out whether Wolf's efforts to program Joan Little had changed all that.

The test began at one o'clock and lasted for over an hour. Using a description of the incident prepared by Paul from his discussions with Joan Little, Furr went through a series of questions as the polygraph instrument recorded changes in her blood pressure, pulse, and respiration. When the session was over, she and Karen Galloway left at once to fly back to North Carolina for a television appearance, while Paul and Miller stayed to talk to Furr. He told them the test was very positive. Paul would say that it "was not border-line." Two days later Furr wrote Miller a letter stating that:

1. Joanne Little is telling the truth about the fact, Alligood brought the questionable ice pick to the jail cell the night of the assault.

2. Alligood, did in fact try to force Little to have sex with him.

3. At no time during her stay in jail did Joanne Little make or have plans to escape.

Paul immediately arranged for a second polygraph test, and this time he went to an acknowledged authority in the field, John E. Reid, one of the authors of a standard text called *Lie Detection and Criminal Interrogation.* On June 27 Paul, Miller, Joan Little, and Richard Wolf flew to Chicago, and she underwent an examination in Reid's office after Wolf had again subjected her to preparatory hypnosis: "Any time a person asks you a question, you will respond in a healthy manner, a healthy way. . . . Every time a person asks you a question, you become more relaxed, more peaceful. You control your mind. You control your body. Your body does not control you. . . ."

On June 30 Reid reported the results in a letter to Paul: "There was no indication in this subject's polygraph records that she brought the fatal weapon, the ice pick, to her cell on August 27th before Guard Alligood arrived and there were no indications in this subject's records that she planned to stab Guard Alligood with the ice pick before he arrived in her cell and there were indications that Guard Alligood did force his sexual attentions upon Joan Little against her will. Furthermore, there were no indications that she had planned to escape prior to the time that Guard Alligood entered her cell."

The validity of these tests, and the accuracy of their results, might have been open to question if the details of Joan Little's preparations had been disclosed. Polygraph experts suspect that the mind-control aspects of hypnosis and meditation can diminish the polygraph instrument's reliability by disrupting the ordinary physiological responses it is designed to record. A controlled or subdued state of mind or a psychologically induced tranquillity can produce confusing test results just as drugs can throw polygraph techniques awry. While an experienced examiner can usually detect the influence of drugs, no procedures have been devised to determine whether a subject's responses are being affected by meditative serenity or post-hypnotic suggestion. Examiners rarely even ask about psychic, psychiatric, or psychoanalytic preparations, since the answers to such questions would be less and less revealing as the particular subject's preparations have been more intense and thorough.

The letters from Furr and Reid said nothing about meditative or hypnotic preparations Joan Little might have undergone for the examinations they had administered, and the defense attorneys did not acknowledge Richard Wolf's role in producing test results they later used to argue that all charges should be dropped. Confronted with the letters in private, William Griffin declined to act on the basis of tests conducted without his prior approval and participation. Instead, Griffin suggested another examination, one conducted by SBI polygraph experts. Paul refused.

For several weeks nothing more was said about the polygraph tests. No information about them was leaked to the press, and no further efforts were made to convince Griffin that he should drop the charges against Joan Little. Then, early in the trial before jury selection had been completed, the defense filed a surprise motion for a dismissal on the grounds that the district attorney had failed to honor a prior oral agreement to "dismiss the indictment" if a polygraph examination "indicated that she was not lying in regard to her contentions as to the events in the jail on August 27, 1974. . . ." The letters from Furr and Reid, attached as exhibits, were released to the press with the motion itself and were widely publicized along with an attack on the prosecutor. In spite of the fact that the results of such polygraph examinations were not admissible as evidence in North Carolina courts, the defense attorneys were able to use the media to broadcast the conclusions of their own paid experts to those jurors not yet selected and sequestered. Griffin composed a scalding answer which accused Joan Little's lawyers of having tried to negotiate a plea bargain during the fall (their affidavit stated that they had consistently maintained she was innocent) but withheld it until all jurors had been sequestered so as not to risk a mistrial by disclosing possibly prejudicial information. After jury selection was completed and the jurors were sequestered, defense attorney Marvin Miller casually clarified the situation for reporters, telling them that no actual agreement on a polygraph examination had ever been reached between the defense and the district attorney.

By the beginning of July, money and time had grown critically short, and the defense team had begun to fragment. Months earlier, before the pre-trial hearings, Paul had commissioned a "psychological evaluation team" from Durham to study the interpersonal relationships of the people working on the case and to recommend changes in the structure of the defense organization. The evaluation results, delivered in a two-page report written with a ballpoint pen, exposed "an unnecessary one-up, one-down arrangement, which commonly leads to passive-aggressive sabotage hindering further communication and decreasing productivity due to energy deployed for resentment, etc."

But Paul ignored the report, even though he had spent several thousand dollars to have it prepared, and by the summer various "passive-aggressive saboteurs" were de-

pleting the morale and determination of a staff the evaluation team had found to have "a high sense of commitment
to the case and a positive attitude of 'not guilty.'" Control
of the Defense Fund had finally been decided by rapacious
squabbling that left Patricia Chance at the top and turned
a number of early volunteers and staff members into exiles.
Among the lawyers there was constant bickering and
strain. Jerry Paul's attention was occupied by a series of
running skirmishes with Morris Dees, who "had to be
shown who's boss" during a meeting in Paul's office late in
June. Karen Galloway resented Dees, at least in part because he seemed to think she was too inexperienced even
for her limited responsibilities. Dees did not like Marvin
Miller and seriously doubted Jerry Paul's capacity to handle the case as he thought it should be handled. This dissension at the top inevitably percolated through the whole
staff, and by late June grumbling and quarreling were commonplace.

Responsibilities for the preparation of the case had been
broken down into eight independent defense-team "projects." But in fact Jerry Paul ran a loose defense effort
without giving much vitality to these various organiza-
tional distinctions, partly because he did not seem adept at
delegating authority and partly because the people he had
recruited were inexperienced and, in a few cases, irrespon-
sible.

The Fair Jury Project was the most effective of the eight
groups, and the most expensive. More than $70,000 had
been spent by early July, according to Paul's rough estimate. Working out of offices in Raleigh near the campus of
North Carolina State University, Courtney Mullin had organized the twenty-three-county survey prior to the pre-
trial hearings and then a similar effort in Wake County just
before the trial. She had also assembled and briefed a team
of experts to assist the defense attorneys with the actual
selection of jurors.

The Joann Little Defense Fund, Inc., constituted a separate project, which included not only fund raising but pub-

licity and efforts to organize demonstrations and rallies. Larry Little was considered a part of this project, as was Pat Chance, who was chiefly responsible for keeping up with correspondence and for serving as a media coordinator for Paul and the others. Public relations, as part of publicity, was assigned to several volunteers, who were given little to do except collect the names of reporters who wanted interviews. The substance of interviews and the information to be disclosed to the press were closely controlled by Paul himself.

The Psychological Evaluation Team had originally been another project, but this team's responsibilities eventually devolved on Richard Wolf. Paul relied on him to smooth out friction in the office. Several physicians and psychologists who were asked to attend Joan Little at various times, and her bodyguard, Russell McDonald, were also considered a part of this group.

Largely by default, the Investigation Project became the province of Morris Dees. Without deriving any noticeable benefits, the defense paid thousands of dollars to a private detective agency in Durham before the pre-trial hearings, and just before the trial Paul hired two half-brothers from California who professed to be trained investigators and criminologists. Like the local detectives, they were unable to make any significant contribution to the case.

As part of a separate Court Reporters Project, Paul had planned to pay trained recorders to produce daily transcripts of the trial solely for the use of the defense attorneys. He was negotiating confidentially with two experienced court reporters, but then Judge Hobgood forbade the use of private stenographers in the courtroom.

The remaining three projects pertained to work done or being done by the legal staff. The Pre-trial Project had been the responsibility of Marvin Miller, who did much of the research on the motions argued in Beaufort County and on those carried over for later consideration. The Trial Research Project was assigned to James Rowan and James Gillespie, who worked on various new motions to be sub-

mitted to Hobgood, and on legal issues that were expected
to arise during the trial. Legal was the project name for the
attorneys who would actually appear in court—Jerry Paul,
Morris Dees, Marvin Miller, Karen Galloway, James
Rowan, James Gillespie, and, by early July, an experienced
criminal lawyer from Greenville named Milton Williamson.

Tall and spare, Williamson wore seersucker suits and
desert boots, chewed gum, and had a bony, intimidating
face that seemed locked in a perpetual scowl. At the last
minute he was brought out of the relative seclusion of his
law practice in eastern North Carolina to give the defense
team something it had lacked in spite of size and depth—
litigation expertise. Paul and Dees had some courtroom
experience but not enough, it seemed, to match the prosecution. Besides William Griffin and John Wilkinson, the
state had added a third skilled lawyer, former Wake
County District Attorney Lester Chalmers, now a special
prosecutor in the North Carolina attorney general's office.
Though Paul intended to employ unique and innovative
trial techniques and had recruited social scientists, body
language experts, psychologists, and an astrologer to assist
him, it was clear the defense would eventually have to rely
on fundamental courtroom skills to win the case. Williamson had spent his entire professional life in the crannies and
corners of criminal court in Pitt County, and as a young
lawyer there Paul had grown to respect his abilities as well
as his aggressive trial tactics. During the spring Williamson
had consented to act as a confidential paid consultant; Paul
had explained privately at the time that for "political reasons" Williamson's connection with the Joan Little case
could not be disclosed. But in July Williamson emerged and
openly joined the defense team. He became, in the football
vernacular Paul was fond of using, its "back-up quarterback."

Until just before the trial the defense preparations ran
laterally, in parallel, and the efforts of the various team
members were not fully consolidated even when court

opened for the first day of motions and jury selection. Milton Williamson remained in Greenville. Rowan and Gillespie confined themselves to legal research. Marvin Miller pursued his own practice in Virginia. Paul and Galloway worked on the case in the office whenever there was time between fund-raising rallies, press interviews, and the public appearances they made—sometimes with Joan Little and sometimes alone—during June and early July. By then it was clear that some attorneys would play a greater role in the trial than others. James Gillespie and James Rowan would take little active part in the proceedings and in fact would not even appear in court every day. Karen Galloway would be there; but as the only woman and only black on the defense team, her role would be essentially symbolic until the end, when she would deliver an emotional and effective closing argument. Marvin Miller would assume most of the responsibility for arguing motions and would handle a few cross-examinations. Morris Dees would conduct the cross-examination of most of the "non-expert" prosecution witnesses he had previously interviewed, as well as the examination of several defense witnesses. Paul, with Williamson's help, would cross-examine the major prosecution witnesses and examine the most important defense witnesses, including the defendant. Everyone seemed satisfied with this arrangement except Morris Dees, who appeared to be growing more and more unhappy about the division of responsibilities and about the direction the case was taking with Paul at the helm.

Jerry Paul and Morris Dees were temperamentally unsuited for their partnership, and the strain brought on by their contrasting styles and goals only worsened as the trial drew near. As chief defense counsel, Paul's judgment was sometimes colored by cynical idealism and a sense of justice that confused football's violent ideology, the gentler wisdom of Martin Luther King, Jr., and the teachings of Chairman Mao. Morris Dees, on the other hand, approached the trial preparations with cold intensity and a lawyerly indifference toward matters that would not contribute directly to obtaining the desired results in the courtroom. He insisted that all the attorneys should focus on the facts and concentrate on finding chinks in the state's case, endeavors that would have conflicted with the heady round of publicity appearances being scheduled for Paul and Galloway. He seemed ready now to disregard the social and political significance of the case, the issues he had touted in order to raise money for the Southern Poverty Law Center and the Joann Little Defense Fund. Paul wanted to establish Joan Little's innocence, in and out of the courtroom, to vindicate his own opinions about the society and the criminal-justice system he scorned. Morris Dees thought it would be sufficient merely to prevent the prosecution from proving her guilt, to secure the evidentiary default which gives a defendant the benefit of the doubt. "The whole point of this case," he had told the others during one of their private meetings, "is to get Joan Little off." To Jerry Paul, however, that was not the whole point at all.

In late June and early July the differences between Paul and Dees developed into delicate antagonism and finally into a raw contest for power and control. Paul accused Dees of being "too caught up in disbelieving Joan," and after Dees had delivered the last SPLC contribution to the Joann Little Defense Fund, Paul began looking for a way to remove him from the case. "I really don't need Dees any longer," he said, "and if I could figure out a way to fire him I would." At about the same time Dees got into a conversation with Ottis Davis, who was angry about a comment Paul had made to a reporter. "Don't worry," Dees told Davis. "When we get to Raleigh, I'm going to be in charge."

Hamilton Hobgood wasted no time beginning to prepare for the trial. Soon after his appointment he had dinner with James H. Pou Bailey, the senior judge in Wake County who had granted bail in the case in September. Together, they agreed that Bailey would be responsible for the security of the courthouse building and for everything that went on outside the courtroom. Hobgood would have autonomy over what transpired inside the courtroom and in chambers.

On June 21 Bailey issued an order banning all "demonstrations, assemblies or other gatherings of people . . . on the grounds of the Wake County Courthouse." The order did not mention the Joan Little trial, but did stipulate that it was to take effect at 8:00 a.m. on July 14, the day the trial was now scheduled to begin. He also soon arranged to borrow an airport personnel scanner and had it installed at the entrance to the courtroom. During the trial several knives and one toy gun would be impounded by sheriff's deputies after being detected by the machine.

At the end of June, vacations were curtailed by the city police and the Wake County Sheriff's Department, and the Highway Patrol and the State Bureau of Investigation placed extra men on assignment in Raleigh. A spokesman for the North Carolina National Guard told reporters that "no special plans had been made . . . and no troops were on standby alert," but guard officers had recently reviewed their contingency plans for civil disturbances and a few guardsmen were informally placed on modified readiness in the event of trouble.

Then, early in July, there was a last attempt to delay the trial. The long murder prosecution in Beaufort County had finally ended in conviction for all the defendants on June 27, and during the following week William Griffin had been able to turn his attention to the Joan Little case for the first time in nearly two months. Time for trial preparation was short, but it was the mystery of Terry Bell's confession that finally compelled Griffin to seek a continuance. The temptation to believe Bell and to use him as a witness was excruciating—his testimony alone could quell the storming publicity and make Joan Little's supporters look like fools—but neither William Griffin nor the investigating officers now believed that Bell was telling the truth. The results of his polygraph test had been negative. The examiner, SBI agent Dave Keller, who would serve as Griffin's bodyguard at the trial, was convinced Bell's story was a hoax, a detailed but elaborate falsehood. Other agents who had questioned Bell agreed, and even Willis Peachey, who had awakened Bell from a sound sleep to inform him of the jailer's death, now thought the young man knew nothing about the killing.

Bell's uncanny familiarity with the crime-scene details and the condition of the body had not yet been explained, however, and although Griffin accepted the judgment of the officers, he could not disregard the possibility that the polygraph results were wrong, not until he knew enough to interpret Bell's statement in its entirety. Jerry Paul had been told about the confession and the results of Bell's test, and he too wanted to know more about it, and about the threat it posed to the version of the incident already being disseminated by the Joan Little defense. Both Paul and Griffin needed more time to deal with this situation, but they would not get it.

Griffin had already tried to obtain a postponement from Judge Hobgood during a telephone conversation a week earlier, but Hobgood had been uncooperative. The trial would begin on schedule, he had brusquely informed the district attorney, unless one of the principal participants was too sick to appear in the courtroom. The case, he said, had become "an albatross around the neck of the state."

To Griffin, who was already suspicious because of the manner in which the appeal of the change-of-venue order had been handled, it seemed that the new judge was under pressure to go to trial as soon as possible. Such pressure, if it was being applied, could have been coming from only one source. After discussing the results of Bell's test with Paul, Griffin placed a call to the offices of the North Carolina Supreme Court and asked to speak to Susie Sharp, the chief justice, the only woman in the country to hold such a position at that time.

At sixty-seven, Susie Sharp was still the same groundbreaker she had been all her life: the only female in her law school class, the first woman special trial judge in North Carolina, the first woman associate justice of the state's highest court, and finally the first female chief judge. A spinster and a skillful politician—her appointive posts in the judiciary had always been followed by election to a term of her own—she tightly administered her professional and her private life with great care but without much humor. She and Griffin did not know each other well, and their conversation was clipped and strained. Pointedly calling him "Mr. Griffin," she scolded the district attorney for even suggesting a delay, despite the fact that both prosecution and defense lawyers apparently thought a continuance was necessary. She brushed aside the significance of Terry Bell's confession, saying that the trial would go on as scheduled and that it should not be postponed under any circumstances. "North Carolina has had all it can stand of Joan Little," she told Griffin. "This case is an albatross around the neck of the state."*

No delay was possible, and the coincidental language both Judge Hobgood and Justice Sharp had used to convey their decisions unnerved Griffin and deepened his belief that the Joan Little prosecution was being isolated from the rest of the state judiciary. John Wilkinson had guessed that the change of venue had been inspired by politicians in Raleigh who wanted to assuage defense supporters and public opinion. Since the abortive effort to appeal Judge McKinnon's order, Griffin had been teetering between Wilkinson's view and his own, which was that there were practical and pragmatic reasons for moving the trial to a metropolitan area. Now he began to wonder whether the power of the judiciary was actually being marshaled

---

*Because Justice Sharp refused to be interviewed, even after all appeals in this case had been disposed of by the North Carolina Supreme Court, it was impossible to ascertain her views on the conversation she had with Griffin, or to know exactly what she had meant when she told him that the state had "had all it can stand of Joan Little." Justice Sharp was the only public official who declined to cooperate with the author.

against him, whether the case was being subverted from within as well as from without. After talking to Susie Sharp, Griffin began to sense that he had only a remote hope of winning. It was possible that the outcome had already been decided by pre-trial publicity and political intrigue, elements long at work in this case by the time the district attorney perceived their significance. In June, ambivalence settled over the prosecution like a fog. Later, looking back on it, Griffin would say that he had felt like "a passenger with his ticket punched, who had nothing to do but hang on for the ride."

Jerry Paul's confidence seemed shaken for the first time. Terry Bell's confession threatened to destroy his case. If Bell testified, there was a good chance Joan Little would be convicted.

But the crisis lasted only a few days. Paul told Morris Dees of Bell's story after hearing about it from Griffin during the meeting in which Paul first disclosed the results of Joan Little's lie-detector tests. Dees soon went to the Beaufort County jail for an interview with the young inmate. Paul, who left at once on a fund-raising trip to California, would later say he had specifically instructed Dees not to contact Bell until he had returned. At first Bell refused to speak to Dees, but then he relented. Their private conversation, held in the deputy's squad room, had an immediate impact on the efforts to find out what Bell really knew. After Dees left, Bell seemed outraged that his statement had been given to the defense attorneys. He began to recant his whole story, saying that he had made everything up because he liked the jailer and wanted to see Joan convicted for killing him. By the end of the day he had impugned his earlier confession with new statements to Ottis Davis and to Griffin, who came to the jail when he heard of Bell's turnabout. But still the young inmate seemed out of touch with the realities of his situation, and still he refused to explain how he had known about the bloody toilet tissues, the jar of Vaseline, and the way the jailer's body had been found lying slumped across the bunk.

The district attorney spent only a short time preparing his courtroom strategy and looking closely at the evidence. On Wednesday, July 9, William Griffin met in the grand-jury room at the Beaufort County Courthouse with Willis Peachey and William Slaughter to go over the state's case and to talk to some of the likely witnesses. John Wilkinson looked in for a moment, but did not take part in the preparations for trial. He wanted more money to go to Raleigh, and the Alligoods had not yet found a way to pay him. "I'm a defense attorney anyway," he chuckled that day. "I'd be more comfortable running with the rabbits than hunting with the hounds." As Griffin reviewed the evidence with Peachey and Slaughter, their long-standing consensus about what had happened between the jailer and Joan Little took solid shape. She had enticed Alligood early in the evening, they reasoned, and later, after obtaining the ice pick, she had invited him to her cell. He had gone there for the last time, after checking to make certain that all the deputies were off patrol for the night. There were flaws in the assumptions they made about the jailer's movements, especially about the reasons he might have had for checking with the radio dispatcher, but the tone of the prosecution had already been set and there would be no turning back for re-evaluation. The jailer's character would not be defended, but it would be argued that he had been weakened by Joan Little's intentional provocation rather than by his own uncontrollable urges. As a theory, this scenario seemed as plausible within the existing framework of evidence as the stories being circulated by the defense. It would be sufficient in any event to get Joan Little to the witness stand, and there the case would be won or lost.

The next day they went over the evidence in more detail, and for a moment they discussed the knife Clarence

Alligood had been carrying in his pocket when he died, agreeing that he would have probably used the knife instead of the ice pick if he had wanted to intimidate his prisoner. But the conversation went nowhere. The knife, along with all of the jailer's personal effects, had been returned to the family and now could not be produced as evidence because no chain of custody could be established. The knife was never mentioned in any of the investigative reports, and it would not be mentioned to the jury at the trial.

Jerry Paul called several times that day to ask whether Griffin intended to drop the case now that Terry Bell had admitted he was lying and once, after Griffin told him he still believed Joan Little was guilty, to arrange for yet another interview with Bell. Even as Paul was on the phone, Bell was in another part of the building talking to Louise Stokes, one of the female deputies. "We're not even interested enough to go in there and find out what he's saying," Willis Peachey remarked, and Griffin nodded as he placed the receiver back on its hook.

They were certain by then that Terry Bell had had no part in the killing of Clarence Alligood. Bell had finally explained exactly how he knew about the tissues and the other items in the cell and how he had been able to describe the position of the body. At 9:00 a.m. on August 27, Ellis Tetterton had received instructions from Ottis Davis to clean the cellblock, and Tetterton had told Terry Bell to do the work. Bell knew about the tissues because he had discarded them, along with the jar of Vaseline, and he knew about the cigarettes because he had pilfered them for his own use. He had tossed the blankets and the bloody sheets into the laundry hamper, and then he had cleaned up the bloodstains on the floor and the wall. Later that same morning, perhaps only moments before Peachey and the two SBI agents arrived, he had wandered into the photo lab in the jail and had seen the pictures of the corpse where Danny Respass had hung the fresh prints to dry. That was how he had learned of the position of the body and of the way the ice pick had been clutched in the dead man's hand.

Jerry Paul arrived at the jail late that Thursday afternoon with the two young criminologists from California. Paul was dressed as he preferred to be when he was not in court —a dark T-shirt, straight-leg blue jeans rolled up at the cuff, and sunglasses, which he kept on while he was inside. One of the investigators, a chubby young man who was wearing high-top tennis shoes, followed everywhere in Paul's footsteps. The other—taller, thinner, dressed in a modish three-piece suit without a tie—lagged behind and continually wiped his aviator glasses with tissues he pulled from the pocket of his coat.

Terry Bell's shoulders sagged and his eyes darted from one person to another as soon as he was brought into the squad room, where the interview would take place. He glanced quickly at Paul and the strangers, then toward William Griffin, then toward Ottis Davis, who sat munching a cigar butt. "Come on in and sit down," Davis said cheerily, pulling out a chair and patting the seat. Bell shuffled over. "Now, Terry," Griffin said, "Mr. Paul wants to ask you a few more questions. Do you mind that?" Bell shook his head slowly from side to side, but said nothing.

Paul walked briskly around in front of Bell, put one foot up on the seat of a chair, and began his interrogation. Bell remained somber and quiet, answering when he could by nodding his head. As Paul kept his attention, one of the investigators carefully took a tape recorder out of a valise and set it down on a nearby table. Griffin stiffened at once, and Davis lifted the cigar butt out of his mouth. "I don't think that'll be necessary," he growled softly, and as unobtrusively as it had appeared the tape recorder went back into the bag. Terry Bell had not even seemed to notice it.

Paul was getting nowhere. Bell stared at the tabletop in front of him, his fingers clenched tightly together, and continued to answer by nodding or with just a short word or two. "Do you remember telling us that you and Alligood talked about sex that night?" Paul asked finally. Bell shook his head slowly and then looked up. "I didn't ever talk to him about that," he said firmly.

Paul wanted the criminologists to hear Bell's original story again. What had he told the deputies? Bell began to explain how sleepy he had been when Willis Peachey woke him in his cell on the morning of August 27. "No, no," Paul interrupted. "I mean the story you told them a few weeks ago, about seeing Joan and moving the body."

Bell looked quickly toward William Griffin. "Go ahead and tell it," the solicitor reassured him. "It's all right."

Haltingly, Bell repeated his earlier confession. "I heard noises . . . saw her at the door . . . went into the overhead . . . saw Alligood on the floor . . . came down." He paused, breathing heavily, then continued. "She asked me to help . . . I came down to help Mr. Alligood . . . I wiped blood off his forehead with toilet tissues and threw it back in the sink . . . when I realized he was dead, I went into shock . . . did what she said . . . took his pants off . . . to make it look like rape."

Momentarily, Bell's attention seemed to drift away. Then his body tensed and his head snapped back. Before going on he looked around as if dazed, as if awakening from a dream. He continued in a slow monotone, telling Paul and the others about cleaning the cell later that day. There had been a "right good bit of blood on the wall," and he had found bloody toilet tissues in the sink, little bits of paper that were "not very bloody, really."

Again there was a pause, a long silence.

"How did you know about the details of the wounds, Terry?" Griffin asked.

"I saw pictures of the body in the ID room," Bell murmured.

There were other questions, but Paul seemed to grow weary of listening to the story again. He wandered away and stood on the other side of the room, while the criminologists pulled their chairs closer to Bell and leaned toward him, concentrating on whatever minute details he could remember about conditions in the cell before he had cleaned up. They seemed especially interested in the toilet tissues and at one point got some paper and made balls out of it in an effort to approximate the scraps he said he had thrown away that morning.

After a while Griffin decided to leave the room. On his way out, he passed by Paul and nodded.

Paul smiled from behind his dark glasses. "You ain't got no case, Billy."

"We'll see in Raleigh," Griffin replied as he went through the door. "We'll see, won't we?"

PART VI

JULY 1975
—
AUGUST 1975

CHAPTER 12

IF THE EVIDENCE IS THERE, THEY'LL CONVICT HER

"How say you, Joan Little, are you guilty of the crime of which you are charged?" The clerk of court was nervous and had stumbled through the arraignment.

"Not guilty," said Jerry Paul, speaking for the defendant. Joan Little stared ahead, wide-eyed and mute.

"How will you be tried?"

"By God and country."

"May God send you a true deliverance."

Joan Little's trial began without fanfare, much in the way it would be conducted throughout the coming five weeks. Courtroom procedures, strictly enforced by Judge Hobgood, would seldom permit theatrics to interrupt the methodical interrogation of witnesses. Lawyers were required to remain in their seats except when handling items of evidence, such as photographs, or when addressing the bench in formal arguments. Witnesses were separated from both the prosecution and the defense by a distance of more than ten feet. Spectators had to remain seated and quiet from the moment court convened until a recess was declared by the judge. Those who slipped out while the session was going on risked losing their places for the rest of the day and, in any event, were not permitted to return to the courtroom until a break. The jury box was emptied frequently during the trial while prosecution and defense lawyers debated points of order or the admissability of certain evidence. When the jurors were present, Hobgood imposed restraint on the comments and actions of the attorneys on both sides. Only in the closing arguments would there be ringing oratory, but nothing said in summation would seem to alter the impressions left by weeks of laborious testimony and fumbling inquisition.

Jury selection began on the afternoon of July 14, the first day of the five-week trial. The morning had been spent on the last of the procedural motions and on acrimonious meetings between the judge and the attorneys in chambers. There had been an overflow of bustling newsmen on the third floor of the Wake County Courthouse, and those reporters not already assigned to available seats had to be accommodated in another courtroom where a sound system had been installed. Desks, chairs, and a bank of pay telephones had been set up in a nearby grand-jury room, which would serve as press headquarters throughout the trial.

Steady rain had been falling since the previous evening, and only a handful of people had gathered to huddle under umbrellas outside the courthouse. Extra police were on duty to control the expected crowd, waiting under awnings and in the doorways of buildings. Larry Little was guiding a group of marchers along a route from Women's Prison to the courthouse, and Golden Frinks, despite having earlier disassociated himself from the case, was defiantly leading his own small band of protesters down Fayetteville Street. Court had convened long before any of the drenched demonstrators arrived. It was a somber and unimpressive beginning for what the Washington, D.C., *Star* had headlined as the "Biggest Civil Rights Trial of [the] '70s."

The process of examining prospective jurors is called the *voir dire*, and it is a crucial stage in all jury trials. Not only does it afford the attorneys their first chance to establish a rapport with the people who will ultimately render a verdict, it also gives them an opportunity to begin molding vague perceptions in the minds of jurors about the evidence which they will later present in detail. The *voir dire* is most important, however, as a method of selecting the panel that will hear the case. The composition of a jury can sometimes be as crucial as the evidence it receives before deliberating, particularly when emotions are running high and the facts are weak. The *voir dire* may be no less significant than the calculus of cross-examination or the eloquence of a closing argument in determining whether a defendant goes free or goes to jail.

The *voir dire* which began on July 14 to select jurors for the Joan Little case threw two different trial techniques against each other, techniques as distinct as the attorneys who employed them. The prosecution's approach was deliberate and straightforward. William Griffin would rely on Lester Chalmers to make an assessment of each prospective juror after asking a few traditional questions. Chalmers knew Wake County and had a reputation for being able to pick juries which tended to be biased toward the state. He had been recruited by Griffin two weeks before the trial primarily to shoulder most of the burden of jury selection. On the other hand, Jerry Paul had decided months earlier to use a complex and relatively controversial system called "scientific jury selection," which involved computer-compiled demographic and personality profiles, psychological interrogation of prospective jurors, and a team of social scientists and body-language experts to aid the defense attorneys in court. Even Richard Wolf was called on to contribute an opinion based on the psychic stimulation he might feel emanating from anyone in the courtroom.

As dissimilar as these *voir dire* methods seemed, however, they were both aimed at reading the minds of the people who would be chosen to sit on the jury. Chalmers and the other prosecutors would use instincts honed from years in court to judge whether a particular individual might be inclined for or against the prosecution. Paul and the rest of the defense lawyers would use the elaborate trappings of science and astrology to reach a similar consensus about the susceptibility of a particular individual to the evidence they knew would be introduced against the defendant. The true difference between the prosecution and the defense was not so much methodology as it was preparation. By the use of thorough pre-trial questionnaires and skillful interrogatories during the *voir dire,* the defense attorneys would be able to identify several people whose predilections about the case would make it difficult for them to weigh the evidence. At least a few of those finally selected would already be sympathetic to the defendant and would be prepared to accept nothing short of overwhelming proof of her guilt, proof that would have to reach far beyond the minimum legal necessity of erasing reasonable doubts. "We sat through the whole trial waiting for a prosecution bombshell," one of them would later say, "and it never came."

The technique called scientific jury selection had been the subject of debate and criticism even before it was used in the trial of Joan Little. Its effectiveness had been argued among attorneys and court officials, and critics had claimed that its disadvantages far outweighed its benefits. While the merits of the system were open to speculation, its defects were readily apparent. It was expensive—costing $40,000 for surveys, tabulations, and computer analyses in this case—and it was laborious. Each prospective juror was subjected to a lengthy series of questions, many of which must have seemed pointless and, in some instances, invasions of privacy.* In state courts, jury selection can take as little as one hour and seldom requires more than a day, but in this case the process dragged on for two weeks and severely tested the patience of the judge, who had hoped the entire trial would not last as long as it finally took to choose twelve jurors and four alternates. Hobgood's patience began to wear thin on the afternoon of the second day, when only one juror had been selected.

"If you were applying for college," Paul asked a young woman, "which school would you most like to go to?"

"I've been pretty liberal," Hobgood interrupted, "but

---

*The proprietor of a vegetarian restaurant was asked, for example, whether she was really a vegetarian.

we can't permit questions about what they would or might do."

"If you voted now," Paul asked a moment later, "how would you vote?"

"Objection," said the district attorney.

"Sustained."

Paul came out of his seat. "Your Honor, we have every right to ask these questions!"

"No, no, you don't"

"We have a scientific jury-selection system worked out."

"Well, I'm busting up your system right now."

In fact, Hobgood did not break up the system and soon backed down from his hasty remark. A confrontation ensued, followed by a compromise in chambers which permitted the defense to continue employing its scientific jury-selection technique. But this issue did raise the first open dispute of the trial, and during their exchange Paul abruptly accused the judge of being unable to give Joan Little a fair trial. So serious a charge might have been discussed in chambers or brought up with some restraint in open court, but Paul hurled the accusation with flailing arms, pointing his finger straight at Hobgood: "To sit there and say like the Queen of Hearts, 'Off with their heads because the law is the law,' is to take us back a hundred years. I don't intend to sit or stand here and see an innocent person go to jail for any reason, and you can threaten me with contempt or anything else, but it does not worry me."

Actually, Paul's bravado exceeded his true zeal. A few days later Hobgood informed him that he would indeed be cited for contempt as a result of his outburst, and that he might be sent to jail after the jury returned a verdict. Paul spent the remainder of the trial restraining himself in open court and trying to soften the judge's bruised feelings whenever they were alone in chambers. But Hobgood was waiting for an outright apology, and it never came, and on the day Joan Little was acquitted he have her chief defense counsel fourteen days for contempt of court.

. . .

It was impossible from the outset to disregard the presence of the news media. Elaborate rules governing press behavior had been promulgated by the judge through the office of the clerk of court, and special facilities for reporters had been set up throughout the courthouse. Nearly one third of the seats in the courtroom had been reserved for the press, and credentials for the reserved seats had been granted to four television networks, one radio news network, three international newspaper wire services, seven television stations, twelve newspapers, one weekly news magazine, and several radio stations. One day before the trial opened, a Durham newspaper called it "a magnet for reporters." The first thing Judge Hobgood did after convening court was to speak to the press. "Because of the immense publicity given this case," he said, "procedures will be conducted to guarantee a fair trial for all concerned. The defendant will be tried in the calmness of the courtroom instead of the spectacle of the arena."

There is an undisguised conflict between the First Amendment concept of free press and the Sixth Amendment guarantee of fair trial.* Currents of contention ebb and flow between them, creating legalistic eddies and shoal waters. It is impossible for media coverage of a court case to be unprejudicial, though the effect and even the target of prejudice raised by publicity is not always clear. The mere publication of an arrest report is sufficient to inspire certainty of guilt in the minds of some readers, while reports that criminal acts were committed for political or

---

*Some aspects of this conflict were ominously skewed in July 1979, however, when the U. S. Supreme Court held in *Gannett Company* v. *DePasquale* that the public, and thus the press, has no constitutional right to attend pre-trial criminal hearings. The court ruled further that judges have a constitutional duty to protect criminal defendants from adverse publicity, saying that various other stages of a trial might be closed to journalists, and even to private citizens with no interest except viewing the proceedings.

social reasons, or in self-defense, can engender sympathy for a defendant in others. Ordinarily the problem is not of consequence; the vast majority of court cases receive so little publicity that no prejudicial influences are exerted on prospective jurors. But when the matter is controversial and press coverage is pervasive, as in the Joan Little case, no trial can be truly "fair." There is no effective compensation for the subconscious baggage of precognition that jurors will inevitably carry into their deliberations, and no measure to determine its impact on the outcome.

Not all pre-trial publicity had been favorable to Joan Little—her record of prior arrests and rumors of her alleged prostitution were often mentioned—but she was frequently depicted as a victim of racial and sexual suppression, as a woman who had finally struck out in self-defense after years of exploitation. This imagery had been carefully cultivated by the defense, which had been working to shape news since the day of the surrender by dealing with reporters in historic clichés and by trading on the paucity of alternative sources of information. While Jerry Paul and the other members of the defense team were always ready to accommodate requests for interviews and background material, William Griffin and the investigating officers grew ever more leery of cooperating with newsmen. In February Griffin had granted a brief interview, only to be accused by the defense attorneys of trying to prejudice public opinion against the defendant. Members of the sheriff's department in Beaufort County felt that publicity about the case had been unfairly critical of them and gradually began to withdraw from contact with reporters. Ottis Davis declared the bottom floor of the courthouse off-limits to the press and stubbornly refused to talk to any journalists. In May a college newspaper photographer with his camera poised jumped at the Sheriff without warning from behind a bush near the courthouse, apparently unmindful of the danger of giving an armed lawman the impression he was being attacked. In June a correspondent who had unsuccessfully demanded access to the women's section of the jail told Davis the press would "get" him when the trial started. Of the prosecutors, only John Wilkinson regularly welcomed the attention of the media, but his comments were often argumentative and he was not an easy man to interview. Even before the trial, therefore, the defense team had established itself as the primary source of factual and interpretative information about the progress of the case. "We know we're being manipulated," said a reporter from the Raleigh *News & Observer* during the pre-trial hearings, "but what can we do?" During the trial, regular briefings would be held by at least one of the defense lawyers to explain to newsmen what had transpired in the courtroom each day.

News coverage of the case had begun slowly, with the *New York Times* story in December 1974, but after the Southern Poverty Law Center's mass appeal for funds and support, a glowing indignation seemed to gather behind nationwide concern for the plight of Joan Little. "She was a creative spark," said a Chicago activist, explaining why so many diverse and potentially competitive forces had joined in this case. "She happened in a time sequence when people were ready to come together." The time had indeed been right. The jailer's death in 1974 had followed by only a few weeks the resignation of Richard Nixon and the end of the Watergate obsession as daily front-page news. The case had stretched into the dog days of the summer of 1975, covering the period of Gerald Ford's first tentative months in the presidency when there was little activity in domestic or foreign affairs to fill newspaper space. The matter seemed fundamental, and reactions often were axiomatic. Here were interracial sex and interracial violence, scented with magnolia and garnished with prejudice, bigotry, and the unseen evil of Southern justice. During the winter and spring a wave of public opinion had washed over the case, sweeping in its path not only sympathizers rallying to a new cause, but also journalists who were building an old story:

· In February, the Hartford (Connecticut) *Times* editorialized under the headline NORTH CAROLINA INJUSTICE, saying that "the white jailer was in the process of attempting to rape Miss Little," that "the Beaufort County medical examiner . . . revealed that there was clear evidence of recent sexual activity by the jailer," and that "Dr. Carpenter was prepared to support the woman's story . . . but he was not allowed to testify before the Grand Jury which indicted her." Seemingly based on the SPLC solicitation material, the editorial called indignantly for a "full investigation, preferably on the federal level, to ascertain all of the facts," and referred to Joan Little as an "apparent victim of Southern bigotry that decrees it only a minor crime for a white man to rape a black woman [who is] fighting for her life."

· In March, Atlanta *Constitution* editor and columnist Reg Murphy informed his readers that the case would "have impact on the history of the South and on the battle for women's rights as well," and added: "What gives it the extra dimension that lifts it beyond the ordinary case is that Washington, N.C., is generally believed to be the North Carolina headquarters of the Ku Klux Klan." There was no factual basis for Murphy's suggestion that Beaufort County had ever been a stronghold of the KKK. Klan activity in North Carolina had always been most prevalent in the Piedmont, the central region to the south and west of Raleigh, the area *into* which the defense would ask that the trial be moved.

· In the spring, Mark Pinsky, a freelance journalist from Durham who claimed to be intimate with the defense, placed stories about the case in *The New York Times* (JUSTICE IN NORTH CAROLINA IS ONCE MORE OLD SOUTH), *The Progressive* (IN THE HEAT OF THE NIGHT), and *New Times* (THE LITTLE WOMAN WHO FOUGHT BACK). "The irony of the case," he said in his *Times* article. ". . . [is that] no county official has come up with a plausible explanation as to why [Joan Little] had not been transferred to Women's Prison in Raleigh." In *The*

Progressive he dramatized in the present tense: "The deputies who discover the body do their frantic best to clean the cell, make explanations, and to find the woman before she can talk." And in *New Times* he put the situation in the following perspective:

> "Down east," they call it. The rich, eastern coastal plain of North Carolina where the main crops are cotton, corn, peanuts and tobacco. It is the only section of the state that boasted plantations and slaves in the antebellum years, and since then it has been the main stronghold of the Ku Klux Klan. The main, non-agricultural export of the region is black people, and within the state's black community "down-east justice" became synonymous with what outsiders used to call "Southern justice," although it applied with equal inhospitality to such outside agitators as labor organizers, civil rights workers and longhairs.

Public opinion was understandably stirred by reports such as these, which seemed to spring from loose assumptions about geography and history, and were often based exclusively on interviews and statements by the defendant and the defense attorneys. Even the local press succumbed to the torque of its own publicity and began to deal in conclusory journalistic justice. "Details of the case are hardly in dispute," wrote Claude Sitton, the editor of the Raleigh *News & Observer.* "Miss Little's attorneys have admitted that she stabbed the jailer, Clarence Alligood, with his own ice pick when he attempted to rape her in her cell." Two weeks later all of the jurors would be drawn from Raleigh and Wake County, but what would be left for them to decide? The pre-trial disclosures of the defense and the selective carping of reporters had, it seemed, settled every question of fact in the case. It was a matter of self-defense. The jailer had been killed *when* he attempted to rape the defendant.

.   .   .

The defense had begun the work of probing for acceptable jurors months earlier, and the effort came to fruition on the third day of the trial. In the spring, opinion surveys had been conducted throughout Wake County by the Fair Jury Project under the guidance of Richard Christie, one of the originators of the scientific jury-selection method. Investigators had sampled attitudes about matters related directly to the trial—capital punishment, blacks, rape victims—and at the same time had gathered background data on income, employment, education, hobbies, reading habits, and religious and political affiliations. By comparing the results of this survey with the answers obtained from a questionnaire prepared by the defense and distributed by the court to the people in the jury pool, Christie and Courtney Mullin were able to deduce the probable attitudes of most potential jurors before the trial. In theory, the lawyers had only to confirm that the juror held such views by asking a series of carefully contrived questions in court.

The thin, serious young man who came to the witness stand on July 16 had asked to be excused when his group was impaneled, and he asked again while under individual examination by the prosecution. But Hobgood refused to grant his request, despite being told that he would almost certainly lose his job if he became a member of the sequestered jury and the trial went on for weeks, as was expected. The young man said he was opposed to capital punishment but could return a guilty verdict if the state proved its case "absolutely." The prosecutors, satisfied of his impartiality and trying to conserve their limited number of peremptory challenges, accepted him.

Jerry Paul jumped directly into the examination without pausing, as he had with others, to explain the purpose of his questions or to introduce the jury-selection team. A decision had already been made regarding this prospective juror, and only bare confirmation was needed. Paul learned

quickly that he subscribed to *Saturday Review* and the
New York Review of Books—periodicals considered to indicate desirable qualities—and that he would "gladly indicate" that he "voted as a Democrat."

"Will you require the state to prove the defendant
guilty?" Paul asked.

"Yes."

"Can Joan Little depend on you to do that?"

"Yes, she can."

"Your Honor, the defense accepts this juror."

His name was Mark Nielsen, and he was a twenty-six-
year-old stereo salesman with two years of college education who would become one of two white males on the
jury. He had indicated on his questionnaire that his
neighbors were white but that he encountered "an equal
number of blacks and whites at work." He was "not a
member of a church or organized religion," and he had
never before served on a jury. He would become the
foreman of the panel that nearly five weeks later would
acquit Joan Little.

"I believed her wholly," he would say after the trial. "She
seemed so guileless and powerless."

The last of the four alternates was not seated until the
end of the second week, and by then some of the newsmen
had grown tired of jury selection and were writing that the
case had "bogged down." An important phase of the trial
had now come to an end, however, and the defense attorneys were content with the panel. It was balanced between
the sexes and the races, and its members spanned several
generations. None of them fitted the defense profile of the
perfect juror—no young black woman had been seated—
but all had qualities of significance to the defense team.
Most opposed capital punishment, and all had expressed
sympathy in one way or another for the various social and
political themes on which the defense had been building its
case for months. "We have a better chance of getting a fair
trial than we thought we would have," Marvin Miller now
told a reporter.

The prosecutors were not so pleased. John Wilkinson, who had finally been authorized to remain in the case and whose fee was being paid by private contributors as well as by the Alligood family, told newsmen he thought the jury was "defense-oriented."* William Griffin refused to comment for the press, but the composition of the panel did little to ease his nagging suspicion that the case was already lost. "The best we can hope for," he told SBI agent Dave Keller, "is a hung jury." Only Lester Chalmers was still confident when the third week of the trial began the following Monday and witnesses were called for the first time. He believed in the twelve jurors and four alternates he had chosen. He had been told by a courthouse source that one of them, a young lawyer, had an application on file for a job in the Wake County district attorney's office. Another, he had learned from an acquaintance, would make "a good juror." A third, he knew, went to a church where the minister was a deputy sheriff.

"They're fine people," Chalmers told the others. "If the evidence is there, they'll convict her."

*The Ethics Committee of the state bar had by then advised Hobgood that Wilkinson's appearance would not be a conflict of interest. The source of his fee was never confirmed, but Wilkinson told several people after the trial that he had been paid by fellow members of the Board of Trustees of the University of North Carolina at Chapel Hill.

CHAPTER 13

TO SEE JUSTICE IS DONE

On Monday, July 28, the state commenced its case. Before calling the first witness, Hobgood granted a defense motion to suppress Joan Little's health, prison, social-services, and juvenile-home records and listened to arguments on a motion to exclude the notes she had written in her crossword-puzzle books and magazines. The debate was intense. The prosecution intended to rely on these notes to establish her state of mind on the night Clarence Alligood had been killed. Hobgood delayed his decision on this motion until the notes were actually offered into evidence.

The defense had arranged for celebrities to visit the courtroom throughout the trial, and on Monday Georgia state senator Julian Bond, the president of the Southern Poverty Law Center, was there. For the first time, too, a few members of Clarence Alligood's family attended the trial. They took seats in the row reserved by the prosecution, which had been empty much of the time. The buzz of conversation subsided almost at once when they came in, and did not resume until they were all seated and staring toward the front of the courtroom.

At 9:45 Hobgood convened court, and by eleven o'clock the first prosecution witness was on the stand. He was Washington policeman Jerry Helms, who had discovered the body. Helms told of arriving at the courthouse to assist Johnny Rose, of finding the jail open, and of looking for the jailer until he found the corpse in the women's section. "He was naked from the waist down except for his socks . . . short-sleeve shirt was open . . . left hand was under his body . . . right hand was hanging over his body down toward the floor and the ice pick was in it." There was "a small splotch of blood on his hip," Helms said, "and a splotch of blood on his right forehead."

As soon as the cross-examination began, Jerry Paul inquired about Helms's education and experience. He learned that Helms had been an officer for eight years but had had no training in police work. "Have you received any formal training in being observant of things?" Paul asked. Helms said no, but that he tried to do the best he could. "Is it not true that a trained police officer often makes a decision subconsciously or because of the training he's had?" Paul asked. The prosecution objected: Helms was not an expert in the routines adhered to by policemen in general.

"Do you have a notebook, or did you make a diagram of the crime scene?" Paul asked.

"No."

"Are you a trained officer?"

"Objection!"

"As a trained police officer," Paul said, "aren't you supposed to make a note of the time often, so that you can later testify?"

"Objection!"

"Sustained."

Officer Johnny Rose came to the stand next, and testified that he had arrived at the jail at about 3:55 a.m. and that Helms had arrived "ten or fifteen seconds" later. They had restrained a woman prisoner in Helm's custody with handcuffs. She was "quite emotional" and uttered "a lot of obscenities and loud noise." Inside, Helms had "called out to Alligood four or five times." A few moments later he had followed Helms into the women's section. On the cell bars he had seen some woman's clothing—a nightgown or night coat—hanging at a height of about five feet off the floor.

After quickly examining the body, he had been sent out to "look for Joan Little."

With Helms and Rose as his first two witnesses, William Griffin had embarked on an obvious strategy. He could not hope to build a solid case of first-degree murder because he had only circumstantial and inconclusive evidence. But Griffin would concentrate on three key points: (1) The dead man had received eleven ice-pick wounds, including seven in the chest, five of which had been clustered directly over the heart, three of which had been driven home with sufficient force to penetrate organs within the chest cavity; (2) Joan Little had fled from the scene of the killing and had remained in hiding for eight days; and (3) she had kept a written record that revealed a pattern of possibly seductive behavior and an intense dissatisfaction while she was confined in jail. With this evidence, and with additional information from the medical examiner and the regional pathologist about the cause of death, the prosecution would force the other side to make a crucial decision. The defense attorneys could rest, hoping there was insufficient proof for the jury to convict, or they could offer evidence to refute the state's case. That was what William Griffin hoped to accomplish—to give the defense no choice except to put Joan Little on the witness stand.

On cross-examination Tuesday morning, Jerry Paul learned that Johnny Rose had taken courses in investigative work and one course to prepare him for testifying in court, and then embarrassed the already nervous officer by easily eliciting hearsay testimony from him before going on to ask about his role in the case. Rose said he was familiar with the rules at the Beaufort County jail for handling prisoners, though he had never received any "comprehensive training" on the subject. Women were supposed to be searched by a female deputy, he said, who was also responsible for escorting an inmate to her cell. He had never been inside the women's section of the jail before the morning Clarence Alligood had been killed.

As he questioned the officer, Paul used a diagram of the

jail prepared by the defense. Rose seemed confused by the drawing and studied it for several minutes after Paul asked whether it was a fair representation of the jail area.

"That's not the way I remember it," Rose mumbled.

"What's different about it?" Paul asked impatiently.

"Well, I'm not an engineering student. Is this a hallway?"

Using a pointer, Paul tapped various spots on the diagram for reference.

"Now that you've explained it to me," Rose said, "it looks like it to me."

"Is that hard for you to understand?" Paul said sharply.

The young officer's gaze passed quickly from the diagram to Paul and then to the judge. "Your Honor, do I have to answer that?" he asked softly.

"No, sir," Hobgood said, "you don't."

Paul returned to his seat and continued to ask about what the officer had observed inside the cellblock. Rose had seen men's shoes on the floor and he had "looked up" and seen "a bra and a nightgown" hanging on the bars. But inside the cell he had been too confused and upset to notice very much. He remembered seeing blood "behind the right eye and several patches of blood on the back of his scalp," but he could not remember the pants, the ice pick, the nightgown, or the blankets on the floor. He had touched the man's neck and nothing else. "I don't mind admitting I was excited. I just didn't see the ice pick. I know he was dead —well, I didn't feel any pulse."

Had he made any notes?

"Notes? No, sir. Patrolmen don't make notes. We don't investigate."

"You've been in law enforcement four years, Officer Rose. As you observed the scene, did you begin to make mental notes?"

"Objection," said John Wilkinson. "How can that possibly be relevant?"

Dr. Harry Carpenter followed Johnny Rose to the stand. Tan and dapper, he had on peach-colored trousers and a dark-blue blazer with a large and ornate emblem on the breast pocket, a Washington, North Carolina, Bicentennial patch he had worn as a "silent protest" against the press because he thought that "in some respects Beaufort County had been maligned." On direct examination, Carpenter recalled going to the jail, confirming that the man was dead, taking note of the conditions in the cell, and performing a cursory inspection of the corpse and a "preliminary examination of the wounds." Blood had been coming from a puncture in the head "about an inch above the right ear," some of it flowing "backwards" and some of it "streaming down over his face." There had been "something less than a teaspoon" of fluid, apparently seminal fluid, on the man's thigh.* Griffin could not seek to impeach his own witness, and was therefore unable to object to Carpenter's conclusions because no sample of the fluid had been preserved and tested.

Morris Dees cross-examined, having Carpenter say that he was an experienced pathologist and that he had conducted or supervised approximately 4,500 hospital autopsies. "In your opinion," Dees soon asked, "did the fluid on the jailer's thigh come from sexual activity?"

"In my opinion, the fluid was significant and had probably been ejaculated at or just prior to death," the doctor said. "I assume it indicated sexual activity."

The state's case was moving quickly, if not well. Carpenter's testimony took about an hour, and there was still time to call Beverly King, the radio dispatcher, before lunch. She testified she had seen Clarence Alligood at 2:55 a.m. when they had engaged in a "general conversation" in the radio room in the basement of the courthouse. Alligood had asked "how I was doing and had I been busy, and then he asked had the deputies gone in yet."

"Now, was there anything out of the ordinary about him

---

*No conjecture about the substance remained by the time Carpenter had finished his testimony. In his jury charge Judge Hobgood would say: "Dr. Carpenter gave a detailed statement . . . that a string of seminal fluid extended from Alligood's penis to his left thigh."

making inquiry about whether the deputies were—
whether any of them were on duty or not?" John Wilkinson
asked.

"No, sir."

"Had he done that many times before?"

"Yes, sir."

"Do other members of the Sheriff's Department make
similar inquiries to you?"

"Yes, sir."

A troubled expression settled over the face of Morris
Dees when he heard this testimony. Before the trial Dees
had become convinced after interviewing Beverly King
that her conversation with Alligood about the deputies had
been unusual, even extraordinary, a clue that his intentions
were to return to the women's cells and rape Joan Little.
Dees had expected the dispatcher to give testimony suggesting that the jailer had wanted to make certain no one
else would be coming to the jail that night, a theme he had
hoped to elaborate during cross-examination. The reason-
ing was flawed and conjectural: Alligood might have made
the same inquiry for reasons unrelated to his female prisoner, or even if he had been invited into her cell. But the
defense would succeed nevertheless in making the point
seem compelling, if only because the prosecutors failed to
challenge it. In working to defend his theory, however,
Morris Dees would make costly mistakes.

After the conflict between Hobgood and Paul during
jury selection, Dees had emerged as the lightning rod of
the defense team, the lawyer who seemed most intent on
provoking confrontations. His feud with Paul had estranged him from the other defense attorneys, but he continued to pick fights with the prosecutors as if he were
riding point for them, and he had already clashed bitterly
with Hobgood in chambers. Warned by another attorney
about antagonizing the judge, Dees smiled confidently and
said, "He wouldn't dare throw me out of the trial."

But Beverly King surprised him when she got to the
witness stand, and he seemed anxious and shaken when he

began to question her. The testimony she had already
given made Alligood's conversation with her seem innocu-
ous and stripped Dees of his opportunity to drive home
what he considered a crucial point. On cross-examination,
he set out at once to correct the impression she had given
the jury, hammering again and again in an effort to make
her say that it was unusual for Alligood to come to the radio
room unless he wanted to request the assistance of an
officer. But her testimony remained unchanged.

"No, it was not unusual," she said once more.

"It was not unusual?"

"No."

"But on this particular night he did not ask you to call
anybody?"

"No, he did not."

"He merely checked on whether the deputies had gone
home, is that correct?"

"That's right."

For a moment Dees seemed perplexed, and the cross-
examination turned in another direction.

"Mrs. King, who have you discussed this case with?"

"Well," Hobgood interrupted before she tried to answer
the question literally, "you mean officials, or everybody?"

"Yes, officially, investigators that have discussed this case
with you?"

"I gave a statement to the SBI that morning—the next
morning I came on, at two o'clock."

"Have you discussed this case with the District Attorney?"

"No, I have not." A more precise question might have
gotten a different answer. Griffin had seen Beverly King in
the radio room a week before the trial and the case had
been briefly mentioned but not "discussed" in the sense of
a formal interview.

"And Sheriff Davis?"

"No, I have not." Dees had reason to believe, however,
that she might have gone over the case in some detail with
Ottis Davis, and an affidavit later filed by the sheriff would

state that she had spoken to him during the investigation.

Now Dees was holding a long sheet of paper in his hand and gesticulating with it. "Did you give a statement to the State Bureau of Investigation?" he asked.

"Yes, I did."

"And in that statement," he said, glancing at the paper in a manner that seemed to imply he was using it to formulate his question,"did you not tell them that it was unusual for Mr. Alligood merely just to check and see if the deputies had gone in, that he usually always wanted the aid of a deputy?"

Beverly King hesitated, and there was an objection, which Hobgood overruled. Then she testified that she could not remember giving such a statement to the SBI. "Would you think for just a moment and try to refresh your recollection?" Dees said, making no move to show her the paper he was holding. Again there was an objection, again overruled, but Beverly King insisted she still could not recall. "Well, maybe I'll use the exact words," Dees went on, glancing again at the paper. "Did you ever state that you thought that was abnormal conduct on his part?"

"I don't remember stating that."

"You don't remember stating that?"

"No, I don't."

Finally, Dees shook his head and sat down, carefully placing the paper on the table in front of him. But he did not give up. When Hobgood interrupted the cross-examination to declare the lunch recess a few moments later, Dees quickly approached Beverly King before she could leave the room. Holding the paper in his hand, occasionally pointing to it and marking it with a red pen, he talked to her in a low voice. They were standing at the edge of the defense table, out of earshot of the judge and the other attorneys. There was disorder in the courtroom as everyone filed out, and in the confusion no one overheard their discussion.

Beverly King returned to the stand that afternoon and underwent further cross-examination without revising her

earlier testimony. Instead of excusing her once the questioning had been completed, however, Judge Hobgood
unexpectedly had the jurors leave the room and then asked
her about her conversation with Dees at the end of the
morning session. During lunch, seemingly on the verge of
tears, she had complained to William Griffin that Dees was
trying to force her to change her testimony. Griffin had
informed the judge just before court reconvened. Hobgood
had given no indication what he might do, but now, after
warning Beverly King that his inquiry was "very serious,"
he asked her under oath whether her accusations were
true. She told him Dees had encouraged her to swear that
Alligood's question about the deputies was unusual. He had
told her, she said, that doing so "would help Joan and
wouldn't hurt the state."

An impromptu hearing went on for the next twenty minutes, with both Hobgood and Dees asking questions. Dees
produced the paper he had been waving while he asked
about the SBI report, but it turned out to be a typed statement he had prepared following his own interview with
Beverly King some time prior to the trial.* He asked her
to read aloud one sentence from the statement: "She said
this was abnormal conduct on his part and that it was
unusual." Then Dees took the paper back to the defense
table and sat down.

"What I want to know is this," Hobgood said. "Did he say
you go ahead and do it anyway, it would help Joan and
would not help the state—would not hurt the state? Did he
say you go ahead, say it anyway?"

"He said, 'Go ahead and say it. It would help Joan,' "
Beverly King replied.

"Your Honor, that's exactly what I said." Dees leaped
from his seat. "I said, 'You go ahead and say exactly
what's in that statement.' Absolutely. I told her to fol-

---

*The brief report of the SBI interrogation of Beverly King on the day of the
killing contained information about the jailer's inquiry but said nothing about
whether his question had been unusual or not.

low the statement that she had given me."

"Regardless of her testimony here today?" Hobgood frowned.

"No, sir," Dees stammered, lowering his head, "not regardless of her testimony. Pardon me, sir."

All further attempts to explain the colloquy between Morris Dees and Beverly King fell short, and Dees only got himself deeper into trouble.

"Mrs. King, didn't I tell you to tell the truth, that the statement you had given me was the truth, and I was insisting on you telling the truth? Isn't that what I told you?"

"I told you I didn't remember."

"Yes. You told me you didn't remember, but didn't I insist and show you the statement and underline the portions in the statement and insist that you tell the truth? I did that, didn't I?"

"And I have told the truth," Beverly King said. "I did not remember."

There may have been confusion now about Beverly King's testimony (it was never clear what she "did not remember"), but there was nothing more to be said about the way Morris Dees had tried to handle the situation. Instead of merely cross-examining this witness on the stand in open court, he had privately urged her to repudiate testimony already given under oath and to repeat instead an observation he had made in his own notes after talking to her some time earlier, an observation he referred to as "the truth."

"All right, Mr. Dees," Hobgood said finally, "you are out of the case as of right now, and I suggest you not say anything to me about it."

Morris Dees had been wrong. Hamilton Hobgood *would* dare to throw him out of the trial, and now he had done so. Later that afternoon a warrant was issued charging Dees with attempted subornation of perjury, a felony with a maximum penalty of ten years in prison.

.   .   .

The trial went on without Morris Dees, even though his expulsion set off a flurry of sideshow activity that eventually reached the United States Supreme Court. A prosecution diagram of the jail and a number of photographs taken by the SBI of its interior were introduced during the testimony of Special Agent James Bailey that afternoon, and the next morning Bailey was cross-examined by Milton Williamson, who appeared suspicious of the angle from which the pictures had been taken and the way some of them had been framed. Later, however, the defense attorneys would introduce photos of their own and a defense expert witness would testify that the angle of a photograph could in no way distort the scene captured on film.

Bailey was followed by Mike Alligood of the Beaufort County rescue squad, whom William Griffin had decided to put on as a witness only to provide continuity in the state's case and to establish another link in the chain of custody over evidence taken from the women's cellblock. John Wilkinson conducted the examination while Griffin was out of the room, however, and Wilkinson's questions soon seemed to take the young man beyond the range of precise recollection. Wilkinson asked Alligood to recall the cellblock, the cell area where the body was found, and the details about what was going on while he was at the jail. Then he asked the witness to demonstrate how the ice pick had been clenched by the dead man. Using a ballpoint pen, Alligood held up his hand and allowed the shaft of the pen to lie loosely in his curled fingers with his thumb extended outward from his palm. Instantly Jerry Paul shouted an objection and jumped up to get the pictures of the body from the clerk of court, and then on cross-examination he ripped apart almost all of Alligood's testimony.

Mike Alligood seemed happy to give specific answers to every question he was asked. The ice pick, he explained again, appeared to have been "laid in the hand" of the dead man. But when Paul produced the photographs of the body introduced by the state, Alligood admitted that none of them "showed the thumb along the side," as he had just described the jailer's grip, and after studying the pictures he assured Paul that none of them accurately depicted how the ice pick had been positioned in the palm of the corpse. It was damaging testimony, impeaching the reliability of the prosecution's evidence and suggesting that the body had been moved before the pictures were taken. Paul went on, asking for a description of the body. There had been blood on the temple and across the face, Alligood said, and also some blood streaming "backwards." Again Paul pointed to the pictures, none of which showed a stream of blood behind the man's ear. Alligood smiled. "I must have been in error. It's been such a long time ago."

Mercifully for the prosecution, Hobgood soon declared a recess, but not before Paul had persuaded Mike Alligood to testify further that he and Ed Mercer, the other rescue-squad volunteer, had raised the body soon after the arrival of the medical examiner and that he thought the state's photographs had been made some time thereafter. At the break Lester Chalmers drew Wilkinson into an office and berated him for departing from the prosecution strategy in a way that had made it possible for Paul to roam freely during cross-examination. Griffin, unaware until then what had happened in the courtroom, looked on in silence. Finally Chalmers turned away and looked sharply at Griffin. "He's too damn busy fighting the other side in the press," he said angrily, jerking his thumb at the private prosecutor. Wilkinson stalked out of the office without making any reply.

There was little the district attorney could do. He decided not to call Ed Mercer, even though there was now testimony suggesting that Mercer had disturbed the hand holding the ice pick when he tried to take the man's pulse, and that he and Mike Alligood had moved the body before any of the sheriff's deputies had arrived. "I'm not going to worry about that," Griffin told the others when they went back into the courtroom. "If the pictures can be rehabilitated, that might not be a problem."

But the prosecution never really recovered from the

blows Paul struck during his cross-examination of Mike Alligood. Later testimony by Danny Respass and Willis Peachey about the condition of the body when the pictures were taken seemed defensive rather than definitive, and on cross-examination Peachey was driven to give what seemed to be vague answers when Paul asked him whether he could be absolutely certain the body had not been moved and then put back on the cot for the photographs. The very orthodox strategy of the defense, which was to discredit the integrity of the investigation, had been successfully launched. A high degree of ambiguity had quickly been suggested, even about the evidence that had not been bungled or lost, and the prosecution's case against Joan Little was already in shambles.

Morris Dees did not easily accept his expulsion. The defense filed a routine motion for reinstatement, which Hobgood denied immediately, and within a few days Dees hired two prominent Raleigh attorneys and brought in American Civil Liberties Union lawyers from Atlanta and Washington, D.C., to get him back onto the case. In no time, motions and affidavits had been fired off to various federal and state appeals courts, all claiming that Beverly King had committed perjury, that Clarence Alligood's inquiry about the deputies had been unusual, that Dees had merely encouraged her to tell the truth, and that the trial judge had no authority to expel a defense attorney. Inevitably, these appeals would fail, not only because Hobgood had correctly interpreted his power to dismiss an out-of-state attorney (who had appeared only because Hobgood granted him discretionary permission to do so) but also because they skirted the essential issue now facing Dees. Because of what he had said in court, the key question for him was not whether Beverly King had been telling the truth. If he believed she might have perjured herself, there were several steps he could have taken—in and out of the courtroom—to rectify the situation. The question was not

even whether it was appropriate under the circumstances
for a defense attorney to talk privately with a prosecution
witness while she was testifying without first alerting the
district attorney. It is not unusual or unethical for an attorney on one side to speak to a witness for the other side
while a trial is in progress, though in tense situations most
lawyers will obtain permission from opposing counsel before doing so to avoid even the appearance of trying to
apply pressure. The question Dees and his attorneys had to
answer was whether he had urged Beverly King to take the
witness stand in the afternoon and contradict what she had
said under oath in the morning. In "Findings of Fact"
preceding his order ousting Dees from the trial, Judge
Hobgood had found that "Mrs. Beverly King stated on
three occasions that Mr. Morris Dees insisted that she testify that it was unusual for Mr. Alligood to ask her where
a Deputy was, and Mrs. King advised Mr. Morris Dees that
that was not true."

But Hobgood's decision to dismiss Morris Dees had been
based on more than the accusation against him by Beverly
King, on more even than the statement Dees had made
during his colloquy with the judge. There had already been
other trouble between Hobgood and the Alabama lawyer.
Dees had been performing on borrowed time since a pre-
trial conference in June when he had met the judge for the
very first time.

Even then, Hobgood had gotten the impression that
Dees was "a very talented and intense young man" and
that he "had a great deal of ability." But he had also
sensed that Dees "always wanted to have everything his
own way," which meant that they would probably clash
before the trial was over. Their conflict had started as an
apparent agreement. Dees had suggested that the motions to suppress evidence should be argued after the se-
questration of the jury, to shield them from publicity
about Joan Little's records and about the magazines and
puzzle books. Hobgood had thought this "was a very good
suggestion" and had made a note of it. In his own notes

Dees had written: "Suppress motions . . . will take up after jury selection."

By the end of the first morning of the trial, therefore, Hobgood had gone into his chambers thinking that all preliminary procedural matters had been disposed of. But when he called in all of the lawyers and mentioned that he was ready to begin jury selection as soon as court reconvened, Dees insisted that the motions to suppress should be considered before any jurors were selected and sequestered. Hobgood reminded him that these motions were to be brought up later, as Dees himself had suggested, but the attorney argued that no such decision had ever been firmly made. "Of course," Hobgood would say later, "that was a confrontation right there."

Deliberately, using his notebook from the June meeting, Hobgood "went over it with him." Still Dees denied suggesting such a procedure and said that all motions should be discharged before the jury selection began. Again Hobgood referred to his notes, but by then Dees was on his feet, pacing in front of the judge's desk, arguing heatedly. Finally, Hobgood lost his temper. He stood up, looked straight at Dees, and called him a "goddamn liar." Later, after consulting his own notes, Dees would apologize. But the damage had been done and as the trial progressed Hobgood's displeasure with him became ever more apparent. "I had never had anything like that happen to me before," the judge would say later. "It put me on guard. It put me on guard."

And then Dees had forced the judge's hand during Beverly King's appearance on an issue that had no substantive bearing on the case. Where Dees got the notion that it was extraordinary for the night jailer to ask about the deputies remained unclear. Beverly King had told William Griffin the inquiry "didn't seem unusual at the time," indicating that it was routine and might have become important only in light of what had happened later. Dees never released a copy of the statement he had asked the radio dispatcher to read from in court, which appar-

ently indicated that she had told him the jailer's conduct
"was abnormal," but notes Dees had made in April during an interview in Beaufort County suggested that it had
been Ottis Davis instead of Beverly King who planted the
idea in his mind:

> *"CA had gone to radio room on many prior times & asked*
> *operator to call a deputy to come to the jail (for some official*
> *purpose) but he had* never *gone there just to ck. & see if they*
> *were all in." Note: Sheriff Davis believes this was unusual*
> *behavior implying CA was up to no good w/JAL.*

Apparently Dees had committed himself to a theory supplied gratuitously by Sheriff Davis and had even managed
to convince the other defense attorneys of its merit. They
insisted in their summations that Clarence Alligood must
have wanted to know whether all the sheriff's deputies
were off patrol so that he could be certain there would be
no interference after he went back to the women's cells, an
argument that may have seemed compelling because none
of the prosecutors thought to point out that the town of
Washington shared jail facilities with the county and that
the town kept at least four policemen on active patrol
throughout the night. Even if all the deputies had
"checked off," any one of the city policemen might have
brought a prisoner to the basement of the courthouse later
that morning. In her early conversations with the defense
attorneys Joan Little had told them she first thought that
Alligood was locking up someone else when she heard the
cellblock door being opened for the third time, but she did
not say this at the trial. Still, the logical weakness of the
point Morris Dees had risked everything to pursue was
self-evident. Jerry Helms and Johnny Rose had been bringing in a prisoner at 4:00 a.m. when they discovered the
body of the jailer only moments after he had been killed in
cell number one.

· · ·

On Wednesday the state's case slipped further out of control. The pathologist who had performed the autopsy, Dr. Charles Gilbert, described the eleven wounds suffered by Clarence Alligood and said that the varying locations and angles of penetration suggested he had been moving as he was being stabbed. The cause of death, he testified, had been bleeding "secondary to a penetrating wound to the left ventricle of the heart." During the autopsy, fluid taken from the interior of the urethra had been examined and found to contain spermatozoa.

"What conclusion did you draw from this finding?" Lester Chalmers asked.

"In my opinion," the doctor said, "he had ejaculated prior to death."

On Thursday the investigating officers began to appear, including Danny Respass, the best of the prosecution witnesses. His direct testimony did, as Griffin had hoped, rehabilitate the photographic evidence of the body and the cell, and he was also able to demonstrate how the ice pick had been clasped loosely in the dead man's hand and how he had "raised it off the fingers and slid it out" to give it to Willis Peachey.

Respass held his ground under cross-examination by Marvin Miller. Armed with a laundry list of technical questions about photo equipment, Miller tried unsuccessfully to confuse the officer and to put a dent in his confidence that the body had not been disturbed until after he had finished taking pictures. Respass, who had had extensive training and had been qualified as a fingerprint expert by the prosecution, testified that he had considered the possibility of lifting prints from the ice pick before touching it, but had decided the surface of the handle would not yield detectable impressions. "Did you make any notes at the scene?" Miller asked. He had "jotted a few notes down" after the body was taken from the cell, Respass said. He still had them, in fact, and had referred to them to refresh his recollection before coming to testify.

Willis Peachey was next, taking the stand at mid-morn-

ing and remaining there under direct examination by William Griffin until court recessed at 5:00 p.m. "The body had
not been disturbed until after Respass had taken pictures,"
he said, and "up to the point the body was moved, all items
in the cell were in the same location as when [he] had
arrived." He and Respass had finally raised the corpse,
resting it momentarily against the wall to confirm that the
bloodstain there was at the exact level of the man's head.
Under the buttocks they had found a multicolored
woman's scarf which had "some form of red substance on
it." On the floor of the cell they had found a "purple nightgown or ladies' night apparel . . . on top of this, a pair of
men's light green underwear . . . under the legs and knees
a blanket which was folded . . . another blanket on the floor
extending partially out into the hall . . . three blankets in
all."

Jerry Paul's cross-examination consumed all of Friday.
Peachey's main concerns at first had been to "determine
if Alligood was still alive . . . free the other prisoners and
find Miss Little." The "pattern of the investigation" had
not been set up until around 11:00 a.m., after the SBI
agents arrived. Until then Ottis Davis had been in charge;
thereafter Peachey had been.

"You were the man in charge of the investigation at the
scene, weren't you?" Paul asked.

"No, sir."

"I believe you said no one was in charge? . . . "

"I happened to be there . . . to be there when Detective
Respass took the ice pick out [of his hand], and I made the
decision to collect the articles of clothing."

"Would you say on that morning the situation was one of
mass confusion?"

"No, sir, I would not say mass confusion. There was some
confusion."

By late Friday afternoon, however, the taciturn deputy
had been forced to admit that no effort had been made to
take fingerprints from the dead man's shoes or glasses, or
from the desk drawer where the ice pick was usually kept;

that not enough photographs of the crime scene had been made; that some of the surviving items of evidence had been handled in a "careless manner"; and that much potentially important evidence had simply been lost. Paul overlooked no opportunity to suggest that Peachey was confused, both during his investigation and during his appearance on the witness stand, and that he had never been cooperative with the defense attorneys. Using notes made in April by Morris Dees, Paul asked whether Peachey had ever said that if he "didn't get a conviction in this case [he] could not hold his head up in Washington."

"I did not. I absolutely did not," Peachey said.

"Didn't you tell Morris Dees that you were tired of people making fun of the way things are handled in the Beaufort County jail?"

"What do you mean by 'making fun'?"

Paul referred to the notes, then rephrased his question. "Have you felt pressure as a result of this case?"

"Yes," Peachey admitted. "Quite a bit." That was not news to Paul, or to anyone else who had spoken to Willis Peachey about the investigation. Beaufort County deputies had become the butt of many jokes, and Peachey seemed especially sensitive to the criticism. In April, according to Dees's notes, he had said that the case had "hurt law [enforcement] in Beaufort County" and that people had kidded him about "going down to the jail to fuck some."

Willis Peachey had been on the stand more than eleven hours when Paul reached the end of his recross-examination. It had been a bad experience for him. "Now let me ask you this question and see if you can tell me the truth," Paul had said more than once. "Your question is vague to the point I cannot answer," had been one retort. But mainly it had been a continuous embarrassment to testify about an investigation that had gone so poorly and produced so little information about the crime. "Isn't it true," Paul often had the opportunity to ask, "that we have lost another valuable piece of evidence forever?" And there had been nothing, really, that Peachey could say.

"Did you give the radio in the jail cell to Joan Little's mother?" the defense attorney asked finally, well after 5:00 p.m.

"I don't recall," Peachey answered.

"Are you aware," Paul snarled, "that that's the one hundredth time today you've said 'I don't recall'?"

Except for the expulsion of Morris Dees, the first week of the trial in which evidence was offered had gone by without any major disruption in the courtroom or outside. A few picketers paraded in front of the courthouse, but there had been no demonstration since the first day, when Larry Little had led a group of marchers through the rain from Women's Prison to the courthouse steps. An effort to overturn Judge Bailey's order banning demonstrations on the grounds had failed, and by the third week even the crowd inside the courtroom had begun to diminish. On a few days there were empty seats during the afternoon sessions, and spectators were now often outnumbered by the deputies and patrolmen. The trial had turned out to be a tight, narrow struggle over the facts rather than the issues behind them, a sluggish examination of inconclusive evidence rather than a spectacle or a circus.

Angela Davis had been in court on Friday, the second of the celebrities who came to Raleigh to lend their presence to the Joan Little movement. In June she had published a polemical article about the case in *Ms.*, a national feminist magazine, and shortly before the trial she supplied a stack of printed copies of the article to the Joann Little Defense Fund for use as campaign literature.

On Thursday the family of Clarence Alligood had appeared in court for the second time. One of the dead man's sons told a reporter that they hoped to be there often "to see our father's name is protected" and "to see justice is done."

On Monday, August 4, the country's premier radical lawyer arrived and took a seat in the courtroom. For several days the defense attorneys had been hinting that William Kunstler would appear and petition to practice before the court in this case. He was coming, they said, to replace Morris Dees.

Judge Hobgood already knew that Kunstler was in Raleigh. When he got to the courthouse that morning, Hobgood called in a bailiff, R. W. May, and reminded him that only authorized people were permitted within the bar. Hobgood "didn't want to see any new faces sitting out there this morning," May would explain. The judge had not mentioned Kunstler by name, but May knew whom he was talking about. Paul would accuse Hobgood of referring to Kunstler as "a bastard" that morning before court convened. Hobgood denied making any such remark, but would confess privately with a smile that someone on the defense team "might have read my mind."

As soon as court opened, Paul stood up and said, "If Your Honor pleases . . . we have a motion to make. We would like Mr. William Kunstler, who is— Mr. Kunstler, stand up."

Kunstler rose and moved forward confidently, an erect figure with wavy grayish hair and ruddy skin. There was a faint smile on his face. He leaned forward, resting both hands on a railing.

"We have a written motion to petition the court to allow Mr. Kunstler to participate in this case for the following reasons," Paul began. "As Your Honor well knows, Mr. Dees was kicked out of the case and we had divided up the case into certain divisions among the lawyers and the removal of Mr. Dees hurt our case irreparably. In order to make some attempt to repair that damage done to Joan Little, our client, we ask the court to allow Mr. Kunstler to participate to aid us in repairing in some small way some of that damage that was done. Mr. Kunstler is a member of the bar of many states and of the Supreme Court and of the Fourth Circuit. He has practiced in this state before and we move the Court that he be allowed to participate in this trial."

"All right," Hobgood said without looking at Kunstler, "do you have it in writing?"

"Mr. Rowan is bringing in the motion in writing."

"Of course, any order I enter would be in response to the written motion which would be filed," Hobgood went on tonelessly. "Now, your motion is denied in the discretion of the court based on the fact that you now have six attorneys representing the defendant, the fact that this is the beginning of the fourth week of the trial, and I do not plan for the prosecution or the defense to add any more lawyers at this late stage. . . ."

"In that case, Judge," Paul said, "we make a motion that we be allowed a hearing on Mr. Kunstler's participation."

"Motion denied." Hobgood set his face in a stern expression and did not take his eyes off Paul.

"But we need to get it in the record."

"Motion denied," Hobgood said again, firmly. "I don't want to hear from you. Put it in writing."

"But we need something in the record. We need a hearing," Paul insisted, even though his motion and the judge's action on it would automatically become a part of "the record" and even though written petitions and affidavits could be submitted later without "a hearing."

"We'll not have a hearing, Mr. Paul."

"But if you—"

For the first time the judge looked beyond Paul. "Mr. Kunstler," he said, "you can have a seat."

Kunstler had been watching with a calm, bemused expression, but now he raised his arms in the air and boomed, "Thank you, Your Honor, I'm glad to see that the quality of justice in North Carolina courts has not improved."

Then he whirled to walk back to his place on the defense row, but as he did Hobgood leaned forward and said, "You make many more statements like that and you'll be up on the fifth floor." William Kunstler could not have known that the fifth floor housed the Wake County jail, but it was obvious that he did not intend to let Hobgood have the last word. He turned back to face the judge. "Take me up there," he said in a resonant, angry voice. "I think what you're doing is outrageous!"

"Your Honor," Paul interrupted, as if the exchange had somehow escaped the notice of the court stenographer. "We would like a hearing so that it might be on the record."

Hobgood did not immediately reply. He looked toward the bailiffs, who had risen to their feet, and pointed to Kunstler. "Take him up there!" he ordered. Then, as the officers were marching Kunstler out of the courtroom, he turned his attention again to Jerry Paul and said finally, "Motion denied."

The advantage the defense had hoped to gain by Kunstler's appearance, or by forcing the judge to exclude him from the trial, seemed obscure. Paul had said he needed Kunstler "to repair [the] damage done" by the removal of Morris Dees, but in fact the defense attorneys—especially Paul—were elated when Dees was expelled. "I don't know what the state of North Carolina is trying to do in its continuing process of intimidation of black leaders and the attorneys who represent them," Paul had said at the press conference after Dees posted bond. But in private he called the expulsion "a blessing in disguise" and boasted of telling Dees's lawyers "not to get him back in at least until after the state had put on all of its evidence." On the day Kunstler was thrown out of the courtroom, Paul told newsmen that the defense needed him to deliver a final summation on the issues in this case of "national importance." On the same day he told several officers at the courthouse he had opposed Kunstler's trip to Raleigh because he feared it would rankle Hobgood and cause him to become harsh with the defense. Rumors began to circulate that Kunstler had edged himself into the highly publicized trial over the initial objections of the defense attorneys, perhaps using his influence as a ranking radical attorney. Several days later Harry Reasoner of ABC-TV called Kunstler a "clown" during an evening news comment on criminal justice in the United States, and the *News & Observer* ran a biting editorial cartoon suggesting that the New York lawyer had flown to Raleigh simply to provoke a confrontation with the judge. Ironically, Paul and Kunstler had met during a seminar at Yale University months earlier, and Kunstler had asked then whether there was anything he could do on the case. Paul had told him his assistance was not needed.

In any event, Kunstler spent only two hours in jail, where he was taken after throwing his arm around a startled black deputy and saying, "Come on, take me to the pokey and get me away from all these honkies." Hobgood had him brought back downstairs, found him in contempt, gave him a sentence of several hours, and ruled that he had already served the sentence imposed. Paul made a last attempt to prolong the crisis, again asking for a hearing and then for a chance to make a statement.

"I have another motion to make."

"Not about this!" Hobgood cut him off. "We're going back to the trial. You got any motion to make, I've told you time and again to put it in writing, then it will get in the record."

But Paul persisted, and finally Hobgood seemed on the edge of his temper. He rose to his feet and pointed his finger at the defense counsel. "Sit down," he ordered, "or I'll begin finding facts on you."

It was over. Kunstler was gone from the courtroom, and soon would be gone from Raleigh, but not before holding a sidewalk press conference during the lunch recess. "I think the man [Hobgood] is determined to see this woman convicted by any means necessary, in violation of his oath as well as the Constitution, and that constitutes in my mind a criminal act," Kunstler said, after observing court proceedings less than fifteen minutes. He told reporters he had spent part of his time in jail reading about the trial of Christ in the biblical Book of Matthew and said that trial had "serious similarities to what is happening here now." He announced that a rotating team of attorneys would be brought in as "judge watchers" to compile information for a possible civil suit against Hobgood. Then he went to the airport. All along Kunstler had been holding reservations on a 4:40 p.m. flight back to New York.

On Tuesday, Morris Dees reached the court of last resort. Former United States Attorney General Ramsey Clark appeared before Chief Justice of the United States Supreme Court Warren Burger and argued that Dees's removal denied Joan Little "her right not to be deprived of her life without due process of law." Burger rejected the request to overturn Hobgood's order.

In Raleigh later the same day, one of Dees's local attorneys met in chambers with Hobgood and the Wake County district attorney, and the following morning Dees filed a motion asking "to be relieved of all responsibilities and duties as associate counsel for Joan Little." Simultaneously, the subornation-of-perjury charge against him was dropped. A few days later, Dees left Raleigh. He took no further part in the trial of Joan Little.

On Wednesday the state rested its case. Jailers David Watson and Ellis Tetterton had by then testified about the defendant's presence in the Beaufort County jail, SBI Special Agent William Slaughter had explained his role in the investigation, an SBI forensic chemist had given testimony about laboratory analyses on the jailer's shirt and undershirt, and an SBI expert had confirmed that the handwriting in the books and magazines introduced by the prosecution was that of Joan Little.

It had not been a good week for the prosecution. Distressed about the progress of the trial and distracted by the antics of the defense, William Griffin had left much of the courtroom work to Chalmers and Wilkinson, who were squabbling openly about how the case should be conducted. John Wilkinson's questioning of David Watson had gone into details which the jailer was unprepared to discuss, making both the lawyer and the witness seem to stumble and grope for the truth. At one point Wilkinson asked Watson to indicate a particular doorway on the jail diagram, but the jailer, who had never seen the diagram before, pointed to one of the cells. Jerry Paul walked over and patiently explained the drawing to him, while Wilkinson slumped in his chair and muttered, "Well, objection. . . ."

On another occasion, during important testimony from an SBI chemist, Lester Chalmers permitted the defense attorneys to interfere with a visual display of the wounds. As Chalmers obliviously questioned the witness, Paul and Milton Williamson stood between the jury and a large easel that had been set up nearby. For a moment Paul moved close to the display and completely blocked it from view. Several of the jurors leaned sideways, straining to see, and then gave up. As a result, the exact location of the wounds, which was crucial to the state's contention that Joan Little had used more force than necessary to repel the jailer when she stabbed him eleven times in various parts of his body, remained unclear. As soon as Chalmers finished his direct examination, Paul and Williamson moved the easel to the other side of the room and turned it away from the jury. It would not be shown again.

During the testimony of handwriting expert D. C. Matheny, however, the prosecution had scored a victory when Hobgood finally denied the defense motion to suppress the books and magazines taken from the women's cellblock. They were introduced, identified, and passed around for each juror to read. On cross-examination, Jerry Paul had Matheny quote certain passages from the pages of the books: "God is a good God, so clean, so pure. . . . God will bring us together. . . . Today is the fourth. Happy birthday, baby. I cried all day. God will bring us back together soon." William Griffin made no similar effort to point out specific passages and did not ask Matheny to quote any of the language of the marginal notes, but he felt confident that the overall meaning of the writings had made an impact on the jurors. They had spent more than two hours poring over each page.

The case was far from airtight, and without the testimony of Terry Bell, the only state witness who might have linked Joan Little with the weapon used to slay Clarence Alligood, the prosecution had relinquished all chance to prove first-degree murder. Even before the trial began Griffin had tentatively decided not to call Bell as a witness because of fears that he might attempt to repeat his "confession," causing a mistrial and possibly jeopardizing any further efforts to re-prosecute the case. The defense attorneys were also reluctant to call Bell because of his conflicting stories and erratic behavior, but they did attempt to capitalize on the favorable aspects of his statements. In chambers they requested and received the SBI photos of Bell's climb through the jail overhead, and during the trial they informed reporters that the young trusty had had "access to the women's section of the jail through the crawl space."

This was vital information from a legal standpoint, since in a case based on circumstantial evidence the prosecution might have been forced not only to prove that Joan Little had killed the jailer but also that Terry Bell had not. The defense attorneys were unable to make use of this ammunition in court, however. Judge Hobgood began to discourage both sides from mentioning Bell in the courtroom after he had studied the young man's statements and after learning that Bell was near a nervous collapse in a prison hospital. The matter was finally resolved when Bell's newly appointed attorney drove up from Beaufort County to say that he would object on grounds of self-incrimination if an attempt was made to put his client on the witness stand.

Even without Bell's testimony, however, the basic goals of the prosecution strategy had been accomplished. There was uncontroverted evidence of multiple stab wounds and of the cause of death; there was evidence that the defendant had been an unhappy prisoner in the Beaufort County jail; and there was evidence that she had fled from the cell where Clarence Alligood's body was found. There was no indication, furthermore, that the jailer had assaulted the defendant or that she had killed him to protect herself from bodily harm. The prosecutors had been careful to avoid raising the issue, and the defense attorneys—because they could anticipate what the answer would be—had not asked the state's witnesses whether there was any evidence that the jailer had been stabbed in self-defense.

At once there was a motion that the case be dismissed, and Marvin Miller and Milton Williamson spent the afternoon attacking the state's evidence as inadequate and inconclusive. By the time they had finished, both Griffin and Chalmers had left the courtroom. Only John Wilkinson sat at the prosecution table, brooding and listening to the defense arguments. "William should be here to refute this," he whispered tightly to an SBI agent, but Griffin did not intend to make any reply at all.

John Wilkinson had not been informed, as had the district attorney, that the issue was already settled. On the preceding Friday, Hobgood had let Griffin know that there was sufficient evidence in the record to avoid an involuntary dismissal, and after resting the case Griffin had learned that unless the defense decided to offer rebuttal evidence there would be a strong charge to the jury on voluntary manslaughter.

"All right," Hobgood said when the defense attorneys had finished. "Motion denied."

Hobgood's ruling ensured that the jurors, not the judge, would decide the outcome of the case. But it remained to be seen whether Joan Little's life would continue to depend on their verdict. The defense attorneys moved immediately for dismissal of the charge of first-degree murder.

It was the prosecutors who argued strenuously this time, even though Hobgood's inclination to reduce the offense had been apparent to both sides for weeks. Lester Chalmers vigorously urged him to let the jury decide the question of premeditation, and John Wilkinson conjured the image of a jailer stabbed so severely that he "bled like a hog and lay there in a pool of blood and died." William Griffin said simply that "the nature of the wounds is sufficient for the jury to consider first-degree murder," and then he suddenly shouted that there was "not a shred of evidence of provocation" and that "without all the publicity and attendant clamor, Your Honor knows as I do that this case would have gone to the jury on first-degree—"

"Well," Hobgood stopped him, "I don't know about that."

But Griffin had chosen the correct tense, even before the judge made his decision known. "I have given this a lot of consideration and I have done a lot of research during the last twenty-four hours," Hobgood soon announced. "There is insufficient evidence of first-degree murder . . . and that charge is dismissed."

The defense attorneys then moved for dismissal of the charge of second-degree murder, not a capital offense but a serious matter nonetheless. The maximum penalty was life in prison.

This time, again as if he knew how Hobgood would inevitably rule, William Griffin declared that he would "submit the issue without argument," and a few moments later he and Lester Chalmers walked quietly from the courtroom, leaving Jerry Paul and Marvin Miller to shadow-box with the judge.

"The court is well aware that there are many questions about the facts in this case to which we do not have any answers—everyone is aware of that," Hobgood said finally. "But the court holds that at this stage of the trial that the motion is denied."

At last it was certain. Joan Little would take the witness stand. She still faced the prospect of spending the rest of her life behind bars.

CHAPTER 14

I GOT TO THE ICE PICK FIRST

Jerry Paul had been suffering throughout the trial and now, the first day of the defense presentation, he came to court looking strained and haggard. His chronic ailments had raged unabated for weeks—a bad shoulder from a football injury, prostate trouble that was painful and disabling, and remorseless migraine headaches that welled up for days at a time. Often he had visited a chiropractor during the lunch recess, and several times during the trial a doctor had treated him at his motel or in a hospital emergency room. To combat the symptoms of these maladies and to keep himself going, Paul took compound dosages of various prescription medicines, and his dependence on these pills and remedies prompted rumors that he was a drug addict and that he was dying of cancer.

Paul had great difficulty with the first witness, Dr. Page Hudson, the chief state medical examiner. He was unable to ask satisfactory hypothetical questions, and often seemed dazed by the answers he got from the doctor. Hudson said that nothing in the medical reports indicated Clarence Alligood had been instantly incapacitated by his wounds, or that he would not have been able to move around inside the cell for several minutes after being stabbed in the heart. But he refused to speculate that a struggle had taken place in the cellblock and discredited the notion that an early laboratory examination of the trousers would have produced dispositive or even important information. Hudson's testimony seemed, on balance, to be at least as beneficial to the state as to the defense, and it rebutted some of the earlier medical evidence that had appeared favorable to Joan Little. But he was not vigorously cross-examined, and his impact on the jury was uncertain and undramatic.

During the afternoon the defense called three former inmates of the Beaufort County jail. Annie Gardner, twenty-six, said she had served time for resisting arrest and destroying public property, and described how Clarence Alligood had tried to pinch her breasts "three or five times, five or six, I don't know." Rosa Roberson, stout and resplendent in dark glasses and a bright pink dress, said she knew all of the jailers and that during her three weeks of incarceration Clarence Alligood had asked her several times whether she needed sex. On cross-examination, she admitted she had tried to commit suicide while she was in jail, and on redirect she said she had wanted to kill herself because she "was tired of being bothered about sex." But it developed that she had first cut her wrists with a knife in the courthouse elevator just after being sentenced for making a threatening telephone call, and that some time later she had slashed herself with the bottom of a toothpaste tube. Neither of the wounds had required a doctor's care. A deputy had talked to her, bandaged the cuts, and told her "not to do it any more."

Phyllis Ann Moore appeared at the end of the day, telling the court that she and Joan Little "used to pray and read the Bible together in the morning and in the afternoon." Her testimony—that Clarence Alligood had twice asked Joan Little "if she missed her man," and that he had frequently gone into the women's section and on several occasions had gone into the women's cellblock alone—surprised the prosecutors. They had no reason to suspect she had told the defense investigators anything other than what she had told the SBI: ". . . Spent several days and nights in jail and was treated well at the jail." But she explained she had not said anything to the SBI about the incidents because she "didn't think it was important," and that she had later volunteered to testify for the defense after being contacted by Morris Dees.

The defense then spent almost a full day questioning Herbert L. MacDonnell, an authority in criminalistics who was their only paid expert witness. He was followed by Dr. Neil Hoffman, the associate state medical examiner, who testified briefly and said the jailer "would have continued to have motor ability" for several minutes after receiving the fatal stab wound. After Hoffman, Gordon Edwards, the television newsman who had taken motion pictures inside the jail, said that he had noticed several spots of blood near the man's shoes inside the cellblock and that the stains "didn't appear to have been disturbed . . . they were round in appearance." By the end of the week the defense attorneys had built a solid foundation for Joan Little's coming testimony. Two doctors had said that the jailer was able to move around even after the deadly blow to his heart. A criminalistics expert had interpreted many of the crime-scene details in ways that would later become pertinent when the defendant testified. Three former inmates of the jail had recalled that Clarence Alligood made suggestive comments or improper advances, either toward them or in their presence. And a television news photographer had introduced color blow-ups of the film he had taken inside the cellblock after the killing.

On Monday morning, the beginning of the fifth week of the trial, Dr. Arthur Finn completed the background testimony. He recalled his trip to Beaufort County almost a year earlier to bring Joan Little back to Chapel Hill and said she had been unable then even to speak of the incident. "She had clearly recovered to some extent," he testified, "but as she began to talk about what had happened in prison [jail] she broke down completely." None of the prosecutors realized until later that Finn was the chairman of the Board of Directors of the Joann Little Defense Fund. On cross-examination John Wilkinson did not ask him anything about his involvement with the defendant or her attorneys except in a professional capacity. At 10:20 a.m., as Finn was stepping down, Jerry Paul paused and pinched the bridge of his nose, then said, "The defense calls to the stand Miss Joan Little."

For nearly a year she had been living on the edges of this moment—enjoying the luxury of stardom, dwelling in the shadow of the gas chamber. At twenty, Joan Little had become someone special, a symbol, the vortex of a swirling political and social movement. Scores of people had flocked to her aid, and thousands had sent contributions for her defense effort. Her case had been the subject of several television documentaries, numerous magazine articles, countless newspaper stories. Her picture had appeared on the cover of *Jet* magazine, a national black periodical, causing people on the street to recognize her and ask for her autograph. Members of Congress had rallied to her side by calling on the United States attorney general to intervene in her behalf, and the Black Panther Party had voted her 1975 Woman of the Year. Through it all, though, Joan Little had been alone in one respect. Only she would face the dire consequences if her defense effort failed. Only she would have to testify before the jury, to answer once and for all the questions that still had to be asked.

Yet Joan Little was not unprepared. Her self-image as well as her public image had been carefully recast during the preceding year and it was now difficult to imagine that she was the defendant in a murder trial, that she had ever before been in trouble with the law. Gone were the miniskirts and the wigs. Gone was the dialect of the slum and the gutter. Gone, except in the records that would not be introduced, was the promiscuous delinquent, the petty criminal. She took the stand fashionably but discreetly dressed, and once there she spoke quietly and confidently of outrages she had suffered. She was the same woman who had written mundane notes in the margins of crossword-puzzle books, but now it was said that she had composed long, complex, and sometimes moving poems in her prison cell. She was the same woman who had stolen from other blacks while they were away at work, but now she had learned to speak of "freeing my people" and of the "fight for human survival."

Only the image had changed, however, and those on the defense team who knew her best, who had been with her constantly, realized that Joan Little had not been transformed. "She really hasn't changed that much, because when she's out of court and away from the press she's not that quiet," a member of the defense entourage told a reporter near the end of the trial. "Her attitude is like she's on one big merry-go-round. She jumps up and sometimes just runs off without anyone knowing where she is. Her ego has gotten so big that she just doesn't relate to other people." Another said, "It has always been the symbol for me. Joan just rubs a lot of people the wrong way, but they stay because their cause is important." In private, the members of the defense team closest to Joan Little spoke even more bluntly. "She's a spoiled, selfish, self-centered little brat," Richard Wolf said. "She's manipulative—she knows how to get what she wants," her bodyguard, Russell McDonald, observed. And Jerry Paul, whose strategy was to insist that she had been the victim of racism and sexism and a lecherous old man, told Richard Wolf before the trial that he thought she was "a nymphomaniac."

Images tend to blur the truth, but seldom really transform it. The maelstrom of activity around Joan Little and the flood of support she received had not seemed to soften her. She was still obstinate, still wary and defensive, calculating and alert, moody but not particularly thoughtful, street-wise beyond her years but immature and blithely naïve. Until the trial she remained distrustful of almost everyone except Paul, McDonald, and Wolf. Often she simply refused to work with other members of the defense team. Even her attachment to Paul was tenuous at times, and he was aware that the real source of his influence was his control of the defense funds, which were spent for her personal needs as well as her legal expenses. For a while

she seemed to harbor special resentment for Karen Galloway, apparently unable to perceive another black woman
as an attorney, or an attorney as another black woman. "It's
a problem," Karen Galloway would say, "that I'll have to
deal with all my life."

Because of the cocoon Joan Little had spun around herself, no one except Paul could have been certain that she
was ready to take the witness stand. In the hectic schedule
of rallies and public appearances during the spring and
early summer, it had been difficult even for Paul to work
with his client. There had been frequent early-morning
flights to distant cities where they were chauffeured in
limousines, adored by supporters, and followed by the
press. Then there had been late flights to get back home,
too tired and haggard to concentrate on the inevitable
moment when it would all come to an end. For a time she
had been reluctant to discuss the case at Paul's office, pre-
ferring instead to gossip idly with members of the defense
team while she sipped soft drinks. At least once she had
dropped out of sight for several days without telling anyone where she was going. Often she was late for appointments, and occasionally she missed them altogether. But as
the trial neared, preparations became more intense. Content earlier to discuss the case on the run or in occasional
late-night conversations at his home, Paul began to spend
more time alone with his client. At the table in his dining
room, away from the bustle of the office and the disquieting
presence of other people, they went over the incident
again and again, fighting fatigue and boredom, until her
recollections had been distilled and a format had been
developed for the testimony she would give in court on
direct examination.

There would be questions from Paul first about Joan Little's background—her family, her schooling, the work she
had done—and about her criminal record. She had been
convicted once for shoplifting and once for breaking and
entering and larceny, and as a result of the breaking-and-
entering conviction she had spent time in the Beaufort

County jail waiting for the filing of her appeal, waiting to get out on bail. "I stayed in the Beaufort County jail from June fourth of 1974 until August of 1974," she responded when Paul asked the anticipated question shortly after she took the stand.

"When in August, do you know?" Hobgood asked, as if it really was not important.

"The twenty-seventh," she said, as if the date had no meaning at all.

There were questions about conditions in the Beaufort County jail, about what she did while she was there, about the jailers, and about which jailers had come into the women's section and into the women's cellblock.

"How many jailers did you know?" Paul asked.

"I knew all of them."

"All of them?"

"Yes."

"Did any of the jailers ever come into the female section?"

"Yes."

"Who?"

"Mr. Alligood."

"Mr. Alligood?"

"Yes."

There were questions about some of the female inmates who served time in jail while she was there, about which jailers and which deputies might have entered the women's section unannounced, and about her efforts to get out on bail. Then Paul reached back to the evening of August 26, 1974, and Joan Little recalled asking Clarence Alligood whether she could use the telephone in the jailer's office and testified that while she was on the phone Alligood had returned Terry Bell to his cell, leaving her in the office with a white man whom she could not identify. On the way back to her own cell, she said, she had asked Alligood "to go to Terry Bell and ask him to send me some cigarettes and he said that he would."

PAUL: Now, did Mr. Alligood go and get some cigarettes?*

LITTLE: Yes, he did.

PAUL: All right, when he came back what did he say to you if anything?

LITTLE: He gave me the cigarettes that Terry had sent me and he told me that he would get me a pack of cigarettes if I didn't have any. I told him no I didn't want him to get me any cigarettes and he said that he would get me some and I could pay him back later and he continued to stand there and he started talking to me telling me how nice I looked again, and that he wanted me, you know, to give him some pussy is what he said.

PAUL: All right, what did you say at that time?

LITTLE: I told him no, and I would really appreciate it if he left and he left.

PAUL: All right, now what happened later, after he left, what then happened?

LITTLE: He came back again with a pack of cigarettes.

PAUL: What kind of cigarettes?

LITTLE: Salem cigarettes.

PAUL: All right?

LITTLE: And a bag of sandwiches and he stood there.

PAUL: Miss Little, what were you doing when he came back with the sandwiches and the cigarettes?

LITTLE: I was laying on my bunk in cell number one. I was reading.

CHALMERS: If Your Honor pleases, I can't hear the witness.

HOBGOOD: Would you repeat just what you said?

LITTLE: I was laying on my bunk in cell number one. I was reading and listening to the radio.

When Clarence Alligood returned to the women's section at about two o'clock with the cigarettes and the bag of

---

*Portions of the trial transcript have been edited here only to eliminate repetitious material. The questions and answers which do appear have been extracted in full, in the correct sequence and, unless otherwise indicated, without editorial revision.

sandwiches, Joan Little went on, he came into the cellblock and into cell number one, where she was reclining on the bunk. "He said that he had brought the sandwiches and that he was going to talk to the dispatcher and that he would be back, and I took the sandwiches and he kept standing there and he said that—by that time I had changed into my gown and he was telling me that I looked real nice in my gown and that he was gonna, you know, wanted to have sex with me again.* And I took the sand-wiches and at that time he left."

Here was possibly significant information that had not been previously disclosed. "He said . . . that he was going to talk to the dispatcher." In spite of Beverly King's testi-mony, attorneys on both sides still thought that Clarence Alligood's conversation with the radio dispatcher might have indicated his intention to go back to the women's cellblock, either for a tryst or to commit rape. Yet Alli-good, an experienced night jailer, must have known that police officers might still come to the jail at any time, even if all the deputies had gone off patrol. Joan Little was not asked if he had said why he was going to speak to Beverly King.

PAUL: All right now, after Mr. Alligood said he was going to see the dispatcher and brought you the sandwiches, when was the next time you saw Mr. Alligood?

LITTLE: When he came back the third time, which was when the incident occurred.

PAUL: Where was he the first time you saw him?

LITTLE: Just standing there just outside the bars of cell number one.

PAUL: Would you describe for me the expression on his face?

---

*No issue was made during the trial about the precision of Joan Little's remark, i.e., whether she meant that Alligood had said he wanted to have sex again, or that he had said again he wanted to have sex. In the context of her earlier testimony, it seemed apparent at the time that she intended her statement to have the latter meaning.

LITTLE: He had a sort of, I'll say a silly looking grin on his face.

HOBGOOD: Had a what kind of grin?

LITTLE: Sort of silly grin.

HOBGOOD: Silly grin.

PAUL: All right, did you notice anything else about him?

LITTLE: No, not at that time.

PAUL: All right, where were you when he came and stood in the doorway?

LITTLE: When he first came into the automatic door and stood at that door, which was the first time that I had seen him, I was up. I had gotten off the bunk at that time and stood up.

PAUL: All right, where were you standing?

LITTLE: Just approximately middleway the bunk.

PAUL: All right, what did Mr. Alligood say to you at that time, Miss Little?

LITTLE: He said that he had been nice to me and that it was time that I be nice to him, and that he wanted—

PAUL: And anything else?

LITTLE: That he, that he wanted to, wanted me to give him some pussy and that, you know.

On cross-examination William Griffin would return to explore this response in detail. He would wonder why the jailer had used a gutter reference to conventional sexual intercourse when he had apparently intended to force Joan Little to perform an oral sex act. The results of Griffin's effort seemed dubious, and the point appeared to have no impact on the jury.

PAUL: Now, how were you dressed at this time?

LITTLE: I had on a gown, a pair of panties, and—

HOBGOOD: Panties?

LITTLE: And a scarf that had a lot of colors in it. . . .

PAUL: Now, Miss Little, what did you say to him?

LITTLE: I told him no, that I didn't feel I should be nice to him in that way and I asked him to leave.

PAUL: All right, now did you continue to stand there or did you move?

LITTLE: He came, he started—he was standing there and he started to take off his shoes outside the corridor.

PAUL: Did he take them both off?

LITTLE: Yes.

PAUL: All right, then what did he do?

LITTLE: He started in towards the cell and I backed off to the back wall.

PAUL: And what did he say?

LITTLE: He said that I may as well do it because if I told it that Ellis or Red or none of them were gonna believe me anyway.

PAUL: What did you do?

LITTLE: I stood there scared, and hoping that he would turn around and leave, and he started feeling all over my breasts.

PAUL: All right, would you describe for me how he started feeling of you?

LITTLE: He just started touching me, fumbling over my breasts.

PAUL: All right, what were you doing at this time?

LITTLE: Standing still, scared stiff. I didn't know what to do.

PAUL: Were you doing—what physical action were you doing, if any?

LITTLE: I had started to cry.

PAUL: What did Alligood say while he was standing there feeling of your breasts and you were crying and he was fondling you, what did he say to you?

LITTLE: He didn't say anything. He just continued and he started—he reached down and pulled up my gown and put his hands between my legs.

PAUL: Okay. Now, Miss Little, while he was doing that and he was feeling between your legs, what did he say to you at that time?

LITTLE: He told me that he knew that I had did it before and then he backed up away from me.

PAUL: All right, what did you say?

LITTLE: I told him no, and I asked him to leave again.

PAUL: What did he say?

LITTLE: He said he wasn't gonna leave and he came more forcefully in what he tried to say.

PAUL: All right, now have you left out anything that he said to you?

LITTLE: No.

PAUL: All right, now, as he came back towards you what did he do, Miss Little?

LITTLE: He just started taking his pants off and when he took his pants off, then he came towards me and he said —he reached for me.

HOBGOOD: Let me ask you, did he take his pants off?

LITTLE: Yes, and he came back towards me and when he came back towards me I told him no I wasn't gonna do anything like that, and then that's when he tried to force me towards him and—

PAUL: Now, as he tried to force you towards him, Miss Little, what did you see about him, what did you notice about him?

LITTLE: That he had his pants off and when he tried to force me towards him I tried to get away and reach for my gown and that's when he snatched it out of my hands and told me that, you know, that I wasn't gonna, you know, going out or going to put my gown back on. And at that point, that's when I noticed that he had a ice pick in his hand.

Here was another point the prosecution would attempt to exploit. Where had the ice pick come from? Why had she not seen it before? Why had Clarence Alligood suddenly produced a weapon, even though she had not yet really tried to resist?

PAUL: Which hand did he have the ice pick in?

LITTLE: In his left hand.

PAUL: All right, now, what did he do then?

LITTLE: He grabbed me around my neck.

PAUL: With which hand?

LITTLE: His right hand.

PAUL: And did what?

LITTLE: Pulled me towards him.

PAUL: Towards him, where was he?

LITTLE: Standing middleway of the bunk at that time.

PAUL: All right, he pulled you towards him and what was he doing while he pulled you towards him?

LITTLE: He had me by my neck, right by the back of my neck holding me, pulling me towards him, and he had the ice pick at my head.

PAUL: Now, did he keep standing up or did he start sitting down?

LITTLE: Started sitting down.

PAUL: Now, Miss Little, will you explain to me when Mr. Alligood took your panties off?

LITTLE: He didn't.

PAUL: All right, now, as he pulled you towards him and sat down on the bunk, Miss Little, would you explain from that point on what happened and what did he do and what did you do?

LITTLE: He pulled me down to the floor.

PAUL: And was he sitting on the cot at this time?

LITTLE: He was sitting on the cot at that time.

PAUL: All right.

LITTLE: He asked—what he was telling me was that he wanted me to suck him, and I told him no that I'm not gonna do it. He threatened me with the ice pick and I then did what he told me to do.

PAUL: All right, let me ask you this, did he have an erection when you began to suck him, as he said?

LITTLE: No.

PAUL: Did he later have an erection while you were sucking him?

LITTLE: Yes.

PAUL: All right, now, where was the ice pick while you were sucking him?

LITTLE: In his left hand.

PAUL: Will you describe the manner in which the ice pick was in his left hand?

LITTLE: At this point he had a grip on it just like this [indicating with her left hand that the weapon was held in a closed fist with the point extending out from between the curled thumb and forefinger, the same manner in which the ice pick had been clasped in the right hand of the corpse].

PAUL: Now, Miss Little, I want you to tell me how long did you have oral sex with him?

LITTLE: Maybe three, four minutes.

PAUL: All right, now, what were you watching or looking at while you were having oral sex?

LITTLE: I was looking at that ice pick because I didn't know what he was gonna do. I didn't know where [whether] he was gonna kill me or not.

PAUL: All right, now, will you tell me what happened after you had oral sex with him for a while?

LITTLE: He loosened his grip on the ice pick and I grabbed for it and it fell to the floor.

PAUL: All right, then what happened?

LITTLE: He went for the ice pick.

PAUL: And what happened?

LITTLE: I grabbed for the ice pick.

For several minutes the defendant had seemed to be losing her composure, and now she broke down and began to cry into the handful of tissues she had taken to the witness stand with her. Hobgood declared a recess immediately, the jurors filed out, and Joan Little disappeared with Paul and some of the other defense attorneys. Fifteen minutes later, when the trial resumed, she seemed fully recovered. This was the only time before the verdict was announced that she showed any emotion in the courtroom. Later Jerry Paul would tell a reporter that the tearful interruption had been intentional, that he had learned during trial preparations how to elicit an emotional response from his client at this point in her story.

PAUL: Now, after the ice pick fell, tell the jurors what then happened?

LITTLE: I reached for the ice pick and he reached for the ice pick. I got to the ice pick first.

PAUL: Speak up please.

LITTLE: I got to the ice pick first and when I grabbed the ice pick up and I hit at him, he fell backwards and I came up with my feet and he was sitting on the bunk facing me and I was standing there facing him.

HOBGOOD: Did you actually hit him with the ice pick when you hit that first time?

LITTLE: I don't know.

HOBGOOD: All right, go ahead.

LITTLE: He was sitting on the bunk and I was facing him and he came up at me. . . . When he came up at me I struck at him. At this time he came at me. Then in the course of that he finally got up and he grabbed me around my wrists and when he grabbed me around my wrists I had the pick in my hand with the point out towards me and the handle in my hand facing him, and I pushed him and he came back up at me with more force and I put my feet on the bunk and he came behind me. When he came behind me he had both my hands and I came over my right shoulder and hit him.

PAUL: Now, did you switch hands with the ice pick?

LITTLE: Yes. And he was in front of me and when I got a chance to push him away with my right hand and got my hand out extended far enough to put the handle in my left hand that's when I changed hands.

PAUL: All right, then, what happened please?

LITTLE: He was behind me. I put my feet on the edge of the bunk so I could place the weight of my body up against him and I hit over my right shoulder and he turned me loose.

PAUL: Do you know whether or not you hit him when you hit over your right shoulder?

LITTLE: Not at that time. He fell forward.

PAUL: All right, now, where and how did he fall?

LITTLE: He fell middleway of the bunk forward with his knees on the floor and just on the bunk but he was raised . . . with his head turned . . . [to] the left.

HOBGOOD: You said his feet were on the floor, didn't you?

LITTLE: No, he fell forward with his knees on the floor, his hands on the bunk with his head turned to the right facing the wall the sink was on.

PAUL: Now, after he fell and turned loose of you, Miss Little, what did you do?

LITTLE: I saw blood on his right side of his face and I turned and went—ran to cell number two.

PAUL: All right, when you got to cell number two, what did you do?

LITTLE: I reached for the first thing that I saw, which was my blue jeans, blue pullover blouse and my pocketbook.

PAUL: Now, did you see him again after you grabbed these articles?

LITTLE: As I was coming out I didn't see him. When I got out into the corridor . . . and turned and looked around and he was standing there.

HOBGOOD: At that time had you put on your jeans and blouse?

LITTLE: No.

PAUL: All right, when you turned here and looked back here where did you see him?

LITTLE: Standing at the doorway . . . outside of cell number one.

PAUL: What do you remember about him as you looked back and saw him?

LITTLE: I just remember seeing his face and seeing that grin that he had on his face when I saw him the first time.

PAUL: Where was the ice pick?

LITTLE: I don't remember having the ice pick any more after I—I don't remember having it any more after I hit over my right shoulder.

PAUL: Now, as you looked back and you saw him standing, what did you then do?

LITTLE: I slammed the automatic door.

That had been the end of it. Joan Little said she quickly fled from the jail and ran down a dark alley toward what she hoped would be sanctuary. "When I got to my cousin's house, Raymond Cobb's, and knocked on the door, he came to the door and let me in and I told him that—that the jailer had come in with an ice pick and [was] trying to make me have oral sex with him, and he told me that I couldn't stay there because he didn't want any trouble with the police. So I asked him could I make a phone call and he said yes. I made a phone call to my mother and then I left."

The remainder of her testimony concerned the entries she had made on the pages of her crossword-puzzle books and on the inside cover of a Bible which had also been taken from the cellblock. Paul handed her the small book and asked her to identify it as her own. "On the inside cover there is some writing," he said. "Did you write that?"

"Yes."

"Would you read it for me please?"

"This Bible was given to me on the fourth of July, 1974, by Mr. Charles Oden, to help me to endure the stress and hardships I was going through. It has helped me to make a lot of decisions and has comforted me when I had no one to turn to, so I called on God. Since the sixth month, 6, 1974, I have really learned the true meaning of faith and prayer. Faith more than anything. St. Luke, 5th Verse, 50th Chapter to 54th Chapter [sic]; also St. Mark, 14th Chapter from the 27th Verse, 32nd Verse; also John 14; also Jeremiah, the 3rd to the 14th Verse [sic]. These are just a few of the readings that have caught my attention during this time. I only pray that more young people can convert themselves before it is too late and turn more toward Jesus Christ for support and strength in these troubled times of today. I am no Christian or anything, but I am praying every day and night that I may get closer to God. To those of you that are without mothers and fathers, just think how blessed you are to have someone to love you and to be there when you really need them. Others, God is your parents for ever and

ever and he'll always be there so you are never alone. Pray
with all your heart and soul and he will answer your prayers. He can help you when no one else can or will. God will
never turn you down. He is a forgiver of all sins. Each and
every day, praise God and the many blessings he gives you
and always believe in God and through God all things are
possible if you only believe. Thank God our Father. Joan
Little."

"All right," Paul said, "can you explain to me what you
meant when you wrote those words, Miss Little?"

"What did I mean?"

"Yes."

"During the time I was in jail this Bible was the only
thing that I had to read and I read this Bible and I have
heard people say that—"

"Objection, if Your Honor please," Chalmers said.

"As a result of what people said," Hobgood prompted.

"As a result of what people have said to me, I was under
the impression that they seemed to think that people can't
change. So I wrote exactly what I felt at that time in this
Bible, the lonely times that I had. I had time to think over
my mistakes and I wrote that down in this Bible."

Jerry Paul said he had no further questions, and turned
Joan Little over to the prosecution for cross-examination.

CHAPTER 15

AND YOU HAD BLOOD ON YOUR HANDS

William Griffin's questioning of Joan Little did not begin until after the lunch recess, and during the break she returned to defense headquarters, where Richard Wolf hypnotized her.

During the past week Wolf had intensified his efforts to help the defendant prepare for cross-examination. Using hypnotism, astrology, meditative tapes, religious symbology, dream interpretation, his own inspirational sense of prophecy, and a telepathic technique called "binding" through which they both attempted to communicate with and to confuse the prosecutors, he hoped to put Joan Little in the best possible frame of mind to withstand what was expected to be blistering interrogation. During the midday break on Monday he kept her in a trance for more than half an hour and told her she would become ever more relaxed while she was on the witness stand, that she would always give the correct answer, that she would never forget anything important. She returned to the courtroom looking calm and confident, and the most dreaded ordeal began.

But the expected onslaught did not come at once. For reasons of strategy, William Griffin had decided to "waste the afternoon" with wearisome questions about Joan Little's activities before the night of the jailer's death. He spent a great deal of time going over her background, even though the range of his inquiry had been severely curtailed, ensuring that the jury would remain ignorant of much of the defendant's past. At the start of the afternoon session the defense had moved successfully to restrict the scope of cross-examination by arguing that Joan Little's direct testimony had not put her character into issue. No questions were permitted, therefore, about her earlier arrests or about the circumstances of her conviction for breaking and entering. Moreover, no information from the various school, prison, and social-services records suppressed by Hobgood could be used even to phrase an inquiry because all such data had been deemed irrelevant to the current charges. Late in the afternoon Griffin began going through the notations in the crossword-puzzle books, asking for an explanation of almost every entry, and then he went directly on to questions about what she had done after she left the women's cellblock and was running away from the jail. When court adjourned at five o'clock, he had accomplished his purpose: He had avoided asking anything about what had happened between Joan Little and the jailer on the morning of August 27, and he had given no clue to the defense attorneys about what his approach to that subject would be. He had denied them the opportunity to prepare her that evening, and he had given her one more night to think about the tough questions still to come.

On Tuesday morning the cross-examination turned sharply to the night of August 26, when Joan Little had made a telephone call and then had asked Clarence Alligood to get cigarettes from Terry Bell. She denied asking Alligood to go back for Bell's cigarette lighter when he returned with "three Marlboros." She had not seen the jailer again, she said, until "about two o'clock," when "he came back with the sandwiches and [a] pack of cigarettes, my pack of Salem cigarettes."

"How did he know to bring you Salem cigarettes?"

"Because when he asked me if I wanted him to buy me some cigarettes and I told him no, and he told me he would get me some cigarettes and I could pay him back later and he asked me what kind I smoked and I told him Salems."

Even though Alligood had brought her sandwiches "every night he was on" during the preceding week, she said, this was the first time he had ever brought her cigarettes. He had remained in the cellblock "ten or fifteen minutes," standing just inside the control door and "talking about how nice I looked in my gown and that he wanted me to have sex with him and I told him—I asked him to leave and he said that he wasn't gonna leave right then because he had something to talk to me about and then by that time he had to leave because I think the doorbell rang or something."

"You think it rang. Are you sure about that?"

"He left in a hurry, I remember him leaving in a hurry."

Here was William Griffin's first and best chance to attack Joan Little's testimony. On direct examination, she had said that the jailer told her he was going to speak to the radio dispatcher when he left the cellblock after bringing the sandwiches and cigarettes. Now she had said he left "in a hurry," either because the outside bell was ringing or for some other reason, and this was a significant, perhaps inexplicable discrepancy, a crucial matter of evidence. The defendant's earlier explanation had insinuated that Clarence Alligood must have had sexual assault in mind for several hours that morning, and it contributed neatly to her version of the incident. Her testimony on cross-examination, however, suggested he might have been startlingly reminded not once—as she had already said—but twice of the danger of being caught inside the women's cellblock even after all the sheriff's deputies had gone off patrol.

But Griffin failed to dwell on this point, even momentarily. He did not mention her testimony about the incident in late June, when Clarence Alligood was also supposed to have been surprised by the jangling doorbell, or her earlier version of the jailer's second visit to her cell. "And when was the next time you saw him?" he asked at once, driving his cross-examination past the only clear chance he would have to raise doubts about the defendant's memory and veracity.

Clarence Alligood had returned to the women's section about an hour later, Joan Little testified, and again he had come into the cellblock. He was fully clothed at the time, and she had seen no ice pick in his hand. "He came in and stood at the door and he said it's time that you be nice to me because I been nice to you. . . . I told him no, that I wasn't going to be nice to him."

There followed for several minutes what *The New York Times* would call "the classic courtroom pattern where allegations of rape are made," although it is not often the defendant who makes such allegations and it is usually a defense lawyer rather than a district attorney who launches an attack on the witness claiming to have been molested. As a prosecutor, Griffin was not accustomed to this type of questioning, but he tried to go over each detail of Joan Little's testimony meticulously, looking for flaws, errors, implausibilities. "Didn't you say what are you taking your shoes off for? What are you gonna do? Get out of here! You didn't say anything like that?" Clarence Alligood had moved toward her, she said, and had "started feeling my breasts." "Didn't you slap him?" "No, sir." "Didn't you knock his hands away from your breasts?" "I just stood there." She had not seen the ice pick yet, not while she stood still, crying, as he used "both hands" to fondle her. "You didn't slap his hands away from you? You didn't push him away from you?" The nightgown had come off over her head. "I was so scared I just let him do that." The gown had been thrown on the floor.

"You never screamed, hollered, shouted, pushed him away, struck him or anything during this period of time?"

"I was scared and I didn't know whether to scream or what, because he could have killed me right then and there."

"He didn't have a weapon?"

"He was bigger than me."

"He had not threatened you at that point, had he? Had he said anything to you at that point except make a proposition to you?"

"He said some things later."

"He had not threatened you. He had not said he was gonna hurt you. All he said to you in effect was that he wanted to have sex with you, is that right?"

"Yes, sir."

"And you didn't resist him?"

"Yes."

"You didn't holler? You didn't scream? You didn't fight him off, is that right?"

"May I say something?"

"No, I want you to answer my questions."

"Yes," Jerry Paul interrupted, "explain your answer."

"Answer the question," Hobgood said, "then you can explain."

"No, I did not."

"Now you can explain."

"But if you had been a woman, you wouldn't have known what to do either. You probably wouldn't have screamed either, because you wouldn't have known what he would have done to you."

After a few moments Clarence Alligood had stepped away from her, toward the center of the cell, and had removed his trousers. "While he was taking his pants off," Griffin asked, "did you run by him, push him, try to go by him in any way?" She had not. Could she recall how he had removed his underwear? She could not. "Well, I'm interested in why you didn't see him take his underwear off?"

"I didn't say I didn't see him take his underwear off. I said I don't remember how he took his underwear off."

"Now, at that point, could you tell after he got his pants off, could you tell whether or not he was erect?"

"No."

"It was light in there, wasn't it?"

"Yes, on the outside, in the hallway."

"Well, there was a light right in the cell, right over the middle of the cell, isn't there?"

"Won't [wasn't] on."

"Wasn't on?"

"No."

"How did that get off?"

"Stayed off. Never been on the whole eighty-one days I been there."

This would be Griffin's only other opportunity to drive a wedge into Joan Little's testimony. On direct examination, she had said that she was lying in cell number one "reading and listening to the radio" when Clarence Alligood entered the cellblock at about 2:00 a.m. Earlier in the trial, however, Dr. Carpenter had testified that the light inside cell number one that morning was poor, and that he had borrowed a flashlight to inspect the body. Now, on cross-examination, Joan Little had stated that the overhead light fixture—the only source of illumination inside the cell— had been inoperative during the whole time she was confined in the Beaufort County jail. If that was so, then there would not have been sufficient light inside the cell to read, or even to see clearly from the bars to the back wall. Had she really been reading in that cell, where the light was worse than anywhere else in the cellblock? And why had she draped a blanket across the bars, diminishing even the illumination coming from other lights inside the cellblock but outside cell number one? Or was her testimony in error? Was her memory faulty about this detail, and if so, could it have been faulty about others that were more important, more crucial to the outcome of the case? The jury would never know. The questions were never asked.

Then came the attack, with the jailer sitting on the bunk and Joan Little on the floor between his legs, the ice pick aimed at her temple.

"He forced me to go down in front of him. . . . He forced me on the floor on my knees."

"Did you strike him, resist him, push him away, say anything at that time?"

"No, I was still crying."

"Why didn't you twist away from him, he only had one hand on you?"

"And a ice pick in the other."

"Did you know what he meant when he said to do it?"

"I did exactly what he told me to do."

"How long did it take? . . ."

"Two or three minutes."

During those two or three minutes she kept her eyes on the ice pick, Joan Little said, and then the jailer's grasp had weakened, his fingers had opened and relaxed. Instantly she had lunged for the weapon, knocking it to the floor, and the jailer had come down on top of her, grappling, struggling, his right arm over her left shoulder, reaching between the bunk and the sink.

"When I grabbed for it, I hit up," she said. "I used my left arm to push him away and I hit him up with my right arm."

"He weighed a hundred and ninety pounds," said Griffin. "Did you push him off of you?"

"I didn't push him off of me. I forced—I gave him all—pushed my weight against his body and he sort of leaned back a little bit but I didn't have enough strength to push him off of me."

"Where did you strike him with the ice pick?"

"I'm not sure I hit him."

"All right, what happened to him then?"

"He sort of moved back and I came up from under him in a upright position, standing, and he was on the bunk sitting. I was facing him, standing up."

"And did he sit back down on the bunk?"

"He never got off the bunk."

"Now, what did you do with the ice pick at that point?"

"Still had it in my right hand and he reached for me. . . ."

"What did you do at that time?"

"I hit at him."

"Did you strike him?"

"I'm not sure."

"How far was he from you . . . two feet?"

"Yes."

"Didn't you feel the ice pick go into his body?"

"No, I was so scared I had the pick gripped so tightly I

probably couldn't even, you know, I couldn't tell whether
I had even hit him."

"He came up with his arms outstretched? . . ."

"He reached for me. . . ."

"And came up . . . he didn't go for the ice pick, he came
up . . . and you stabbed him in the belly?"

"I can't say I hit him in the belly."

"Did you hit him or not?"

"I'm not sure."

Clarence Alligood had managed to grab her wrists, Joan
Little said, and in the struggle he came up off the bunk to
get around behind her, between the bunk and the wall. "I
pushed him with my arms when he was facing me and he
came around beside me and I put my feet on the bunk
. . . and placed my hands with the left one and came over
him."

"You mean that he stood up in front of the bunk, grabbed
your wrists and you switched hands, you switched the ice
pick from one hand to the other?"

"No."

"You didn't?"

"No, that's not what I said."

This was perhaps the most speculative point in the story
Joan Little told as a witness, and it was one the prosecution
had anticipated and now hoped to exploit. Clarence Alligood, a man twice her size and reputed to be powerful
enough to lift a 250-pound boar, had stood facing her with
his hands on her wrists. Instead of crashing her against the
nearby wall or hurling her out of the cell, she said, he had
circled her, risking more blows from the ice pick, and had
somehow managed to get behind her in the tiny space
between the bunk and the wall. While he was moving, she
had been able to shift the ice pick from her right hand to
her left and then had pressed her feet on the edge of the
bunk, pinning the man behind her while she struck at him
over her right shoulder.

Why had the jailer failed to use his advantages—power
and bulk? How had he managed to get around the woman

and the flailing ice pick in the confined space inside the cell? Why had he released his grip on the hand holding the ice pick? At the core of most skepticism about the way in which Joan Little claimed that Clarence Alligood had died was a suspicion that the jailer's superior strength and size could have saved him from any real harm in a fight with a woman inmate half his stature.

"He was a big man, wasn't he?"

"Yes."

"Weighed a hundred and ninety pounds, about that?"

"Yes, sir."

"Did he fall on top of you when he went over the top of you?"

"No."

"How was it that he didn't just fall on you and mash you on the floor?"

"There was a bunk and the sink that were almost smashing me and he was putting his weight on top of me from the top so I was between the two, the sink and him."

Yet Joan Little had risen up with the ice pick, pushing the jailer back and striking out at him to keep him sitting on the bunk.

"He was a powerful man, wasn't he?"

"He was fairly large."

Why, then, had Clarence Alligood failed to use his natural advantages to subdue Joan Little, or at least to get away from the flashing ice pick? Why had he treated her almost delicately even as he was fighting for his life? Why had this brutal struggle been played out in such a very strange way? Why had the jailer held back, almost as if he did not really want to hurt her?

Then, Joan Little went on, "he turned me loose and fell to the bunk."

"Fell like a tree? You got out from under him and he toppled like a tree, right onto the bunk?"

"That's not true."

"Well, you had to get out of his way. It was the only way he could have fallen from the position you have described, onto the bunk. You had to get out of his way, didn't you?"

"A tree falls with no life," said Joan Little, "and he didn't fall in that way."

"Did you walk out from under him and let him fall?"

"He loosened his grip and I turned and I just moved."

"You moved?"

"Yes."

"What did you do with the ice pick?"

"I don't remember having it any more after that."

As mysteriously as it had appeared, the weapon was now gone, perhaps dropped on the floor in haste. Joan Little said she ran to the adjoining cell and gathered her clothes, then bolted from the cellblock. Instead of fleeing from the women's section, however, she stopped and turned around. It was then, she said, that she first realized the jailer was back on his feet.

"I didn't even see him, not until I got outside the corridor and turned around and looked in and he was standing there," she explained.

"Did he make any effort to stop you?" Griffin asked.

"No, he [was] just standing there with a funny facial grin on his face."

"Standing there, smiling at you, silly grin, I believe you called it?"

"Mr. Griffin, as I tell it to you now, I see him the same way in my mind."

"I'm asking you if he had a silly grin, is that what you said?"

"Just exactly what I said."

"When you passed him going out, did he lunge for you, did he reach for you, did he do anything to try to stop you?"

"No."

"Didn't make any of them?"

"No."

"Didn't say a word?"

"No."

"And you slammed the door shut, is that right?"

"That is correct."

"And you had blood on your hands?"

"Not that I can remember."

The trial seemed to end there, on a note of ironic uncertainty. The strategy of the district attorney had failed, and it was clear he was going to lose. "If Griffin found any inconsistencies in Ms. Little's version of how she stabbed Beaufort County jailer Clarence Alligood during the sexual attack, they were not evident," Bob Hodierne of the Charlotte *Observer* would report, and the jurors would have much the same reaction. "I thought about it last night," one of them would say after the verdict was in, "and I decided these people hadn't shown me anything to convict her."

But it was not over when Joan Little stepped down from the witness stand after seven hours. A question remained, and the answer still might have been revealed. How the killing had occurred was not really the issue, but why. What was the motive? Had Clarence Alligood entered the women's cellblock to commit rape, or had he been lured there as part of an escape plot? The only other witness who might have had an answer was yet to appear.

The defense had been ready since early spring to have Roger Bernholz corroborate Joan Little's testimony, unaware apparently that he had information which could also severely damage the credibility of their case. In May, Jerry Paul had confidently predicted in private that Bernholz would be "our surprise witness," the one whose appearance would be the key to the defense strategy. The prosecution had not yet discovered the name of the lawyer who had called Beaufort County regarding Joan Little's situation just a few days before the jailer's death. Paul hoped to keep his identity a secret even though court rules required both sides to submit witness lists before the trial in order to give opposing counsels a chance to prepare for cross-examination and to eliminate the calling of so-called surprise witnesses. Bernholz was, nevertheless, a "surprise" to the prosecution. The defense attorneys omitted his name from all witness lists, then submitted a motion after Griffin had rested his case asking for special permission to call the Chapel Hill attorney.*

Even so, Bernholz's appearance made little impression and seemed less a turning point than an unspectacular denouement. The trial had exhausted everyone, and the outcome had already been determined. Scant attention was paid when he came to the stand and responded in tight, professionally precise phrases to the questions posed by defense attorney James Rowan. He testified that on August 23, before calling the defendant, he had spoken to Bessie Cherry, the Beaufort County clerk of court. "She advised me concerning when the judgment in [the larceny] case had been entered," Bernholz said, "and that was important to me in terms of time limits pertinent to appeal in that case, which was the primary purpose of my representation of Miss Little."

Here was a final point of peril for the defense. The procedural time limit for filing an appeal in the breaking and entering case, potentially an important bit of circumstantial evidence, had not been mentioned before. A few moments later, with Griffin again absent from the courtroom, Lester Chalmers returned to it during his brief cross-examination.

"Mr. Bernholz," Chalmers said, "did your investigation

---

*Modern pre-trial discovery practices have virtually eliminated disruptive tactics such as the production of unknown witnesses and previously undisclosed evidence, but the burden of prior disclosure can be far heavier on the prosecution because of the constitutional guarantees of fair trial and due process accorded to every defendant. During this trial the defense attorneys successfully blocked prosecution attempts to call a witness who had been listed by title rather than name, but were permitted to call three witnesses of their own who had not been mentioned on any list. Their motion said that "the third witness is attorney Roger Bernholz of Chapel Hill who will be offered by way of corroboration. Although physically known to the defense, his testimony in a professional capacity was not determined to be necessary for presentation during the defendant's case in chief until after the jury had already been selected."

reveal that the time for perfecting the appeal to the appellate court had expired under the rules of the court?"

"As I recall, the time for perfecting the appeal in that case had not expired."

"Do you recall whether or not it had expired on August 23, 1974, when you last made your contact?"

"My recollection is that it had not. . . ."

Chalmers seemed puzzled by these answers. He apparently assumed that the time limit for filing an appeal had run from June 6, the day of Joan Little's conviction, because he had not been informed of Judge Martin's order starting the sixty-day period on June 29. Ordinarily the deadline would have passed several weeks before August 23, cutting off the appeal and the opportunity for bail. If that had been the case, Joan Little could not have expected to get out of jail soon and might even have been informed by this attorney that her situation was hopeless. But Bernholz had said that an appeal was still possible and that she could still have gotten out on bond. Chalmers let the matter drop there, unable to consult with Griffin without asking for a recess and not wanting to give this surprise witness a further chance to substantiate the defendant's testimony. No more would be said about the time limit, and the jurors were never informed that the appeal deadline would have expired on August 28, one day after Clarence Alligood was killed and Joan Little escaped from jail.

"I was surprised," Roger Bernholz would say later, "because I thought my testimony would be pretty important." He could still recall the visits Julius Rodgers had made to his office, where afternoon sun had poured through floor-to-ceiling windows while they discussed the case and then telephoned Beaufort County. News of the jailer's violent death had burned in these recollections, especially since Bernholz had thought during the week Joan Little was at large that she might contact him for help. He and Julius had spoken to her twice during the summer of 1974, and a year later he was still certain he had said nothing to make her think she was going to get out of jail immediately. In fact, he remembered informing her on August 23 that un-less something could be done within a few days her last chance to avoid going to prison would be lost.

Bernholz had talked to her briefly that day, only to re-mind her he could not represent her until the $1,000 re-tainer was paid, and he had been careful to avoid making commitments because he still did not consider himself to be her attorney. "I don't recall either me or Julius saying that we were going to have her out soon," he would state after the trial. He was certain he had never said anything about sending documents to Beaufort County for Joan Lit-tle's signature, and he knew he had never offered to help her raise the money she needed for bail. "I don't recall discussing the necessity of her signing anything," he would say. Had he ever told her he could get her out of jail on bond? "No," he would answer, "I never do that."

But Roger Bernholz had tried to clarify Joan Little's situ-ation when he spoke to her on August 23. "I had talked to Mrs. Cherry beforehand," he would explain. "I was inter-ested in discharging whatever obligation I had to [Joan] to at least let her know what her status was at that point." Bernholz had already learned that the August term of Su-perior Court in Beaufort County was over. If Joan Little had mentioned anything about getting a new trial before the end of the month, he was certain he would have told her it could not be done. But Bernholz could not remem-ber that the subject had even come up during their conver-sation. He had also learned that the sixty-day limit set in Judge Martin's order was due to expire the following Wednesday and that Bessie Cherry was already making plans to have Joan Little transferred to Women's Prison in Raleigh. If Chalmers had questioned him further while he was on the witness stand, Bernholz would have revealed that Joan Little had been told it would be necessary at least to file for an extension some time during the next few days if she wished to pursue her appeal and if she hoped to make bail under the existing order, which was also due to termi-nate the following Wednesday. Bernholz could not have

been certain that the young woman understood everything he had said to her, but he would have testified that
she had been informed her temporary reprieve from
prison would end soon, not that she would shortly be getting out on bail. "I'm sure Joan knew something was getting ready to happen," Roger Bernholz would say. "I
wasn't going to do anything until I was employed, but I'm
sure I let them know that something had to be done right
away."

By noon Friday it was over. The courtroom had been packed
with spectators all week and long lines had been forming
outside the courthouse. Author and civil-rights activist
Dick Gregory had been there several times, the last of the
celebrities the defense brought to the trial. Members of
Clarence Alligood's family had been present on the first
day of Joan Little's testimony and his daughter had cried
softly, trying to ignore hecklers who whispered behind her
while the defendant told her damning story. The outcome
of the trial now seemed certain, even to the jailer's survi-
vors, and they would not be back "to see justice . . . done."

There was no debate among the twelve people gathered
in the jury room. The summations had consumed another
full day, and Hobgood's charge had taken most of the
morning. Now the verdict was theirs to render, a verdict
which would speak the truth. "It would have been nice to
have all the evidence," Mark Nielsen, the foreman, would
later say. "In my mind there's always going to be some
question." But the others were less uncertain. There were
no hard issues to resolve, no real shadows to dispel. Each
of the jurors spoke in turn, some mentioning that they
were troubled by the number of wounds or by the unexplained telephone calls, but there was no dissension and no
delay. As soon as the last of them had made his feelings
known, about an hour after their deliberations began, they
took a single vote. Then one of them got up and tapped
lightly on the door.

CHAPTER 16

I CAN CREATE
ILLUSION, ANYTHING

The movement that bore Joan Little's name proved to be as fleeting as the spoken words "not guilty." A few supporters, like Black Panther leader Larry Little, had dropped off the defense team even before the trial was over. Now others began to depart, some complaining about the manipulative politics of the case, others about not being paid. The verdict had fallen with surprising finality, blowing out the candle of commitment. Stinging proof of injustices had not emerged during the methodical trial, and the euphoria of victory gave way steadily to a sense of disillusionment.

The defense attorneys continued to insist that they had proved something about bias in the judicial system and the denial of basic rights to women and blacks, but even they seemed unsure what larger purpose had been served by the costly trial. They had won the acquittal of an individual, but in winning they had lost rather than gained credibility. The Southern Poverty Law Center went on using Joan Little's name to raise money, taking credit for the verdict but never mentioning that Morris Dees had been kicked out early in the trial. Dees would boast months later that he had been congratulated by fellow attorneys for "standing up to the judge," and indeed the expulsion did not prevent him from expanding the activities of the SPLC or from becoming the chief fund-raiser for the presidential campaigns of Jimmy Carter in 1976 and Ted Kennedy in 1980. Unlike the Southern Poverty Law Center, the Joann Little Defense Fund did not survive. Chartered as a permanent organization to assist minority inmates in jails and prisons, it withered as soon as the trial was over and finally disappeared when Karen Galloway moved from her smaller office into the room it had once occupied.

The law firm of Paul, Keenan, Rowan and Galloway remained intact for a while, only to break apart later. James Gillespie, hired as an associate for the duration of the murder case, soon began to look for another job. One of the people he contacted was William Griffin, to whom he had written a letter on firm stationery early in September expressing "regret" about "a number of incidents" which had occurred during the trial. Jerry Paul spent months away from his Durham office, lecturing, talking to reporters, discussing plans for a movie about the case. James Rowan had obtained Paul's release from jail five days after Judge Hobgood sent him there, but the appeal of his contempt citation was unsuccessful. Late in 1977, after a last petition had been denied by the United States Supreme Court, Paul served the remaining nine days of the sentence he had received at the close of the Joan Little trial two years earlier. By then he was practicing law alone in Durham, still struggling against those he viewed as adversaries, but with a deepening concern that his own idealistic commitments were waning in the face of both professional and personal setbacks. His former law partners had drifted away one by one to other pursuits, and he and his wife were estranged. His twelve-year-old son David had died of leukemia earlier in the year.

Other protagonists, the judge and those who had opposed Paul and the defenders, slipped quickly back into anonymity. Hamilton Hobgood continued to ride the Superior Court circuit, becoming an advocate of measures to shield jurors from trial publicity and to prevent courthouse demonstrations. William Griffin resumed his regular duties in the Second Judicial District, trying to put the Joan Little case behind him and insisting to incredulous reporters that he had "no regrets." Lester Chalmers became head of the special prosecution section of the state attorney general's office. John Wilkinson returned to his private practice in Beaufort County, still grumbling about political influence. Eight months later he and Jerry Paul were both cited by the state bar for making "unprofessional and prejudicial" comments to the press during the trial.*

In Beaufort County the verdict had been anticipated and came as a relief but not a surprise. The case had been endured, and in endurance there was the satisfaction of knowing that things could go on much as they had before. "Now the decision has been made," wrote Ashley Futrell in the Washington *Daily News.* "It behooves those of us living here in this Pamlico area, Black and White, to seek honestly every possible means now of living together in peace and goodwill." Don Alligood, one of the jailer's sons and a family spokesman, told reporters he was "disappointed" by the outcome. "I don't think it was fair due to the publicity, politics, and money behind her," he said. "I'll always believe that." Ottis Davis did order a few changes at the county jail. The television monitor showing a portion of the women's section was repaired and moved to the communications room where it could remain on twenty-four hours a day, and a woman replaced the only male radio dispatcher. But no matrons were hired and no females were stationed inside the cell area. Women were

---

*The North Carolina State Bar sued Wilkinson and Paul in similar but separate actions, accusing both lawyers of violating various provisions of the Code of Professional Responsibility during and after the Joan Little trial. Bar rules permitted a choice of forums in which the cases could be heard. Wilkinson asked for a secret review by a panel of attorneys; Paul asked for a jury trial in Superior Court. The belated complaints seemed petulantly conceived and poorly drafted, but a state court judge refused to throw out the case against Paul when his lawyers attacked the suit in early procedural skirmishes. In April 1978, however, three of the six charges against him were dropped by another judge and his trial was continued pending action by the Fourth Circuit Court of Appeals in Richmond on a similar case involving violations of the rule limiting out-of-court comments by lawyers to matters which appear in the court record. A day later it was revealed that Wilkinson had received a "reprimand" on December 19, 1977.

still routinely confined there, guarded only by men. There were no further efforts by any of the attorneys who had represented Joan Little to bring court attention to bear on practices inside the Beaufort County lockup. Even where the killing had occurred, the impact of the case in terms of changed circumstances and improved conditions would be negligible.

Joan Little emerged briefly after the trial, not as a symbol but as a celebrity. She made a round of publicity appearances, announced intentions to marry a soldier from Beaufort County, and said she wanted to become a journalist because "I can write exactly what I feel, what I see, exactly the way it is. . . ." But she too lost credibility when she began to make contradictory and outlandish statements and to miss appointments without explanation. By October her marriage plans were off and her publicity tour had been cancelled. In December she became a fugitive again for several days when the appeal from her conviction for breaking and entering failed in the North Carolina Supreme Court. By the end of the year she had surrendered to authorities in a motel room in Durham and was back in Women's Prison to begin serving her seven-to-ten-year sentence. In 1976, after being denied parole, she was assigned to minimum-custody activities. Early the following year she joined the prison work-release program and got a job with a Raleigh dentist. Having become a Muslim, she petitioned in Wake County Superior Court in July 1977 to have her name changed to Hadiyah Joan Nadir, choosing Arabic words which mean, respectively, "valuable" or "great person" and "rare find."

"One reason is for religious purposes," she told an interviewer who asked about the name change. "Another reason is that it is a new start, a change or break with the past."

But the past was never far behind Joan Little, and within a few months it overtook her once again. On October 15, 1977, she escaped from Women's Prison in Raleigh and fled from the state. She was captured seven weeks later in New York, and confined at Rikers Island jail to await extradition.

William Kunstler, emerging temporarily as her chief defense counsel, embarked on an intensive effort to block his client's return to North Carolina. "I think it will be a big fight and a long fight," he told reporters. Months later Joan Little was still in New York, free on bail despite the fact she was an escaped felon, awaiting the outcome of Kunstler's attempt to prevent her from being returned to prison in the South. On February 21, 1978, New York Governor Hugh Carey signed an extradition order, signaling the beginning of the protracted legal battle Kunstler had predicted. Kunstler called the governor's decision an act "not only of sheer racism but of political cowardice as well." Several weeks later he commenced the extradition fight with a petition in state court for a writ of *habeas corpus.*

"Petitioner asks," the motion read, "only that this court recognize that it has before it a unique opportunity to prove to petitioner and millions upon millions of black people that the law is capable of understanding that human rights must be the national security. Otherwise petitioner will be just another tragic victim of the elemental racism that is our most unfortunate heritage."

It would be difficult to calculate the economic costs of the Joan Little murder case, and impossible to determine whether the investment in time and money had been worthwhile, or even necessary. Her attorneys said some time after the trial that at least $350,000 had been spent and 175 people had been employed in the defense effort. Expenses to the state were estimated at over $100,000, and may have run as high as $250,000. Even so, the courtroom confrontation had seemed to raise more questions than it answered. Skepticism about the reasons for the prosecution's insistence on bringing charges of first-degree murder to the jury abounded after the trial produced only inconclusive evidence against the defendant. At the same time, resentment toward Jerry Paul and criticism of his defense extravaganza intensified when he began to suggest that the verdict had been "bought" rather than won and that the news media had been hoodwinked into sympathetic coverage of the case. "You must orchestrate the press," he told Wayne King of *The New York Times*. "This country works that way . . . and that is this country's weakness."*

These comments, and others similarly provocative, kept alive public interest in the case during the fall of 1975, but also revealed for the first time latent doubts about the merits of the defense effort. "I can create illusion, anything. . . . I can win any case in this country, given enough money," Paul boasted, knowing perhaps that his remarks would prompt stormy responses. The Raleigh *News & Observer*, which had endorsed the change of venue and criticized the expulsion of Morris Dees, said then that Paul had "spent a great deal of money winning a case that the prosecution probably would have lost in any event." Mark Pinsky, even as he took credit for helping to "break the story in the national media," finally asked himself in print whether there had been two sides to the case, whether the defendant had been guilty after all of "cold-bloodedly killing an old man with a family who loved him?" Claude Lewis, a black columnist who had attended the trial and thought Paul's performance "absolutely magnificent," called him a "publicity-seeking sycophant" and said that if he had manipulated the media he had "manipulated justice in the process."

Misgivings such as these arose continually in the after-

---

*In the same interview Paul criticized the prosecutors for overlooking a newspaper clipping with biblical references to the story of Jael, a woman who lured the leader of an opposing army into her tent, lulled him to sleep, then killed him by driving a spike through his head. Paul claimed the clipping had been inside Joan Little's Bible and might have been introduced at the trial as circumstantial evidence of premeditation. But the origin of the clipping was unclear. William Griffin denied having ever "heard of its existence," and even Joan Little said she did not remember it. In fact, the clipping had not been a part of the evidence gathered by investigators when they collected the books and other materials left behind in the cellblock where the jailer's body was found. A few days after the *Times* article appeared, Paul told a local reporter he had misplaced the clipping, then said he had thrown it away.

math of the trial to challenge earlier assumptions about the facts of the case and about its intrinsic importance. Critics of the defense regularly emerged in the press, and disaffected supporters swamped Paul's office and the Southern Poverty Law Center with letters of regret or protest. Still a view persisted that the trial had been a sound vehicle for the expression of profound social and political concerns, that Joan Little had, as Kunstler's petition implied, been saved at least temporarily from the snarl of "elemental racism" and sexist prejudice. In spite of her acquittal, one nationally syndicated columnist referred to Joan Little several years later as "the most celebrated victim of North Carolina's unusual system of justice," and another writer described the outcome of the trial as "a modern verdict suited to a modern age." But if assumptions about the case had been wrong, what of such conclusions? If the defense had been a sham and justice itself manipulated, what did this trial really stand for and what truth, if any, did the jury really see?

Jerry Paul had kept constant pressure on the press and the courts to find unique and momentous implications in Joan Little's plight. Fundamental factual questions about how and why the jailer died were likely to be troublesome for the defendant, especially since she had apparently emerged without physical harm from a struggle in which the dead man had been stabbed eleven times. As remote as the possibility was without an eyewitness that Joan Little might be convicted of first-degree murder, there was always the chance even in Raleigh that she could be found guilty of unpremeditated homicide or voluntary manslaughter. Essential to the defense was a need to cloud rather than clarify the actual circumstances of the jailer's death, to quash any hint of Joan Little's complicity in the dead man's presence in her cell.

In concept, Paul's strategy was not original. Deception and distraction are tools used by most trial lawyers, and others had laid the groundwork for his attempt to overwhelm legal and factual issues with psychological and sociological theories. The genius of the strategy lay in its implementation, in its successful appropriation of a host of social concerns and in its use of pre-trial publicity to affect substantially what went on once the trial began. The defense did a better job in court than the prosecution, but even the defense team had experienced perilous lapses, especially in its misassessment of the evidence about the telephone calls from the jail and in its failure to explore beforehand the information Roger Bernholz might have disclosed on the witness stand. Paul's success ultimately rested on conditions over which he had little or no control: the defendant's race and sex, the absence of an eyewitness, the reticence of the chief prosecutor. But another, more conventional attorney might not have seized the opportunity, as Paul did, to infuse these seamy circumstances with seemingly epic importance. Whatever truth the jurors saw in this case was largely born of Jerry Paul's own bold conscience and nihilistic sense of higher justice.

The defense strategy succeeded because many people wanted to believe the defendant's version of the incident in the Beaufort County jail, and because it was easy for them to do so. Stereotypes pervaded press coverage of the case—the pitiable defendant, the crusading defense attorney, the malicious prosecutor—but its very setting was perhaps the most stereotypical aspect of all. Joan Little's story had a certain historical vitality, and it appeared to confirm a suspicion held in other parts of the country that things had not changed very much in the so-called New South. An early magazine story about the case was illustrated with photographs of a lynching in Mississippi fifty years earlier, and Joan Little was often favorably compared with Emmet Till and the Scottsboro Boys, and with Inez Garcia, whose trials in California were seen as a watershed in women's liberation. Interest in the case spread nationwide but money to support the defense effort came chiefly from the Northeast and the Far West, from New Englanders just then facing the prospect of school desegregation, from New Yorkers living in the shadow of Harlem and the South

Bronx, from Californians whose treatment of Chicano laborers had yet to be documented as well as the condition of blacks in Dixie. Notions of regional superiority and enlightenment were strongly stimulated by this defendant and from them she acquired identity as a geographical cliché.

Through the relentless effort of her attorneys Joan Little did become a symbol of many and diverse social causes even though her case legitimately raised few social issues and had a lasting effect on none of them. Paul and his defense team welded together support from people and groups concerned about everything from capital punishment to civil rights, women's rights, black power, judicial bias, rights of the poor, court reform, prosecutorial reprisals, prison reform, Southern justice, and Southern history. Except in an abstract sense, however, Joan Little was neither the inevitable product of her environment nor a hapless victim of society. Though she was poor, black, and deprived as a child, her background was not so unique as to account for all the difficulties she encountered. Cultural experiences might have explained some of her actions, but could justify none of them. She had rebelled first not against racism or sexism but against her mother's efforts to keep her off the streets. Her earlier troubles with the law involved no hint of racial motivation, and her serious offenses occurred only after she had overcome the impecunious disadvantages of her adolescence. Her police record indicated not that the courts had been too harsh with her but if anything that the authorities had been too lenient. Many people who knew her, before and after the jailer's death, regarded her simply as a cunning, unprincipled and thoroughly self-centered individual. Only a cynical and sophisticated publicity campaign erased the person Joan Little was and made her seem to be someone else. Myth eventually swallowed truth in this case, and she became a symbol without substance.

It was the success of the defense attorneys in this regard, the intensity with which they promoted her as a symbol and their reasons for doing so, that ultimately made Joan Little a victim not of her time and place but of those who had clamored to help her. As costly and disruptive as the trial was, it did not accomplish very much in the way of judicial or social reforms, in part because it did not settle the one issue upon which all others depended for legitimacy. Jerry Paul failed in court to prove that Joan Little was *not* guilty, just as William Griffin failed to prove that she was, and Paul's failure seeded a suspicion that the defense had been merely a victory of persuasion over proof, vindicating neither the defendant nor the causes with which her name had been associated. Paul's later inflammatory insights only confirmed what had been earlier perceived, if not acknowledged, and dashed once and for all the expectations he had aroused with his sweeping defense. The Joan Little case had resolved no questions of public policy, had settled no issues of public concern. It would neither provoke judicial reform nor stimulate serious reconsideration of the plight of blacks and women in jails and prisons and courtrooms around the country. The institutions brought under attack by the defense attorneys would survive without apparent damage. The places touched by Joan Little's episodic life would go unchanged, as would many of the people. For a while she became a folk heroine, but even her fame was dubious and transitory. The movement soon moved on, leaving her behind. The Joan Little case would have a legacy not of benefits and accomplishments but of bitter memories, disappointments, and broken spirits.

EPILOGUE

On June 9, 1978, Joan Little was returned to North Carolina, and one month later she went on trial for prison escape in Courtroom Number One at the Wake County Courthouse in Raleigh. The trial lasted three days, though it had been expected to go on somewhat longer. There were no restless crowds on Fayetteville Street this time, and the 112 seats in the courtroom would never be more than half filled. Only Jerry Paul sat with Joan Little at the defense table, and on the bench behind them were officers of the North Carolina Department of Corrections rather than a jury selection team. Most of the spectators were local reporters, few of whom had attended the five-week ordeal in 1975. Seated among them on the first day was a bearded man wearing a faded "Free Joann Little" T-shirt.

Joan Little had told reporters while she was at Rikers Island in New York that she escaped from Women's Prison because she feared for her life, and she had said she would "rather die" than go back. The Associated Press distributed the story nationwide, including her claim that she had been harassed by North Carolina prison officials, but did not ask those officials whether they would comment on the accusation. *The New York Times* reported in February that her "allegations that she fears for her health and safety if she is extradited from New York have been given wide currency." In May, William Kunstler argued before the New York Court of Appeals that two Women's Prison inmates were willing to testify about plots to murder Joan

Little and that an unnamed prison official would swear she would never be granted parole. On June 5, the United States Supreme Court turned down Kunstler's last request for a delay in her extradition. On July 10, in Raleigh, Joan Little pleaded not guilty to prison escape.

It is a summer Wednesday, hot and humid even before 9:00 a.m., when court is to convene. In Courtroom Number One there is no indication that the trial for prison escape is about to end. Pre-trial motions have been heard and five jurors have been selected and sequestered since Monday, the day William Kunstler appeared to ask once again for permission to represent Joan Little in a North Carolina court.

"The motion is denied," Judge James H. Pou Bailey had said after Jerry Paul told him: "We have a defense team prepared to defend Ms. Little. Without him, we cannot defend her."

Bailey's decision provoked an outburst from the New York attorney, as had a similar decision by Judge Hobgood three years earlier. "It looks really as if you've prejudged it," Kunstler muttered, causing Bailey's lips to buckle in anger. "It's a disgrace not to permit it," he went on as he walked toward the door, and as he left he shouted, "It's a great state!" Later that day, carrying a sheet of paper, Kunstler re-entered the courtroom at the lunch recess and rushed toward Bailey. Deputies restrained him as the judge disappeared into his chambers, then put him under arrest. On Bailey's orders, he was released immediately. Later Kunstler explained that he was merely trying to serve legal papers on the judge, though personal service had been unnecessary.

Except for Kunstler's intervention, the escape trial has been uneventful. Paul has looked haggard, and sometimes bored. His client has constantly whispered questions to him, urging him to ask potential jurors about their religious beliefs and their views on the Muslim faith. There have been no altercations between the defense attorney and this judge. "Do not interrupt," Bailey ordered menacingly during legal arguments on Tuesday, and thereafter Paul did not. Bailey is known for imposing strict discipline in the courtroom and is one of several Superior Court judges in North Carolina who have occasionally worn pistols under their robes.

Now, on Wednesday, court is quickly recessed so that Paul can confer with his client. The trial is not going well for them. Motions to dismiss the charges and to change the venue have been denied, and Bailey has made it difficult for Paul to excuse unwanted jurors without using peremptory challenges. The outcome already seems inevitable unless Paul can produce witnesses who will testify that Joan Little was harassed and threatened with imminent violence while in prison. Her case rests on the theory of justifiable escape, which Paul, not the prosecutor, must prove. It is one of the most difficult defenses to establish, one that is seldom successful, although Joan Little has a good chance if the charges she and her attorneys have made can be substantiated. If not, she will automatically receive a sentence of from six months to two years in prison.

Sitting in a small office near the courtroom, the defendant and her attorney are uncertain about what to do. Paul's aim now is not to avoid Joan Little's conviction for escape but to have her serve her remaining time behind bars in a federal institution rather than in Women's Prison. She insists on calling Ramsey Clark's law office in New York for advice, over Paul's objections. It is evident that she has changed in some ways, that she has emerged. During the past two days she has strode the halls of the courthouse, flanked by guards, smiling and speaking to people she has not seen since the murder trial three years ago. Occasionally she has signed an autograph. No longer sullen and withdrawn, she appears more poised, more assertive, more aware and confident than she ever seemed to be then. She is the center of attention again, and this time she seems to like it.

Paul, too, has changed. For the first time he appears irresolute about his defense of this woman, not indifferent but somehow defeated. During the morning break he has plea-bargained with the district attorney and the judge, and through an intermediary he has contacted prison officials in Raleigh to find out whether a transfer to a federal women's facility can be negotiated in exchange for Joan Little's admission of guilt. His efforts have failed. A hard decision must be made.

At 11:40 a.m., court reconvenes. Joan Little stands and faces the judge. "In view of everything that has happened here," she says, "I want to change my plea because I want to get this over with and proceed in a more positive aspect with my life." Her words ring clearly in the courtroom, unlike those she barely whispered during the murder trial. But there is an echo now of what she said then, a nonchalance about the implications of the past for the present and the future. In some ways, she has not changed at all. This will be yet another new beginning.

"The sad thing is," Jerry Paul had told an acquaintance the day before, "we won the murder trial but Joan Little lost her life."

INDEX

A NOTE ABOUT THE AUTHOR

Fred Harwell is Executive Director of the North Carolina Center for Public Policy Research in Raleigh. Born in Washington, North Carolina in 1944, he is a graduate of the University of North Carolina at Chapel Hill and its law school. He was a reporter for the Raleigh *Times*, the Durham *Morning Herald*, and United Press International. He practiced corporate law in New York City before returning to North Carolina just before the trial of Joan Little.

A NOTE ON THE TYPE

The text of this book was set, via computer-driven cathode-ray tube, in a film version of Caledonia, a typeface designed by W(illiam) A(ddison) Dwiggins for the Mergenthaler Linotype Company in 1939. Dwiggins chose to call his new face Caledonia, the Roman name for Scotland, because it was inspired by the Scotch types cast about 1833 by Alexander Wilson & Son, Glasgow type founders. However, there is a calligraphic quality about Caledodnia that is totally lacking in the Wilson types. Dwiggins referred to an even earlier typeface for this "liveliness of action"— one cut around 1790 by William Martin for the printer William Bulmer. Caledonia has more weight than the Martin letters, and the bottom finishing strokes (serifs) of the letters are cut straight across, without brackets, to make sharp angles with the upright stems, thus giving a "modern face" appearance.

W. A. Dwiggins (1880–1956) began an association with the Mergenthaler Linotype Company in 1929 and over the next twenty-seven years designed a number of book types, the most interesting of which are the Metro series, Electra, Caledonia, Eldorado, and Falcon.

Composed, printed, and bound by
The Haddon Craftsmen, Inc., Scranton, Pennsylvania.
Typography and binding design by Virginia Tan.